C000164376

JOSEPH
NUTRITOR/DOMINI

JOSEPH
NUTRITOR/DOMINI

Roger Zimmermann

To order additional copies of this book, contact:
Xlibris
1-888-795-4274
www.Xlibris.com
Orders@Xlibris.com
697906

This work is dedicated to my wife Sarah who fills the roles of wife, advisor, editor and friend. Assisting her were the Trappist Cistercian nuns, Abby of St. Joseph in Arizona and the mirad of others who came to my rescue in my hour of need.

The following is a work of fiction based on facts.

NOTE: With the exception of biblical and other Germaine quotes, all other verbiage is in the vernacular.

PREFACE

In the days of Caesar Augustus, Emperor of Roman Empire, and when Herod was King of Judea, events would take place that changed the world.

• •

EVERYTHING THAT IS known about St. Joseph, the husband of Mary and the surrogate father of Jesus, comes from the first and third Gospels, and that knowledge is underwhelming. To add to the problem of not knowing enough about Joseph, some apocryphal writings – such as the second century *Protevangelium of James*, and the fourth century *History of Joseph the Carpenter* – did nothing to clarify the situation. The development of the child Jesus is left untouched by the canonical writings.

St. Joseph is profoundly respected as a saint in all of the Christian sects. He is believed to be the corporeal father of Jesus Christ. He, arguably, is the most important man in many of the gospels without one word of his recorded by any of the four Evangelists! His first appearance was in the Gospel of Matthew[1] as father of the Messiah, the Carpenter of Nazareth, the Lord of Mary, a man who was with us for a short time, and then disappeared. He is often confused with Joseph of the many-colored coat who became a force in Egypt. Our Joseph is a man who accomplished so much, but so little is recorded about him. So eager was the church to emphasize the mission of Jesus, and his divine paternity, that Joseph, his surrogate father, had been consigned to the shadow lands.

Joseph appears in the Gospels of St. Matthew and in St. Luke, and both agree in the nativity of Jesus, but from different perspectives. They come together in the passion and crucifixion but then go their separate ways. There are significant differences however, between the two versions that reflect the theological interests of these two Evangelists. And yet, everything we know

---

[1]   Genealogy of Jesus Christ, son of David, Son of Abraham... Matt. 1:1

about Joseph, the foster father of Jesus Christ, that can be documented, comes from the Bible. Any mention of this highly venerated man, are, at the least, inadequate. For instance, in the thirteen New Testament epistles written by Paul, he makes no reference to him at all, nor does the Gospel of Mark, the first of the Gospels written. Joseph makes his debut in the Bible in the Gospels of Matthew and Luke[2]. Both of them, Matthew and Luke trace his lineage to King David, but by different paths.

Both writers agree that Joseph and Mary were betrothed when Mary was discovered to be pregnant. In Luke's version he follows the perspective of Mary. When an angel of the Lord appears to her and informs her that she will bear a child by the Holy Spirit, she responds, "Behold, I am the handmaid of the Lord; let it be done unto me according to your word."

In Matthew's gospel he tells the story from Joseph's perspective. In his gospel the discovery of Mary's pregnancy precedes any divine assurance. As a result Joseph is presented with a most horrific dilemma. The discovery of Mary's condition, he was unaware of the mystery of the Incarnation, his tender and delicate feelings would not allow him to defame his betrothed. He would, he thought put her away privately.

The eternal father chose Joseph to be the guardian and protector of his greatest treasures, his son and his spouse, and Joseph fulfilled his calling with perfect fidelity.

In *Nutritor Domini,* we have used the Gospel of St. Matthew as our guide. Saint Joseph, the patriarch of the Holy Family, descended from the greatest kings of the tribe of Judah. He was also descended from the most distinguished of the ancient patriarchs. His true nobility, however, comes from being considered a just man, and a man endowed with unparalleled virtue and humility. Into his hands God entrusted the protection, upbringing and education of his divine Son, Jesus. He was also given the Blessed Virgin Mary to protect her chastity, to keep her from false accusations upon the birth of the Son of God, and to assist her in her perilous journeys, numerous fatigues, trials, and disappointments. Both were awesome tasks and responsibilities he accepted and undertook without demur, willingly, unquestioning, and so completely such that the church has since declared him the patron saint of the family and workers, among numerous other patronages.

Joseph was what the Greeks called a *tzaddik* that is, a righteous man, who brought the Old Covenant to its completion and was used by God in such a remarkable way to bring about the New Covenant.

---

[2]   "To a virgin espoused to a man whose name was Joseph..." Luke 1:27. In Jewish culture of the time, genealogies of women were not recorded but it is recorded that step fathers had all the rights and privileges of the natural father.

In some the Gospel accounts of Matthew, Mark, Luke, and John tell us very little of the childhood of Jesus, his formative years. We only know a handful of events: the family's flight into Egypt and return to Nazareth and in Luke, His increasing wisdom and His visit to the temple in Jerusalem.

In *Nutritor Domini* we have used the Gospel of St. Matthew as our guide. Saint Joseph, the patriarch of the Holy Family, was descended from the greatest Kings of the tribe of Judah. He was also descended from the most distinguished of the ancient patriarchs. His true nobility, however, comes from being considered a just man, and a man endowed with unparalleled virtue and humility. Into his hands God entrusted him with the protection, upbringing and education of his divine Son, Jesus. He was also given the Blessed Virgin Mary to protect her chastity, to keep her from false accusations in the birth of His Son of God and to assist her in her perilous journeys, numerous fatigues, trials and disappointments. Both were awesome tasks and responsibilities he accepted and undertook without demur, willingly, unquestioning, and so completely such that the Church has since declared him the Patron Saint of the Family and Workers, among numerous other patronages.

Joseph was what the Greeks called a *tzaddik,* that is a righteous man, who brought the Old Covenant to its completion and was used by God in such a remarkable way to bring about the New Covenant.

In some the gospel accounts of Matthew, Mark, Luke, and John tell us very little of the childhood of Jesus, his formative years. We only know a handful of events: the family's flight into Egypt[3] and return to Nazareth[4] and Luke[5], His increasing wisdom and His visit to the temple in Jerusalem.

One wonders why so humble a man, a man of his stature, who is a model and inspiration for all men, is only briefly mentioned in the Gospels of the Bible.

In Matthew,[6] "And Jacob begat Joseph, the Lord of Mary, of whom was born Jesus who is called Christ . . ."

Again in Matthew,[7] "Then Joseph her Lord, being a just man, and not willing to make her a public example, was minded to put her away . . ."

In Matthew[8] "Behold, the angel of the Lord appeared unto him in a dream saying, Joseph thou son of David, fear not to take unto you Mary your wife; for that which is conceived in her is of the Holy Ghost . . ."

---

[3] Matthew 2:14

[4] Matthew 2:23

[5] Luke 2:40

[6] Matthew 1:1-17

[7] Matthew 1:19

[8] Matthew 1:20-21

In Luke[9] "And Joseph went up from Galilee, out of the city of Nazareth, into Judea, unto the city of David, which is called Nazareth; because he was of the house and lineage of David."

And, finally in Matthew,[10] "And when they were departed behold the angel of the Lord appeareth to Joseph in a dream saying, arise, and take the young child and his mother, and flee into Egypt, and be thou there until I bring you word; for Herod will seek the young child to destroy him."

Apostles Mark and John make no mention of these events.

Even more remarkable is the fact that Joseph, a silent figure throughout the Gospel, not one word of which Joseph spoke, the foster father of Jesus, is recorded by the Evangelists and Gospel writers! And yet no other human being was closer to Jesus.

We know the Holy Family went into Egypt. We do not know how they got there where they stayed or how they survived from day to day. We are not told how Joseph accomplished this task as Nutritor during Jesus' formative years in Egypt. We learn, from the Bible, that an angel spoke to Joseph after three and a half years, and told him it was safe to go home. Nothing is documented of the Holy Family's homeward survival nor of their life in Bethlehem before Jesus is lost and found in the temple. Then, after Jesus is found in the temple, none of the Gospels mentions Joseph as being present at any event during his son's ministry.

An important omission is that period of Jesus' formative years when Joseph's teaching had to have the most influence on the development of his character.

The last recorded mention of Joseph is in the twelfth year of Jesus' life, when He left the caravan after the Passover celebration in Jerusalem. Many have asked why he left and why he did not tell anyone. When found by his mother and asked, why he did not tell his parents what he was going to do, Jesus replied, "How is it that ye sought me? Wist ye not that I must be about my Father's business?"[11]

Following this encounter, Joseph disappears from the scene to dispel any confusion that may be present as to whom Jesus was speaking about. Finally, there is no word on when or where Joseph died, and there is much uncertainty about where he is buried.

Conjecture yes, but certitude no.

The gospels mention him by name, *"Joseph"* means "God adds" or "God gathers" fifteen times. For whatever reason Joseph appears briefly in connection with the early life of his son, Joseph then disappears without listing a cause of death, a traditional burial ground, nor relics of any sort.

---

9   Luke 2:4

10   Matthew 2:13

11   Luke 2:49

Whereas it is true that the Gospel's focus is on the mission of Jesus Christ, and rightly so, but should a man who is asked much of, who nurtures God's son through his formative years, merely vanish?

In preparing *Joseph-Nutritor/Domini* the source materials regarding Joseph possess certain unusual characteristics the dearth of documentation regarding Joseph and his son, Jesus, working together before and after their flight to Egypt and the complete lack of information on the Holy Family's stay in Egypt, where certainly much of the molding of the Christ child had to have taken place. All of his formative years, a vital history of the Holy Family, is unrecorded.

Information was therefore sought through a number of sources primarily among which include the King James version of the Bible, the Gospel of Matthew, numerous books, documents and writings of the Coptic Orthodox Church, the chief religious sect in Egypt, the essential writings of Josephus, and Internet sources.

The writings and documents of the Copts were researched primarily because the Apostle Mark evangelized in Egypt and he was the author of the Gospel of Mark. He is venerated by the Coptic Orthodox Church as their founder and first pope.

That the Holy Family was present in Egypt is evident. There are temples, monasteries, statuary, shrines, and monuments that attest to their presence. However, there is no such documentation about their return except for the angel's announcement, the episode at the temple, but nothing thereafter.

What follows is the result of those efforts made seeking enlightenment.

INTRODUCTION

AT THE TIME of the Bible, in the rolling, rocky hills of the Judean Mountains, there was a small city called Bethlehem, which in Hebrew means "house" or "place of bread." It was in an unwalled city five miles from Jerusalem, the birthplace of King David, a man of God's own heart,[12] and an area where shepherding sheep and farming were common occupations.

Approximately one thousand years after King David's reign, a descendent, Joseph, son of Jacob, was also born in Bethlehem. It was here that Joseph learned and practiced his trade as a *tektons,* traditionally translated as a carpenter, but also an artificer in stone, iron, and copper. Numerous of these *tektôns* were builders, engineers, and highly skilled craftsmen. Joseph fell into this latter group with his own workshop and employees at a time when there was a paucity of artisans.

Throughout his life he was taught his father's trade and learned to deal with people honestly, and fairly. He lived as he had been taught and had become known as a just and a righteous man.

As an adult, Joseph, about forty years of age, took as his wife Salomé, also known as Melcha. They lived forty-nine years as lord and wife having six children Judas, Justus, James, Simon, Assia and Lydia. They lived in Bethlehem where Joseph plied his trade, devout in his faith and follower of the Law of Moses.

In telling the story of Joseph, and the Holy Family, it was undertaken in three distinct aspects: their life in Judah, their flight into Egypt and subsequent stay, and return to Nazareth and life afterward.

While making this journey, parallels revealed themselves. The flight of the Holy Family into Egypt brings to mind Jacob and his family's flight from famine to live in Egypt. Also, the Holy Family's actions to save Jesus from Herod's wrath recalls Moses' mother protecting her son from the pharaoh.

In point of fact, it is the greatest story never told.

Here is how it came to pass.

---

[12]   1 Samuel 13-14

CHAPTER ONE

WHEN SCRIBES PUT pen to paper telling stories of Saint Joseph, they roughly classify the man under four headings; Joseph's obedience and devotion to his God; his personal virtue as pious, righteous and just; his unique position with respect to his betrothed wife; and his position with respect to his foster son as his Nutritor/Domini.

This was quite a unique and magnificent mission bestowed upon him; that of protecting the Son of God and giving Him wisdom and knowledge, the added mission of protecting the virginity and unblemished holiness of Mary, as well as the mission of cooperating in the Incarnation and Redemption; in other words, a protectorate of those entrusted to his care. He received these missions so that he might take the place of a human father in the care of the Holy Family, and he hesitated not a moment!

Let us take a closer look at this embodiment of a true man.

Nazareth, is a small city in the Judean hills, forty miles from Jerusalem. It was a little village on a plateau north of the Plain of Esdraelon, and one thousand feet above it. The name in Hebrew was Nazareth which meant "verdant." Nazareth, a small town on a caravan route through the country, had a center for temple priests in which they could pray and fast when not on duty at the temple.

In this small town, there lived a quiet humble man. His name, given him by his father, was Joseph he went from day to day working as a *tektôn*, a carpenter, eking out a living for himself and his family. Everyone in Nazareth knew him, respected him as a religious and a just man. However, Joseph was no ordinary man.

God looked favorably on the person of Joseph. He had chosen him because of his humility, his honesty, and his virtue. Because of that God entrusted him with the care, upbringing and education of his Divine son, His word made flesh. He was endowed so that he had the ability for the protection of a chaste spouse, the Blessed Virgin Mary, to be the protector of her chastity, to safeguard her from the slander and degradation upon the birth of the Son of God, to assist

---

1

her on their journeys, her education, fatigues, and persecutions. With all this, Joseph will accept what his Lord has given him without demur.

There is no one on earth so good, so great in understanding, or so excellent, as epitomized in Joseph. Added to this is his unparalleled humility and outstanding virtue. He keeps to himself the privilege that has been given him. He lives as an obscure man, makes no inquiries, leaving the future to God to manifest them at His own time. He is content with his condition, devoting himself to the charges and missions he has been given, knowing that they have come from his Lord and God.

Joseph recognized that he would soon become the earthly father of the Son, not merely an ordinary Son, but the Messiah himself! A myriad of questions came to his mind. What should he teach the Messiah? How would he care for him? What should his education consist of? Women usually were tasked with the education of their young, but this would not be the case with their son. They would share that task but he had, he thought, the greater responsibility. There were so many questions he would face, but so few answers immediately apparent.

In addition to that, he would be given a bride barely more than a child herself, and a pregnant one at that! What else should he do but trust in the Lord? Whenever there was a problem, he had gone to his Lord in prayer. That is what he did now. "Oh, Almighty God and Father, your humble servant Joseph beseeches you to guide him. Give him the knowledge to teach your Son what has to be learned. I can only teach him man's ways and the words of scripture. Is that enough?"

Since he was a boy working at his father's side, Joseph knew he could be the Royal family lineage of David and was also aware of the promise that one day the Messiah would come and that he could be the Royal family of David.

Jacob, his father, as did his father before him, told him about God and the enslaved people, the Hebrews. He was told of Moses and the pharaoh and the tumbling of the walls of Jericho, about the shepherd King, David and his son Solomon. He also learned of the law that Miriam had a brother, Moses.

One of Joseph's favorite stories was about his ancestor, also called Joseph, who was sold into slavery by his jealous brothers who could not stand the special treatment that he received from their father, as his favorite. When the young Joseph was given a very expensive multi-colored coat that was the last straw! On top of which Joseph interpreted a dream he had had. In the dream his brothers bowed down before him. They sold him into imprisonment and slavery where he turned his plight into a situation that not only got him released from prison but allowed him to become the person in charge of the food in Egypt and also, afforded him the opportunity to save his family from starvation.

Another of the stories that was Joseph's favorite was the story of the great flood and how Noah saved not only the animals, but also the human race by building an enormous ark. It was this story that helped him to become a *tektôn* and help him people by building and repairing things they need.

His mother, Rachel, taught him to count to ten, to count his blessings. But most of all, he should cherish the trees that gave fruit, that gave songs in the gentle breezes, wood for fires and for carpentry. From his father he learned that because trees were so scarce in their homeland, each one was to be prized. From his mother he learned much, he gained in wisdom, understanding, and learning.

Joseph enjoyed watching his father work with wood. For more generations than anyone could remember, Joseph's family had been carpenters and craftsmen, known locally as *tektôns*. His father told him that the smartest person is the one who enjoys and takes pleasure in his work. Like most children, he had many questions. What type of wood was his father working with, where did the wood come from, why was it used to make a plow, how were the tools made that his father was working with, and how much would a table and chair cost to make? Craftsmen, at that point in time, did not make the ordinary, crude items that were ordinarily expected. Rather, they crafted such things as yokes that were custom-made to fit oxen and the plows that were used to cut furrows for planting, wooden locks and keys and wood carvings. They also put roofs on houses.

Joseph developed his skill to match that of his father and like his father, he matched his skill with his kindly disposition and his personal integrity. He was also a skilled builder, a smith and a stonemason, which stood him in good stead since. Stones were plentiful and most houses were built with them. His skill as a mason could be put to good use. Long hard work, paying attention to details, which are some of the attributes.

He absorbed all that was needed and at the same time he developed a kindly disposition and personal integrity. As he grew into manhood, he became tall, strong, with a well-developed and powerful body. His demeanor was proud, confident, upright and honest. He respected others, accepting each person as being unique. Joseph was also mild mannered, faithful to the religious conventions of his people, displaying wisdom and learning. It came as no surprise that he became known as "Joseph the Just."

His clothing consisted of a tunic, covered by a leather smock and cinched at the waist by a leather belt. He wore sandals on his feet and a cap on his head. He was a man of self confidence evincing a bearing of old nobility. He deservedly earned the name of "Joseph the Just."

When Diogenes, a Greek philosopher was carrying a lighted lamp everywhere he went, people would ask what he was looking for. He replied, "I am seeking an honest man." Undoubtedly his search would have ended when he came upon Joseph the Just of Nazareth.

Joseph was also well schooled in his religious convictions, believing firmly in the prophets. He lived his beliefs, and the Law of Moses.

The Lord God, in seeking a man who would soon be the guardian for His son who would soon be man's redeemer, found Joseph of Nazareth. He was a quiet man with great purity of heart, and above all, was in obedient and humble.

In sum,

"Blessed is the man who walketh not in the counsel of the ungodly,
nor standeth in the way of sinners, nor siteth in the seat of the scornful.
"But his delight is in the law, doth meditate both day and night. . . .
"For the Lord knoweth the way of the righteous. . ."[13]

The Roman Empire controlled most of the known world at the time of Joseph. Roman legions conquered the Greeks, the former rulers, and wisely incorporated their great accomplishments into the social, political, economic, and educational structures of the empire. To live according to the Law of Moses required a tremendous amount of composure in this Hellenistic culture. Many Jews found it easier to make accommodations in order to survive. Joseph had to walk a narrow line between to follow what he believed rather than the beliefs of the world around him. But that was what made Joseph the man that he was.

---

[13] Psalm 1

CHAPTER TWO

NAZARETH, IS AN OBSCURE village in Galilee that had given birth to King David, Jacob, and his son, Joseph. The village is situated on the southern ridges of Lebanon on the steep slope of a hill about 9 kilometers from the Sea of Galilee and about sixteen kilometers west of Mount Tabor and it lies in a shallow basin lower down than the ancient city.

Housing began as soon as the area was made suitable for agriculture, followed by towns wherever there was arable land. At first tents provided housing but was replaced by houses and villages, bringing the nomadic way of life to an end.

When permanent structures appeared, a basic floor plan was used, followed by floor plans more suitable to the needs. There was now a central courtyard surrounded by rooms that faced on to it. There were few windows and those that there were were covered by lattice work or shutters.

Room size was determined by length of the beams used to support the roof. These beams were roughly shaped reaching from one wall to another, covered by a mixture of branches and clay, smoothed over by a stone roller.

The streets wind narrowly and haphazardly laid out, the blank walls of the houses facing the outside world. Intermittently the walls have small windows covered by lattice work or shutters and wooden doors, all hand crafted. This was also the burial place of the Old Testament Rachel (Jacob's wife) and she was also known because of the prophets.

The houses had been built close together, so close that people, if they needed or wanted, could walk from house to house. It made for a close knit community. The houses of craftsmen were usually identified by the goat skin awnings covering the front entrance. The craftsmen themselves wore identifying badges: carpenters wore a wood chip, sandal makers wore a strip of leather, and so on.

Normally there was little foot traffic on the cobbled or dirt streets in Bethlehem, even donkeys when carrying large loads would often block the roadways. However, three times a day groups of noisy children took over the streets on the way to and from the synagogue for their Torah lessons.

The houses in Bethlehem, for the most part, were constructed of stone and mud-bricks with wood supports in the roof made of woven branches and clay smoothed over by a stone roller. Stairs or a wooden ladder led to the roof, which was used as an outdoor room, partially shaded by a tent-like superstructure with a stone or brick wall providing outside supports. Rooms within the building were small and dark making the courtyard and roof important parts of the house. These two areas were the most frequently used because good lighting was needed for food preparation, and spinning. An additional benefit is that the flat roof provided an area for sleeping, drying textiles and bathing.

Inside the house where Joseph grew up and raised his family, there was a *mikveh,* clean rain water used for ritual bathing. The stone based stove for cooking was in the courtyard area. Mary, she had been taught, kept a fire going constantly, near the fire items for cooking, clay and stone implements, and her cooking utensils. This area Joseph built shelving for the storage of olive oil, spices, and other ingredients.

Outside the homes looked drab and uninviting but inside, it was quite different. They were cool, comfortable and quite pleasant. It was oftentimes larger inside than outward appearances would indicate. Many homes had inner courtyards that were paved with an open drain at the center.

The house was built so that the stones could be rinsed clean and rainfall would not flood the yard. The inner walls were covered with plaster, flattened with a smooth stone. In one room there was a raised platform where the occupants sat and slept on cushions and mats. A second room was used as a kitchen and dining area when inclement weather prevented going outside. In the interior small niches were cut into the walls for storing bedrolls, small food stuffs, clothing, dishes if available and pots. Grains and the indispensible olive oil were kept separately. There was usually space set aside for animals and their food-troughs called mangers.

Twice a day, early morning when it was cool and in the evening when it was not, women carried large earthenware pitchers to the village well. They pulled water from the well with a leather bucket tied to the end of a rope. At the well the women exchanged pleasantries and gossip then carried the buckets home on their heads.

To the Jews, the home was critical to family life. Both the home and synagogue were places of prayer. In the synagogue, the rabbi or scholar had charge of prayer but in the home, each individual woman was in charge of a household and had the responsibility for prayer services held in the home.

Many of the houses in Bethlehem were, in most cases, both a home and the workshop of the artisan in residence. The house and workshop where Joseph and his family lived had been constructed of limestone rock and brick on a flat plain. The shop at the front of the house was opened in order that others might watch his craftsmanship and to ventilate the shop and home as well. Tacked to the front door was a sample of the trade goods. In Joseph's case it was a chip of wood letting everyone know that there was a carpenter within. The upper floor could only be gained by use of a ladder, and that level was given over to living quarters.

The city had a temple and that became the center of city life.

CHAPTER THREE

JOACHIM, WHOSE NAME in Hebrew means "Yahweh prepares," was an extremely wealthy, member of one of the Twelve Tribes of Israel, born in Nazareth. Anne, his wife, was born in Bethlehem. Both are descendents of King David. Joachim was a regular donor to the poor and to the synagogue in Sepphoris. They lived for a time in Galilee and later settled in Jerusalem. Anne and Joachim, although advanced in age, desired to have children but could not since Anne was barren.

For twenty years Joachim and Anne devoted themselves to daily prayer and fasting, in isolation from one another and from society. The couple fervently prayed to the Lord to allow Anne to bring forth a child and promised to dedicate their first born to the service of God. They felt their inability to conceive, because Anne was barren, was a sign of shame among the tribes of Israel.

One day Joachim went to the high priest in the synagogue to make a sacrifice and speak with Rabbi Reuben.

"Rabbi," Joachim began, "Thou knowest that Anne and I want to have children. I am here to offer a sacrifice as a show of our intent and devotion. Would you accept my sacrifice?"

"No Joachim I will not!"

"Why not rabbi? Surely you are aware of our faithfulness and devotion to the Lord God Jehovah. Why do you refuse?"

"The fact that Anne is childless is a clear sign of divine displeasure with you, or Anne, or the both of you. Do not make a useless sacrifice!"

"I will look in the history of the Twelve Tribes of Israel," Joachim said, "and see whether I am the only one who has not conceived a child." He reminded himself of the patriarch Abraham and that the Lord God gave him a son, Isaac.

Undaunted, Joachim retreated into the desert where he continued his prayers, fasting and doing penance for forty days. At the end of that time an angel of the Lord appeared to him and told him that Anne would conceive.

Anne, grieved by Joachim's disappearance, became extremely frustrated and went down into a garden to walk around and pray. She seated herself beneath a laurel tree where she prayed to the Lord saying, "God of my ancestors, bless me and hear my prayers." Anne, in her despair cried out, "Why was I born Lord?"

An angel appeared to her saying, "Thy Lord has looked upon thy tears, thou shalt conceive and give birth and the fruit of your womb shall be blessed by all the world."

According to ancient belief, a child born of an elderly mother who has given up hope for an offspring was destined for great things. And then she gave birth to Mary. In thanksgiving Anne promised to dedicate her child to God. Mary, when she was of age, was placed in the temple to continue her education and learning.

Joachim and Anne taught Mary to walk in God's way and cleave unto him,[14] who is merciful and gracious,[15] full of compassion and an abundance in goodness and truth. They also told her to choose life by loving God, obeying Him, and that Scriptures tell the children to listen to and obey their parents.[16]

---

[14]   Deut.11:22

[15]   Exodus 34:6

[16]   Proverbs 4:13, 8:33

CHAPTER FOUR

JOSEPH AND HIS sons, Simon, Judas, and James were in the workshop similarly dressed, belted tunics, sandals and caps, their hair, arms and legs covered in sawdust, the floor covered with wood shavings. Joseph was at work on a piece of wood, moving his plane forward smoothing the surface of the wood. The sleeves of his tunic were rolled up. His back and neck and skull cap were darkened by his sweat. He stopped, stood erect, arched his back then raised his arms over his head. He sat heavily in the chair shaking his hair through his fingers to remove dust and shavings then breathed a sign as he brushed off his tunic.

"James," Joseph called out, "my work is done. Put the finishing touches to this table with my adze making the sides of this piece of wood as smooth as you can. My aching back is starting to twitch."

"It has only been six hours since you started with this piece of furniture. Maybe you are getting old, old man."

"Show some respect for your elders," he warned smiling. "I have to go to the temple to speak with Rabbi Lowe. He wants some work done on the doors, and someone else needs to do the hard work while I am gone."

He left the workshop and began walking to the synagogue. As he walked up Rabbi Lowe was there at the doors to greet him.

"*Shalom*, Joseph," he called out.

"*Shalom Aleichem*, rabbi."

"Come sit with me. Your work prospers?"

"Enough to keep bread on the table."

"Your children are well?"

"Yes, rabbi, praise God,"

"Do you have the time to do some work for the synagogue?"

"Always, rabbi. What is it thou needs to be done?"

As the two men spoke, priests, cantors, doorkeepers and servants milled about them. The work in the synagogue was quite busy.

———

Joseph noticed the rabbi wore no sandals. Probably a synagogue custom, he thought.

"The doors to the main entrance of the synagogue do not give sufficient praise and glory to Yahweh. Is there anything you can do with your skill and craftsmanship to show His love and devotion for His people?"

"Do you want carvings in the wood or plates attached to the door itself?"

"Is there a difference?"

"Oh, yes. To carve in the wood the door would have to be removed and worked on in my shop whereas wooded plates can be carved in the shop and attached when finished. Another option would be to carve the doors without removing them. That, however, would be more expensive."

"We can't have the synagogue without doors. Is there no way you can work here at the temple?"

"As I said, it is possible, but more difficult, more expensive but possible. Let me think on how it can be done. I will also show you renderings of what is proposed. Of course a panel will be given over to David the leader of our tribe and former resident. I will also work out our costs for such an undertaking."

"Joseph, Joseph remember we are poor so be generous."

"As are we but I will ask for guidance, but rabbi, please keep in mind I will have to take on help to build the scaffold, erect the platforms and assist me in the carvings. I will also have to purchase and hang drapes to protect us from the sun.

"*Tzohora'im Marcusim,*" Joseph said. The rabbi said cutting short Joseph's litany of requirements.

"Good afternoon to you, *shalom.*"

Joseph returned to the shop shaking his head and smiling. That old man never changes, he thought. He is always pinching pennies. He would do the work for less money than he would charge others but it would also be at a fair price. There were unfinished chairs, wooden bowls to be carved, a cabinet for the procurator, and a yoke to be made for a local farmer. Most of the carving for the door he would have to do himself.

"Father," James called out, "what are we giving to the synagogue this time?"

"Respect my son, respect, "which has two meanings. One meaning of respect is for the man and the position he holds and the second form of respect is for the service we provide to the temple. Come," he called to the others, "let me tell you and show you what is wanted. Simon, please bring some parchment with you."

Justus observed, "Cash payments would help us pay our heavy taxes. Respect is not an accepted form of currency."

"Shall we discuss what needs to be done," Joseph inquired ending the conversation?

The youngest of the men, James, who had been sweeping up wood carvings to be used later in the interior stove, joined the gathering.

The sons gathered about him as he laid the parchment on top of the table being worked on. As he spoke he sketched renderings of what he had in mind.

"The good rabbi would like to have the main doors of the synagogue dedicated to the praise and glory of Yahweh. As I describe and show you what I have in mind, please make any suggestions and changes that come to your mind. As I see it there should be four panels instead of just one. That way we can provide each of our different approaches. King David should be represented in one of these, then perhaps Solomon, Isaac . . ."

The sketching and discussion went on for a half hour. Changes were offered, and some were made, along with suggestions and recommendations. When finished, Joseph lay down his charcoal.

"There is still work we have to do and it is my recommendation that I undertake the door carvings while each of you complete the work we have in progress. I will need your help in putting up the scaffolding, braces, platforms and drapes at various levels."

"What do we do," Judas inquired, "about new work that comes in?"

"We will have to be selective in what we take on. Work that can be done in a short period of time would be best. Larger work we will have to discuss."

"How about repairs," asked James, "that are daily occurrences."

"We keep up with them," Simon recommended, "as best we can."

"What will you charge for this master work," Simon asked?

Joseph clasped his hands to his head, "Everything must be purchased separately and an accounting kept of what those purchases are. We must include expenses for materials and labor.

I believe that this undertaking will take three or four months, perhaps more. Therefore, I will take an average of my daily wage multiply it by ninety, plus whatever the materials cost. That is, I think, a fair price."

"Why not add 10 percent for shop costs," Judas suggested. "We should make some profit from this."

"I will do as you suggest but only as a bargaining gambit. If the rabbi balks, then I can reduce the cost by 10 percent."

Justus asked, "When will you begin this, father?"

"This is midweek. I will begin after the Sabbath."

And so it was that after the Sabbath, Joseph and his sons began work on the temple doors. The scaffold was in place, the platforms laid in place and the curtains covering all to protect him and others from the scorching sun. Joseph climbed to the top, dropped a plumb line dividing the door in half then stretched another across the center. That being done, he began sketching views of Yahweh, David and Solomon surrounded by angels and floral patterns in each quadrant. When the doors were laid out, he began his work.

Joseph and James were to purchase the lumber and wood panels to bring back to the temple. His next task was to sketch in charcoal renderings to be carved.

Days followed with the sound of hammer and chisel bringing those sketches to life. Each night Joseph returned home tired, covered with sawdust, wood carvings and shavings. Each day the noon meal and water was brought to him by his daughter, Lydia.

The next day he was back at work again. Slowly his visions began to take shape and villagers stopped to gaze at the work in progress.

At home there was hardly time to brush himself clean, inspect the work that his sons had done before collapsing on his palette.

Isaac, the goat herder and one of Joseph's clients, stopped him one morning on his way to the temple.

"*Shalom* Joseph, you are doing too much and it is beginning to show in your face. Canst thou not slow down?"

"*Shalom*. Wish that I could, Isaac old friend. The rabbi inspects the work every day and is always disappointed at the slow progress. He has no idea of the work involved in creating the carving."

"*Alav Shalom,*" Joseph.

"*Shalom*, go with God."

In their home in Galilee, Joachim and Anne sat at the table discussing the future of their daughter. Anne was saying, "Mary is at an age when she can no longer stay at the temple. She has sworn to remain a virgin but I do not think that will be possible."

"You are quite right, but looking over the selection of young men her age, there are none as pious as she, nor are there any into whose care I would trust her. There is however, one man who is hard-working, righteous, and to whom I would have no hesitation going into contract for marriage."

"I have no idea about whom Joachim speaks. Tell me who it is."

"It is Joseph the carpenter" Joachim said, a smile crossing his face. "There is none better in Bethlehem."

They thought of a plan whereby Joseph, if he agreed, would be placed in close proximity to their daughter Mary. They had looked over the eligible bachelors, and by far Joseph stood out of all those available. He knew that Joseph was a contractor, and approached him to put his plan into action.

Joachim met with Joseph outside the synagogue. "Joseph," he began, "I am building an extension to my house and I would like you to do the work, if you are available. Will you come to my home and give me an estimate for its costs?"

"We will be finished with the temple doors by week's end. I will come to your home after that is done. I will give you a cost estimate. And we can go from there."

As promised, Joseph went to his residence quoted him a fair price and the next day began to work. Joseph had seen Mary in the synagogue and about the village square. The nature of the work to be done was such that it would require that Joseph would stay with Joachim for its duration.

He met with Mary during that stay, and every day at meal time when she brought him water and something to eat. It was during these daily exchanges Joseph became impressed by Mary's piety and devotion to her faith.

The next Sabbath Joachim and Anne went to the synagogue to speak with rabbi Reuben Lowe about their daughter, Mary.

CHAPTER FIVE

IN THE SYNAGOGUE in Nazareth, Joachim, spoke with the high priest, Reuben Lowe. "Are you aware rabbi, our daughter, Mary is of marriageable age, a temple maiden, devoted and dedicated to the service of the Lord, and prays every day. She has been well tutored in household responsibilities, cooking, baking and making bread. She is also of an age where she should be betrothed before we are gone to our reward. We are aging and need to have her betrothed and under the protection of a worthy and deserving man. We have come to you for help.

"We know of Joseph, the Nazarene carpenter, who is a widower but he is also a pious, just, and a righteous man. We have taken measures to bring Joseph and Mary into each other's company so that they might get to know one another better."

"What measures have you taken Joachim," the rabbi asked?

"I hired him to build an extension to our home and we have seen to it that Mary would bring him water and his meals every day."

"As I recall, your daughter has repeatedly said that she would like to remain chaste. Have you spoken to Joseph about getting married?"

"No we have not."

"It would then be my recommendation that you announce that Mary has come of age and it is your wish to give her in marriage. We will ask all eligible men in Bethlehem to come to the synagogue with their walking staff."

"And this," Joachim said interrupting, "is what is needed to get Mary betrothed?"

By way of answer the rabbi continued, "I will have all the eligible men come to the synagogue place their staff on the altar, and according to tradition, the staff that flowers with the Lily is the one selected to be her betrothed. All of this I will explain to them before they cast their staff on the altar."

"Is there anything that I need to do," Joachim asked?

"Yes, be sure to have Joseph participate. Otherwise, Mary may continue being chaste."

Thereafter the temple priests sought a husband for Mary because she was one of the temple virgins. Joseph was among those being considered even though no previous agreement had been tentatively reached.

The rabbi told Joachim that "a prenuptial ceremony is unnecessary. However, in keeping with tradition, a test usually used under God's providence will be used by priests and insisted upon by the rabbi. He would have "each eligible man present themselves with his staff to the temple. They would put their staff on the altar and prayers would be prayed over them. Over time, it varies from ceremony to ceremony, whichever staff blossomed with the lily that would indicate which man was to be considered to be the lord for the temple virgin since he was destined by the Lord."

Joseph was given a dry staff by the priests because he was so much older than the others, They did not want him to be chosen, even though Joachim desired otherwise. But the dry branch miraculously bloomed. The blooming of the lily on the dry branch was foreshadowed by "A rod shall come forth from the root of Jesse, and a flower shall ascend from its root. . ."[17]

The rabbi met with Joseph and Joachim to discuss the ritual and the flowering staff.

"Joseph," the rabbi began, "you are familiar with the ritual as a means for selecting a lord. As you have seen, your staff flowered and, it is ordained that you should be the lord of Mary."

"Yes rabbi, I am familiar with the ritual and the results. However, and I apologize to you Joachim, but it is impossible for me to marry your daughter. She needs someone who is the same age as she, someone who has the same interests as she, not a man much older than she. But let me say this, if Mary is willing to go forward with the betrothal, then I shall do so as well."

The rabbi agreed to the stipulation, and Joachim did as well. He went to his home where Anne and Mary were waiting. Joachim told them what had happened, and of his conference with Joseph and the rabbi, and Joseph's response as well.

"Mary," the choice is yours. Your mother and I think you could do no better than Joseph. He is a righteous and honest man, faithful to his Lord. What is your response?"

With little hesitation, Mary agreed and the arrangements for the betrothal were set in motion. The following day rabbi Lowe met with the principles and began negotiations.

"With regard to the *mattan* (dowry) to Joseph, what are thine intentions Joachim?" Joachim turned towards Joseph saying, "We will be generous Joseph as Mary is our only daughter. We will furnish your home to make it comfortable for you both. We will. . ."

---

[17]   Hebrews 9-4

CHAPTER SIX

GOD SENT THE angel Gabriel to Nazareth to speak with a young girl named Mary, approaching fourteen years of age, was visiting at her parents' home in Nazareth preparing the afternoon meal. She knelt at her sandstone rotary mill grinding flour for bread. As she worked at the bit of honey to the mix a faintness came over her. She sensed a presence. The angel came to her saying:

"Greetings you who are highly favored! The Lord is with you."

Mary was greatly troubled at his words and wondered what kind of greeting this might be. How was it possible for the Lord to be with her? But the angel said to her:

"Do not be afraid, Mary, you have found favor with God. You will be with child and give birth to a son, and you are to give him the name of Jesus. He will be great and will be called the Son of the Most High. The Lord God will give him the throne of his father David, and he will reign over the house of Jacob forever; and his kingdom will never end."[18]

"How will this come about," Mary asked the angel, "since I am a virgin?"

Gabriel answered, "The Holy Spirit will come upon you, and the power of the Most High will overshadow thou. So, the holy one to be born will be called the Son of God. Even Elizabeth your relative is going to have a child too in her old age, and she who it is said."

Mary said to the angel, "How shall this be, seeing – I know not a man?"

And the angel answered her saying unto her, "the Holy Ghost shall come upon thee, take you and the power of the Highest shall overshadow thee; therefore also the only thing which shall be born of thee shall be called the Son of God.

---

[18]   Yahweh is Salvation

"And, behold thy cousin Elizabeth, she hath also conceived in her old age; this is the sixth month with her, who was barren. For with God nothing is impossible."[19]

And Mary said, "Behold the handmaid of the Lord." And the angel departed from her."[20] When the angel had gone, Mary sat in the kitchen stunned. She was trying to come to grips with the news that she had just received: she was to be the mother of the Son of God! Unbelievable joy filled her. Then reality struck. How was she to tell her betrothed? She was going to become pregnant, she had not been with a man, and how was she to tell him she had conceived in a dream. It was also unbelievable. The Law of Moses came to mind, specifically the passages in Leviticus; "The adulterer shall be put to death."

"If I were to tell Joseph," she thought, "that I was with child, and yet have not lain with him, I must have been unfaithful. Therefore, I have committed adultery." Mary was confused as to who could she talk to about this? Her mother or the rabbi? Then Mary recalled the angel saying that her cousin was with child. The one person she knows who will understand, was her cousin Elizabeth. Perhaps if she went to see her of her good news and its ramifications, together they could decide on a proper course of action.

All other discussions were put into writing in the form of a marriage contract prepared by Mary's parents. It was signed by the principles and witnesses. Such a contract was immediately deemed binding, the couple considered married even though the actual ceremony and consummation of the marriage would not occur for as long as a year afterwards. Rabbi Lowe asked the Lord's blessing on this union. Before parting Joachim said, "We give you our daughter Joseph and will deliver her to you tomorrow morning. We embrace you as a son and wish you both God speed."

---

[19]   Luke 1:36
[20]   Luke 1:28-38 The Magnificat

CHAPTER SEVEN

IMMEDIATELY AFTER THE visitation and annunciation, Mary departed in haste into the hill country then into Judah, a city 183 kilometers distant. She was anxious to speak with the cousin. When she came to the house of Zachariah, she dismounted and called out, "God bless all in this house! It is I Mary your kinswoman."

Mary's purpose for the visitation was twofold: she wanted to discuss her situation with her, and she wanted to bring divine grace to Elizabeth and her unborn child. For the first time she was exercising the function as a mediatrix between God and man.

Elizabeth and Zachariah, a devout elderly couple was living in the hills of Judea, had been childless, even though they were both righteous before God walking in all his commandments and ordinances, they were blameless. Yet, she was childless and a woman's infertility indicated God's displeasure. Elizabeth lived daily with the sign of divine reproach. It might well have been on her mind and she might have lost all hope.

The Holy Prophet Zachariah and the Righteous Elizabeth were descended from the lineage of Aaron: Zachariah, son of Barach, was a priest in the Jerusalem temple, and Elizabeth was the sister of Anna, the mother of the Most Holy Theotokos. The righteous spouses, "walking in all the commandments of the Lord[21] suffered barrenness, which in those times was considered a punishment from God.

Zachariah doubted that this prediction would come true, and for his weakness of faith he was punished by becoming mute. When Elizabeth gave birth to a son, through the inspiration of the Holy Spirit she announced that his name was John, although no one in either family had this name.

Zachariah, was in the temple burning incense. Suddenly an angel appeared and announced that Elizabeth would at last conceive. She would give birth to a

---

[21]   Luke 1:16

son "filled with the Holy Spirit." The child would be named John, would have the spiritual gifts in the Old Testament prophet Elijah. As pious as Zachariah was, his natural reaction was disbelief. To have some proof, since common sense told him that Elizabeth was too old and she had been barren. She could only become pregnant by a miracle. The angel revealed himself as Gabriel saying as a sign against his lack of faith he would be struck dumb until his son was born.

Mary was unaware that this had happened.

When Elizabeth heard her cousin's greeting, the baby she was carrying leapt in her womb; and Elizabeth was filled with the Holy Spirit. She cried out as she ran to greet her.

"Blessed are thou among women, and blessed is the fruit of thy womb," she exclaimed! "Why are you here, Mary?"[22]

Mary responded, "My soul doth magnify the Lord and my spirit hath rejoiced in God my Savior. For He hath regarded the low estate of his handmaiden: for behold, from henceforth all generations shall call me blessed."[23]

"Elizabeth," Mary replied, "you are too kind in your welcome. When I heard that you were six months with child, I knew I had to be with you. Do you mind if I stay with you and Zachariah until you deliver your child?"

"Yes, of course you can stay. I can use your help. What about Joseph? Does he mind you staying with me?"

"No, he does not mind. Besides there's something I want to talk to you about."

Zachariah came into the room and embraced Mary saying nothing.

"Lord," Elizabeth said, "Mary will be staying with us during my pregnancy to help us out where she can."

Still Zachariah said nothing. He did however, smile at them both. He embraced Mary once again.

"Come Mary," Elizabeth said, "let us get you settled and we can talk at length. Zachariah has not spoken from the time we learned that I would have a child."

"How did this happen," Mary asked.

"We have been childless for many years, as you know. We prayed, and made offerings but nothing happened. One day an angel of the Lord appeared to him saying, "Fear not, your prayer is heard; and your wife will bear you a son, and thou shalt call his name John."

"I too had an angel of the Lord appear to me, but I will tell you of it when you are finished. Please go on."

"But Zachariah, asked the angel, how he should know this since he is an old man and I was well stricken in years. But the angel answered him saying, "I

---

22   Luke 1:42
23   Luke 1:42-48

am Gabriel and I stand in the presence of God; sent to speak to thee and show to thee these glad tidings. And behold thou shalt be dumb, or else not be able to speak until these things shall be performed."[24]

"He has not spoken since. But come, let us get you settled and you can tell me all that has happened."

When they had Mary settled, they went to the courtyard where they spoke.

Mary began. "Joseph is not the father of the child I am carrying."

Elizabeth's hand went to her mouth in shock and disbelief. "Mary," she stammered, "you have not been with another man have you?"

"No, of course not," she said indignantly!

"Then how can you to be the way you are, carrying a child?"

"Several days ago while I was making bread . . ."

Mary went on to tell her of the angel that appeared to her and telling her that she was to be the mother of the Son of God. "He said that his name was to be Jesus," Mary continued. "My soul doth magnify the Lord and my spirit rejoices in God my Savior, for he has been mindful of the humble state of his servant. From now on all generations will call me blessed for the Mighty has great things done to me-holy is his name."[25]

Elizabeth listened carefully before saying, "You are truly blessed. Does Joseph know about this?"

"No, I have not told him yet. I wanted to speak with you and Zachariah first seeking your wisdom and counsel."

"Zachariah has not spoken a word," Elizabeth said by way of explanation, "since we learned that I was to have a child. However, let us speak with him and you can tell him what you have just told me."

It was almost time for the evening meal. The two women set about preparing the food. When it was done, all ate in silence afterwards, Elizabeth told Zachariah that she had come seeking his counsel. Mary began. . .

Zachariah picked up a slate and upon it he wrote, "Deuteronomy."

"Are you referring," Mary asked, "to the passage about the unfaithful wife?"

Zachariah nodded his head. He picked up the slate to write, "He can't put you out of the house." Mary nodded.

"He can bring you before the synagogue and accuse you," Zachariah wrote, Mary nodded.

"He can divorce you quietly," he continued, Mary nodded.

Elizabeth spoke for the first time. "What you are telling us Lord is that Mary could be put to death or ostracized, or humiliated, or . . ."

---

[24]   Luke 1: 19-20

*   Luke 1:31 Jesus means "Yahweh is Salvation

[25]   Luke 1:46-49

"Joseph can understand what has taken place and agree to marry me," Mary filled in. The matter remained unresolved.

When Elizabeth was to deliver her child, she told Mary that instead of naming her son Zachariah, as custom dictated, she had been told by the angel his name was John.

Zachariah spoke for the first time affirming that his son would be named John.

"Blessed be the Lord God of Israel; for he hath visited and redeemed his people, and he raised up a horn of salvation for us in the house of his servant David; as he spake by the mouth of his holy prophets, - - - that we should be saved from our enemies, and from the hand of all that hate us; to perform the mercy promised to our fathers, and to remember his holy covenant; - - - and thou, child, shalt be called the prophet of the Highest: for thou shalt go before the face of the Lord to prepare his ways; to give knowledge of salvation unto his people by the remission of sins - - -[26]

---

[26] Zachariah's prophecy Luke 1:68

CHAPTER EIGHT

Adultery is any unfaithfulness to ones betrothed that constituted adultery. The same law stated that the betrothal to be as binding as a marriage, and could only be terminated by her betrothed giving her a certificate of divorce allowing her to marry someone else.

• •

COMING FROM THE synagogue, Asa Kahn asked if he might have a word with Joseph. They found a bench and sat. "Joseph," Asa began, "I am having a problem with erosion of my farm land up in the hill country. Every time there is a heavy rain, we spend the next several weeks putting the soil back. And that is time that can be spent to better uses."

"How can I be of help, Asa?"

"I would like you to build a retaining wall, about three feet high, covering 2400 cubits made of rocks, that are set in place."

"That could be quite expensive, Asa. First, the land would have to be surveyed and cleared, rocks would have to be gathered and brought to the site. Then they would have to be individually set in place, leveled, and secured. That would be time consuming."

"How much do you estimate it would cost? I can have my sons and farm hands gather and transport the rocks."

"That would help greatly. I would have to talk with my sons to give you an accurate estimate on costs. We will do the work as economically as we can. I can tell you now that the work will take at least three weeks to complete, but I will have that all worked out for you in a day or so. If acceptable, you can pay me at the end of each week, or in one lump sum, whatever is convenient for you"

"Thank you Joseph, I knew I could rely on you. We will speak again."

Several days later Joseph left his workshop to meet with and welcome Mary home from Hebron. Upon seeing her, now three months pregnant, he became immediately aware of her condition. He assisted her dismounting from the donkey and unpacking, then looking at her dumbstruck. He could say nothing, he mused pensively, until they could meet privately. In spite of that, when they were alone, he turned to her saying, "Mary, Mary thou art great with child! Why have you done this to me? We have not lain together as Lord and wife, and yet you are as you are. Have you been attacked by Roman soldiers? Have you been raped? Are you adulterous? Have I been a fool?"

"None of these," Mary replied. "I am a servant of the Lord. I had a vision..."

"Mary, Mary," Joseph cried out in bitter anguish. Mary stooped to pick up a stone, which she handed to Joseph. "Cast me out as the law requires," Mary sobbed.

Joseph tore himself away from her presence hurt, bewildered, and betrayed. Mary was pregnant! Conflict raged in his soul. She was also his espoused, yet he had to admit to her appearances. Had she been unfaithful? What other possible explanation could there be? Near his house, he fled into the woods. He had to think these things over. He sat against the tree, His head in his hands. Under the Law of Moses, he mused, Mary could be put to death, but he did not want her to be stoned to death; could not bear the thought of it! And, because he was a righteous man, he did not want her humiliated or shamed. He was, he thought, a just man, that is, a strict observer of the divine law which was his guidepost. He was tormented and quite confused on what the proper course of action should be. Questions came to mind. Could he, as a just man continue with the marriage to Mary when by all appearances she was guilty of a grave fault. If, on the other hand, he went to say that he was the father of the child, then he would be subject to punishment for laying with a woman not yet his wife.[27]

"Have I been betrayed," he asked himself once again? Through his loving eyes, he had expected the best from Mary. Now, what was he to do? He could put her away quietly, he thought. No, that was no solution! He threw himself across his bed in exhaustion and drenched the bed with his tears of sorrow. He cried himself to sleep that was at once fitful but then fell into a deep sleep wherein he became calm.

This internal conflict produced the opening through which God aims to elevate Joseph's human thought. The angel came to him in a dream not only to explain how Mary came to be with child but to offer Joseph a part in God's saving plan.

When he dreamt about these things, an angel of the Lord did appear to him in a dream saying,

"Joseph, thou son of David, fear not to take unto you Mary for your wife: for that which is conceived in her is of the Holy Spirit. And she shall bring forth

---

[27]   Leviticus 20:20

a son, and thou shalt call his name Jesus: for he shall save his people from their sins." [28]

Joseph had come to realize that the child Mary was carrying was conceived by the Holy Spirit: by the Lord God Himself! He was overwhelmed by the holiness of the situation, and the responsibility of being the foster father to God's child, Lord of His mother and yet, he felt so unworthy. He was being given the honor of being the foster parent of God's child, the Messiah! But in addition to that, he thought, what happiness would be his not only to see Jesus, his foster son, also to hear what he had to say, to speak with him, to carry him in his arms, to lead him from place to place, to embrace and caress him, to feed him, to direct him on the path of righteousness, and to be privy to all the great secrets which were concealed from the princes of this world. When he awoke he was still drenched with perspiration, but his mind was at ease. Oh, what bliss! What a joy! His agony was ended and he was at peace. Unto himself he said, "I delight to do your will, O God, your law is within my heart."[29]

In a dream the angel had told him what he must do; he would do it! It was as though he had no other choice. He could hardly wait to tell Mary of his decision. He found her in the kitchen once more grinding meal for bread. They looked at one another and when Joseph smiled, Mary did too. She knew everything would be alright. She ran to his open arms and they embraced.

"Mary," he began. She hugged herself fearing what he might say. "I had a dream wherein an angel spoke to me saying that I should not fear to marry you. I am the Lord's servant and I will take you unto my wife."

She ran to him and they embraced once again. Joseph whispered, "His will shall be done."

---

[28]   Matthew 1:19-21

[29]   Psalm 40:6-8

CHAPTER NINE

JOSEPH HAD ASKED his sons to meet with him in the courtyard of their house. He had laid out the work bench with parchment paper pinned to it. As they gathered there was a natural convergence around the table. They looked to Joseph for explanation. With a charcoal taken from the fireplace, he outlined a rectangle.

"This will be a working draft of Asa Kahn's field," he began. "Let me begin at the beginning. Asa Kahn has asked that we build a retaining wall for him to halt the erosion of his southern fields. He is experiencing a major problem every time it rains. He must replace the lost soil and lost crops every time. He would like us to build a permanent wall that will eliminate that problem."

Judas, the practical son asked, "How long a wall does he want and how high?"

"That is why we are here," Joseph said, "To discuss those items and there relevant costs."

"We need to discuss a lot more than that," Simon added.

"What more do we need to talk about?" Joseph wanted his sons to be fully aware of the undertaking, and Simon's statement opened the way.

James began, "How long is the wall going to be?" He took the charcoal from his father to make a notation on the parchment of the length.

"He said he wanted it 2400 cubit in length and three feet high," Joseph said; James made the notation.

"That is about 3600 feet," Justus noted! "That would take tons of rocks. Where will they come from? If and when we find that many rocks, how will they be brought to the site?"

"Now you know why I asked you to take part in this project. James, since you started as note taker continue, when we have a listing of everything we will need, we can put a time line and price to the project.

Justus spoke up. "Our first task will be to have Asa have his people put the soil back where it came from. A second task will be to find a quarry or a location with enough stone for our needs. Once we locate them, our third task will be to transport them."

James wrote quickly.

We cannot carry them by hand," Justus continued.

"No," Judas interrupted, "we have to get drays and horses to pull them, at least two for each dray."

"Have you forgotten," James offered, "plum lines, levels, shovels, mortar...?

"List everything James," Joseph urged.

When they had finished, Joseph added, "Asa tells me he will provide what manual labor we need, or at least some of it. That will cut into expenses. My calculations tell me that the work will take at least three days, once we have the materials on site. Add another two days for that and three of us on the job each day. The others, when not working on the wall, will run this shop. Let us put a reasonable estimate together and I will give it to Asa for his approval."

James interrupted. "Father, you and Mary will wed in a week's time. How will we work that out as well?"

"Good point James. Tomorrow is the Sabbath and I will speak with Asa afterward. If he agrees we can make our schedule accordingly. It was never my intention to work every day on the wall with you. You have been trained all your lives to do this job. Judas, as the eldest you will help me with the wedding when you are needed.

We have our supply list, our work schedule and our estimate contingent on expenses. You all have done yourselves proud putting this together."

Asa and Joseph spoke together and it was agreed that four field hands would assist in stockpiling material, expenses would be determined and agreed to, and work begun on the third day.

When the Sabbath ended, work on Asa's wall began.

On the day of their wedding, friends of Joseph went out at night to bring Mary and her attendants to Joseph's home. Although it was a time of great joy, Mary, as tradition directed, sang songs of lamentation. This part of the ceremony was done at night to allow for a more spectacular display of lights and torches. Together they moved on to the synagogue where Joseph blessed her seven times saying, "Behold, you are made holy for me according to the religion of Moses and Israel."

Joseph and Mary were clad in festive wedding garb standing before the High Priest in the synagogue. They met at the foot of the altar in preparation for the ceremony. Unknown to the priest the woman standing before him was carrying the *Lamb of God*. On either side of the couple attendants knelt, holding large candles further illuminating the ceremony.

Off to one side Joachim and Anne were nervous and excited about their daughter Mary marrying Joseph. Their years of searching for the right man to be the Lord of Mary had been brought to fruition. They milled about the gathering, smiling broadly and Joachim shaking hands with anyone who would allow him to do so.

In Joseph's mind, his marriage to Mary, was more than merely taking a wife, it was to be his second act of obedience to his Lord concerning his bride-to-be; an act of protection to Mary and for her unborn child. That which was going to happen, filled him with fear, awe and unknowing. He has accepted the mantle given him but how does one nurture the Messiah, how does one teach Him who is all-knowing, how does he adjust his life style to merge with Mary's, how should he care for her, how . . . They went on and on.

Rabbi Lowe concluded the wedding ceremony, Joseph declared: "Mary is my wife and I her Lord." In so doing, Joseph accepted that they were legally and spiritually bound together forever before witnesses.

With the ceremony over, Lord and wife were escorted to Joseph's home. He had ordered a banquet to be prepared and they joined with the wedding party in celebration. Joseph's righteousness to bring this all about had nothing to do with the law or the pursuit of justice. Instead, it allowed Joseph to demonstrate his compassion and mercy. When God chose to find the father of his Divine Son in Bethlehem, not only was the prophecy fulfilled that the Messiah would come into the house of David in the town of Bethlehem, it also showed that He chose the humble, hard-working and meek people to accomplish His work.

Joseph was saying, "Today we have accomplished *Kiddushin* and *Nissuin* as required by law which means Mary, you and I are Lord and wife."

"I do not understand those terms that you used. Please explain them to me."

"I keep forgetting that you are still young, but anytime you have questions please do not hesitate to ask me. Those terms are not the most frequently used except during feasts and celebration. *Kiddushin* means the sanctification that is to set apart as holy, all betrothal and *Nissuin* was our wedding feast. You and I are legally married as well as being blessed by the Lord God Jehovah.

"No one will make accusations against us. The rabbi had no idea you were with child. Only you and I will know."

"Husband, are you forgetting my parents know that I am with child along with my cousin Anne and her husband, Zachariah?"

"That knowledge does not matter. We have married as everyone wanted us to be. And all of our wedding rituals have eliminated any question about your purity. What we must now do is to make preparations that are called for, and do what must be done for the child you are carrying. I am with you Mary, and the child, and I will be forever. You are the tabernacle of the Lord and I will always respect your chastity. I give thanks to the Lord, the Most High God for favoring me to be your Lord. He has shown his mercy to me, and I hope and pray that will help me in serving Him, you and the child."

Mary responded by saying, "You are my Lord and I shall be your wife. I am fortunate that the Most High has chosen me as to serve you. Let us give thanks to Our Lord for He is good."

Later that night when all of the celebrants had left, Mary and Joseph discussed all of the things that had taken place, and how their lives have been changed. They sat before a small fire sipping wine and basking in the memory of the celebration.

"Our lives, blessed virgin, have gone and will continue to undergo enormous changes. I will respect your chastity. I give thanks to the Lord, the Most High God for favoring me to be thy husband. He hath shown His mercy to me and I hope and pray that will help me in serving Him, you and the child."

Mary responded by saying: "I am fortunate that the Most High God has chosen me to serve thee. Let us give thanks to the Lord for He is good!"

CHAPTER TEN

JOSEPH AND MARY went about their household duties, he was busy completing the temple doors, and Mary, now living with Joseph, was busy keeping his house, obtaining water from the well and preparing their meals. With each passing week Mary grew in girth, her feet swelled, her nipples enlarged, her steps became slower and more labored. She was frequently ill and her back was causing pain. Now and again she felt the babe kicking and moving. Her time for delivery was close at hand.

Both Joseph and Mary had experienced dreams and angelic appearances. One night after the meal, they decided to speak of them.

Seated in the patio at the back of the house they looked toward the heavens still trying to absorb everything that had taken place. They had not spoken of it at length, but tonight beneath the stars and the moonlight they decided it was time.

"The vision that I had," Mary was saying as they sat in their courtyard, "was a ghostly figure; a specter without form. Suddenly the room was filled with a bright light, there was a form of the man who was and was not. His voice however, was calm and soothing. I was unafraid. I felt that what the specter was saying had to be believed. He called me by name. 'Hail Mary full of grace,' the voice said, 'the Lord is with you.' I was then told what was about to take place. I knew in my heart it was true. What was your vision like Joseph?"

"Much the same as yours Mary, except it was more like a dream. It was, I believe, an angel who was speaking to me, and like your angel, he had to be believed. I was upset and distraught before that, but it immediately ended. I knew what I had to do, and the future was clear.

I found it difficult to believe, at first, that you were with child and that child was the Messiah and although it was difficult, I'm sure it is true and that you are blessed. All work from now on has been ordained and you must be dedicated in raising this precious child. Just think, you will be able to nurse our child.

We will be able to hold him in our arms, and be with us as we watch him as he grows. What a blessing!"

"As I have been thinking about it, I can understand why you were chosen to be the mother of the Messiah. Where after all, temple raised, the child of very pious parents and I do not believe that sin has ever fallen your way. Piety and a devout way of life have been your calling."

"Now, when I tried to fathom why our Gracious Lord has selected a lowly carpenter, a rough, gruff laborer, the mantel does not seem to fit. Surely there is a more suitable, humble man for the role. I do not understand His choice for a foster parent."

"Perhaps husband, our dear Lord did not want to select from the high and powerful, but from ordinary people as you and I certainly are."

"You are wiser than I have given you credit for," Joseph observed.

The very next day their daily life had returned to normal. However it was disrupted and interrupted by a decree issued by the Emperor Caesar Augustus[30] and was being posted throughout Judea. Three Roman soldiers rode into the town square and one read from a parchment before nailing it on a tree...

> "Hear ye, hear ye! The ruler of the Roman Empire, Caesar Augustus, orders all male subject people of Palestine to return to the place of their family origin for census and assessment of taxation!"

This decree required that everyone return to their ancestral home and be registered. This decree would place a burden on the newlyweds because Joseph's ancestral home was in Nazareth 111 kilometers distant, and he must return there.

Gently, when it was time to leave, Joseph placed Mary on the donkey, saw to her comfort and warmth. Mary smiled at him saying, "Be not concerned Joseph. I have seen to our foodstuffs and have packaged them. I have some fish and bread, beans, lentils cucumbers and onions, and some garlic. I have also included dates, figs and honey, as well as the sweetened wine you like."

"You have done well Mary. Although this journey may be hard we certainly will not want for food."

"My time is near Joseph and the road is rough and uncertain. Do you think there will be enough time?"

"It will be an arduous journey Mary and I will make you as comfortable as possible. I only pray the Lord gives us enough time to get you there safely."

---

[30]   Luke 2:1 "And it came to pass that a decree went out from Caesar Augustus, that all of the world should be taxed, each to his own city." This accomplished two things, a census was taken and money raised.

Soon people were on the roads coming in every direction. Joseph and Mary would be heading south to Bethlehem since both of them were from House of David. The journey would take them three days through Samaria and over the rugged Judean hills to Jerusalem and then onward to Bethlehem. Some of their fellow travelers went into cities along the way, while others joined them.

That first night they were fortunate to find a Shepherd's cave. Joseph quickly prepared bedding for Mary, tethered and fed the donkey, and built a small fire to keep them warm. As Mary prepare the meal, consisting of bread and fruit, Joseph set about gathering firewood.

The following night, they were fortunate to find a small escarpment coated with bushes and shrubs. Joseph made a shelter of his cloak and tree branches, he made Mary comfortable and once again built a fire. The nights were bitter cold causing the donkey to lie down so that they might take advantage of his body heat. The animal seemed to sense what was being expected of her. When, at last, they reached Bethlehem, the city was overcrowded with people. Only available rooms had been filled by people who had come to register.

After dusk they arrived at the outskirts of Bethlehem. They entered at one of the caravansary's enclosures. It was a rectangular structure, walled in with stone and sun-dried brick to keep out the brigands. At the center was the source of water, a deep cool well, and palm trees.

A kindly innkeeper noticing Mary was in an advanced stage of her pregnancy, offered them a room in the hills that was also a stable used by shepherds.

"You will find," he said, "it is little more than a cave, but it is warm, clean, and well stocked with feed, and there is water available. The shepherds keep it well stocked with firewood. You can stay there."

"Thank you, you are most kind," Joseph said. Joseph was pleased with these arrangements since it took them away from the bleating of animals and the stench of their droppings.

The innkeeper gave him directions and then left. Joseph found the cave and found it to be a stable just as described. Joseph assisted Mary from the donkey, made her a pallet of straw, and made her as comfortable as he could. He went about finding fire wood. There were several niches in the stone wall and a blazing fire immediately heated the cave. He tethered the donkey close to some feed, and to keep her clear of Mary. Then he turned his attention to Mary and her comfort. Then he placed their foodstuffs in the niches.

Their spirits went soaring, knowing what the angel had told them, knowing that the time was near for Mary to give birth to God's son, and knowing also, they were taking part in God's plan to save mankind from sin. They had trusted God and He had provided for them.

An experienced midwife was called, at the request of the innkeeper to help Mary through her labor. Joseph went out and found two large stones. He broke up some straw, covered that with a cloak, set the stones about ten inches apart on either side of a small pallet. Not long afterward labor pains began. Joseph went to get some water from a nearby well to cool Mary as she labored, and for cleaning up afterward. As Mary began delivering her child she was squatting on the stones. The donkey wandered into the cave, a curious onlooker. Suddenly there was a cry of anguish and pain as Mary delivered their son. The cord was tied and cut by the midwife, she bathed the child to avoid infection, and rubbed his body down with salt, after which Joseph took the infant and returned him to Mary who wrapped him in swaddling clothes then allowed him to suckle.[31] As the infant ate, Joseph covered them both with his cloak after which he built up the fire to keep mother and child warm, then he cleaned the stable. He had just about finished when he turned and found mother and child nestled together, both of them sound asleep. He knelt and gave thanks to his God for delivering them both safely. He also praised God for giving him wisdom to listen to his Lord and do what was asked of him. Before anyone was allowed to see Mary and the infant Jesus, this time together and alone allowed the Holy Family to experience a newfound intimacy in that Mary's full attention was toward the child and Joseph joined with them in this precious moment of intimacy.

And so it came to pass that Jesus was born in Bethlehem, even though his parents' home was in Nazareth. This fulfilled the prophecy of his birth, "But thou, Bethlehem Ephratah, though thou be little among the thousands of Judah, yet out of you shall he come forth unto me that is to be ruler in Israel; whose goings forth have been from of old, from everlasting."[32]

---

[31] Luke 2:7 Swaddling clothes were bandage-like strips of cloth wrapped around an infant to ensure that the limbs would grow straight. This wrapping would allow the shepherds in identifying Jesus.

[32] Micah 5:2

CHAPTER ELEVEN

"AND THERE WERE, in the same country shepherds abiding in the field, keeping watch over their flock by night. And, lo, the angel of the Lord is upon, and the glory of the Lord shone about them: and they were sore afraid."

And the angel said unto them, "Fear not: for, behold, I bring you good tidings of great joy, which shall be to all people. For unto you is born this day in the city of David a Savior, which is Christ the Lord. And shall be a sign unto you; ye shall find the babe wrapped in swaddling clothes lying in a manger."[33]

And suddenly there was with the angel a multitude of the hosts praising God, and saying, "Glory to God in the highest, and on earth peace, good will toward men."

And it came to pass, as the Angels had gone away from them into heaven, the shepherds said to one another, let us now go into Bethlehem and see this thing which is come to pass, which the Lord hath made known to us. And they came with haste, and found Mary and Joseph, and Jesus lying in a manger.

This constellation of the Messiah moved to these astrologers such that they had to follow and see the fulfillment with their own eyes. And when they succeeded, they made known abroad the saying which has told them, concerning the child. And all that heard it wondered at those things which were told them of the shepherds. And the shepherds returned to their flocks, glorifying and praising God for all things they heard and seen and as he was told to them.[34]

With the arrival of the shepherds at the manger; after they bowed before Him and had paid homage to the infant Jesus, as he lay quietly in the hay. They spoke with his parents.

---

[33] Luke 2:8-16
[34] Luke 8:8-20

NOTE: The announcement of Jesus' birth to the shepherds was in keeping with Luke's theme that only the lowly are to be singled out as recipients of God's favors and blessings.

"You are wondering why we have come here" Eleazer said.

"Yes we were," replied Joseph. "It is not every day that shepherds come in from the fields to pay homage to an infant."

Mary looked at the shepherds in amazement. "Why have you men come," Mary asked. "And why have you knelt before Him, praising Him as you have?"

The oldest of the shepherds, Elijah by name, a wizened, white bearded old man said, "An angel of the Lord appeared to us while we were tending our flocks, and told us the news and an angelic choir sang praise to God."

"I am the leader of this group and they have given me the honor of speaking for them. It has been prophesized that the Messiah would come, and there would be signs indicating where he would be. While we were in the fields, a bright star appeared telling us that what had been prophesized. We followed a very bright star until it led us to you and your child."

"Know you this," Joseph was saying, "your quest has been satisfied. We have not seen a bright star instead we were visited in dreams that my wife, Mary, was to give birth to the Messiah, where the birth would take place and what he should be called."

"We heard a voice proclaiming His birth, Christ the Lord. It must have been the angel you had in your dreams. May we give Him all praise and honor?"

Joseph turned aside, extended his right arm pointed toward the manger and its divine occupant.

The shepherds left them and made camp nearby, allowing the sheep to graze and they could continue watching over their new born Messiah and sing his praise.

Joseph and Mary felt quite strange having these men come to worship their son. They were uncertain about how they should act.

When it was time for the shepherds to leave, they paid homage then went about through the streets of Nazareth telling anyone and everyone in the city of the coming of the Messiah and giving Him praise.

"Husband," Mary said quietly, "Joachim sent me off to sleep each night with a story. Could you do the same?"

"I know no bedtime stories. What I know are tales my father passed down to me. No, wait, I remember one but it is for little children. Would you like to hear it?"

"Yes, please Joseph."

"Now the light has gone away; Blessed Lord, listen while we pray. Asking Thee to watch and keep and to send us quietly to sleep."

"Praise be the Lord! Thank you, Joseph," Mary said with heavy drowsy lids.

CHAPTER TWELVE

WHILE THEY WERE yet in Bethlehem, and eight days had passed, the proud parents reentered the City of Jerusalem. In spite of the fact that Joseph and Mary were the parent and foster parent of the Messiah, their deep-rooted beliefs compelled them to follow the dictates of the Law of Moses. They went immediately to Jerusalem, and the temple, to have their son circumcised; the time for *brit milah* had come. It was just past midday when they arrived.

Mary, with the infant Jesus in her arms and Joseph at her side. In compliance with the law, she had walked the last several miles carrying the infant, symbolically giving Him to the temple. The three of them waited at the temple gate. As they waited, they purchased two pigeons as an offering, not a sin offering but one in compliance with the Law of Moses.[35]

The temple itself, an immense structure of cream-colored limestone was adorned with marble colonnades, golden gates, and multicolored hangings. The temple was swarming with hundreds of paid priests, sacrificers, musicians and treasurers.

Joseph and Mary had taken the option provided for the poor people, that is those that cannot afford lamb, sacrificed a pair of pigeons. Within the temple designated *kvatters,* male and female, serving as messengers, bring Jesus from Mary's arms to the location where the *brit* ceremony will be performed. When the High Priest, Simeon joined them at the site, he was dressed in a black and white robe, a yarmulke on his head and covered by a hood. Mary handed him the child who then bade them enter. They went to the temple courts where they were met by Anna, the prophetess, joined them. Simeon had received into his arms the object of all his desires and sighs.

He held the infant aloft saying, "Lord, lettest thy servant depart in peace, according to thy word, you may let your servant go in peace according to thy word, for mine eyes have seen thy salvation, which thou hath prepared before

---

[35]   Leviticus 12, Exodus 13:12-15

the face of all people, a light to the Gentiles, and the glory of your people Israel."[36]

Joseph and Mary begin to hear the startling prophesy that Jesus' significance will extend to all the Gentiles. Then Simeon blessed them and said to Mary: "This child is destined to cause the fall and rising again of many in Israel; and for a sign which will be spoken against; (Yea, so that the thought of many hearts will be revealed. Yea a sword will pierce through your own soul, so that the thoughts from many hearts may be revealed."[37]

The elderly prophetess Anna, the daughter Phanuel of the Tribe of Asher was also in the temple and offered prayers and praise to God for Jesus, and spoke to everyone about Jesus and his role in the redemption of Israel.[38]

The ceremony of the circumcision was practiced according to the "Mohel" in Joseph's presence.

The infant Jesus, who had been conceived by the Holy Ghost, and Mary who had remained a chasted virgin, did not fall under the law, but no one else knew of this. Therefore, Mary submitted the humbling experience with devotion and seals to God her part in the law. There followed a benediction, then came the circumcision and that was followed by a celebratory meal.

On their return trip to Bethlehem, Joseph and Mary spoke of the revelations of Simeon. They were overcome with wonder and awe at what he had predicted.

"Is there anything that we should be doing for our baby?" Joseph asked. "As you have told me, and you were told by the angel, the baby you were carrying is the Messiah! Perhaps Simeon could have advised us."

Mary gave it some thought as she placed her hands to her abdomen. "No, let us do what we have been doing. The Lord, our God will provide and give us guidance caring for his son."

They Holy Family felt as though they were not the same newly wedded couple that had set out on this journey.

Commentary

Did Mary come to the temple to be purified? Was she not already pure? Had her son defiled her in His most wondrous birth? No, certainly He did not! In being born of the virgin, Jesus did not harm to her virginal integrity, but rather consecrated it. Mary had no need for purification but she humbles herself to follow the precepts of the Law.

NOTE:

Mohel, a person who performs ritual Jewish circumcisions. For Jews, male circumcision is mandatory, as it is prescribed in the Torah. In the book of Genesis, the mark of the

---

36   Luke 2:29-31

37   Luke 2:34

38   Luke 2:38

Covenant between God and the descendents of Abraham. Throughout all generations, every child, come circumcised when he is eight days of old... This shall be my covenant in your flesh, an eternal covenant. The uncircumcised male whose foreskin has not been circumcised, shall have his soul cut out from his people: is broken my covenant."

CHAPTER THIRTEEN

HEROD THE GREAT, the tetrarch of Galilee, held the throne in Judea, was born about 74BC in Idumea or Edom, to a Nabatean woman and his father was an Idumean, in the region south of Judea originally inhabited by the reputed descendents of Jacob's brother Esau. He was a member of the Roman Army. He practiced Judaism and adopted their customs. He gained notoriety is his rise to power by being made the Governor of Galilee, a posting given him by his father Antipater.

He demonstrated his brutality by ruthlessly crushing a revolt in Galilee by killing many of its citizens. He initially ruled four provinces: Juda, Galilee, Peraea, and Idumaea. In 36BC, he with his Roman legions, captured Jerusalem whereupon he took the title of Basileus or king for himself. One of his first tyrannical acts was to execute several members of his family, including his wife Miriamme - the granddaughter of Hyrcanus II, an Hasmonean princess whom he had loved greatly. With her they had two daughters and three sons. The youngest was sent to Rome to be educated but died there. His brothers were treated as royalty once their father declared himself Basileus. However, the problem was that Miriamme detested Herod as much as he loved her, primarily because of what he had done to her brother, Aristobulus. Herod appointed Aristobulus to the position of High Priest at the age of seventeen years. He then watched in his paranoia and with trepidation as the youth became quite popular. This should have been understandable since he had a legitimate right to the position he held as High Priest - a bona fide Jew and a genuine Cohen - Jewish priest. Overpowered by his paranoid feeling of threat to his rule, he had his son drowned to put his mind at ease. Miriamme who had helped him legitimize his position through her family position, was put to death at the instigation of his sister Salome, and Mariamne's mother, Alexandra. Herod had her put to death charging her with conspiring to have him assassinated. Later, he also executed her other son Alexander. Contrarily Herod was well known for spending lavish sums of money on numerous building projects and extravagant gifts to Rome.

Among the better known buildings he had constructed was temple Mount and a harbor in Caeserea.

However, in order to complete these many projects, he used the Hasmonean model of taxation in that he employed professional tax collectors rather than using the aristocracy that had been empowered to collect taxes under the Seleucids and Hasmoneans. This disempowerment of the aristocracy probably led to a great deal of resentment of Herod. He relentlessly had built a remarkable chain of cities, palaces and fortresses, replete with dungeons, huge cisterns and aqueducts. The fortress at Masada was built on the top of a rock plateau in the desert. It had an incredible water supply system that fed gardens for growing agriculture staples and three bath houses; the port city of Caesarea, was a supreme achievement. It became a center of trade and the Roman administrative capital of Judea;

Twelve kilometers south-east of Jerusalem, Herod had built a sumptuous palace within a circular fort calling it Herodium. Among his other building achievements, he rebuilt the temple Mount, an edifice that was supposed to stand as the center of all national life - a governmental, judicial and religious structure. It was significant to the Jews in that the first temple was supposed to have been built by Solomon the son of David. The second was destroyed by the Roman Empire. The third, and the one he had built was considered the holiest site in Jerusalem and the place where Jews turn toward during prayer. He had it covered with gold; the walls and columns of the other buildings were white marble; the floors were covered with Carrara marble, its blue tinge giving the impression of moving water; the curtains and tapestries of blue, white, scarlet and purple thread. Herod finished it off by placing at the main entrance an enormously large Roman eagle, it was sacrilegious to pious Jews. It was supposed to demonstrate the unity between Rome and the Jewish people. When completed a group of Torah students smashed the emblem of idolatry and oppression. They were hunted down, dragged in chains to Herod's residence in Jericho, where they were burned alive. Although he claimed Judaism as his choice of faith he showed an insensitivity to the Jewish laws in that he introduced foreign forms of entertainment and had a golden eagle erected at the entrance of the temple indicating that he represented not only the Jewish people but the Roman Empire as well. Two major Jewish sects developed during his reign, the Pharisees and the Sadducees who demonstrated their opposition to Herod. Pharisees were angry because of his disregard for the demands they had made for the construction. Additionally, the Sadducees, known for their priestly responsibilities in the temple, opposed Herod's replacing high priests from Babylonia and Alexandria in his attempt to gain support from Jews in the despora, the historical exile and from the region of the Kingdom of Judah and

Roman Judaea and what further infuriated the Jews was his tyrannical authority demonstrated by a number of his security measures aimed at suppressing Jewish contempt toward him. Specifically, it was widely believed that he used secret police to monitor and report the feelings of the people towards him. Many of those that did express negative sentiments against him, were taken away by force. As the years went by the King became more and more powerful and at the same time paranoid. It was not surprising that Herod was not a beloved ruler but a feared one.

CHAPTER FOURTEEN

THREE WISE MEN, Melchior who had long white hair and beard and wearing a golden cloak, is the king of Arabia, Gaspar had brown hair and beard wore a golden crown with green jewels on it, was the king of Sheba and Balthazar, had black skin, no beard and wore a purple cloak, was the king of Tarse and Egypt. Each was a King in their native lands, and among the priestly caste of Persians.

They were considered experts in the study of astronomy. They were also educated in the prophecies of the coming of the Messiah. In their study of the heavens they saw a star that outshone all of the others. Immediately they knew that this was the sign that had been predicted and the one they had been waiting for so long. Together with their entourages, they began following the star knowing full well where it would lead them, to the Christ born King of the Jews. They traveled westward in their quest until they came to the city of Jerusalem, the royal capital, whereupon they sought out Herod, the most likely place to find the King was in the palace.

When they entered the city of Jerusalem they took immediate notice of the temple and the king's palace. It was in the palace, they were certain they would find the Messiah. A Centurion guard directed them to the court of the Gentiles where they dismounted. The building ahead of them, they observed, had been built on an elevation and the palace itself, they estimated, was at least 1000 feet long running north and south, and 180 feet east and west. They were admitted through the city gate in front of the two main buildings, in the center of which were gardens, porticos, groves, canals, and ponds fitted with bronze fountains.

They dismounted and were immediately surrounded by praetorian guards who asked the reason for their visit. They informed the Captain of the guard their reason for their being there, a quest to find the Messiah. The Captain took them into the palace.

Asa, the King's advisor, was talking with Herod in the throne room telling the King about a group of shepherds who had seen the star that was forecasting the coming of the Messiah.

As the Magi walked through the palace they noticed that the hallways had a distinctive style of stone dressing that featured *meleke* limestone. The interior had inlaid mosaics, pillars, winged lions made of gold and golden statuary. Their overall impression was massive, impressive and expensive.

In the throne room, Herod sat elevated over his subjects and visitors. The thrown itself was draped with purple damask and gold. The inlaid floor consisted of mosaics depicting many of the king's building accomplishments.

Herod had asked his advisor to move closer. "Tell me about the shepherds, what do they have to say, what is this about a so-called Messiah?"

"Well, Majesty, it seems that the shepherds were going about in Bethlehem speaking of a miraculous star they had seen. It seems they were in the hills tending the sheep when someone, they claimed was an angel, told them that the Messiah had been born."

"Was it about a child?" Herod wanted to know? "A newborn infant that is to be the Messiah, a usurper to my throne?"

"They were saying Majesty that this child was to become the King of the Jews."

"What!" Herod had exploded?

Trying to soothe his King, Asa said calmly, "Surely you do not believe that any child born of poor parents, could become the King of Jerusalem."

Herod sat back, his fingers tented and in a calm voice he said, "King David was a shepherd boy and he became king."

"Do not trouble yourself Majesty. This is mere gossip."

As this exchange was taking place, three men in the courtyard, regally dressed entered the palace bearing gifts. They were accompanied by their entourage. The Captain of the Centurion guards went before the King. When he entered the throne room he made himself prostrate before the King. "Majesty," he proclaimed, "three Kings from foreign lands have entered the temple grounds. They are waiting outside under guard. Do you wish to see them?"

"Three Kings you say. How were you able to tell?"

"They came into the court of the Gentiles on camel back. They were accompanied by an entourage of servants, who were also regally dressed."

"Bring them before me."

The Captain stood, struck his breast plate with a closed fist, turned and left. A short time later he ushered in the three Kings. They stood before the King.

"What brings you kings from foreign lands to our palace? What brings you to Jerusalem," he asked?

Balthazar stepped forward and saying, "We came here following the star," he explained.

"Where is the child who has been born King of the Jews," asked Gaspar another of the Magi? "We have seen this star at its rising and have come to pay homage."

King Herod, ever paranoid about a usurper and his being overthrown, became frightened. Ever the diplomat however, he had the Kings made comfortable. He told them to dine while he made some inquiries. He summoned together his chief priests, advisors and scribes.

Herod left his throne and entered a side room. Without being told, the priests and scribes followed.

Herod asked these religious leaders of Israel where the Christ was to be born. They quoted Micah's prophesy,[39] given 700 years before, naming Bethlehem as the place from which the "Ruler of Israel" was to come.

Herod returned to the throne room and when seated he said: "I have met with three Kings from Persia," he began they have asked me where the child was born that is to be the King of the Jews." He turned to his counsels asking, "Could such a thing be governor. Rule my people Israel?"[40]

Asa told him once again of the prophesy: "And thou Bethlehem - - - out of thee shall come a Governor, that shall rule my people Israel."

After he learned what the priests and scribes had to say, Herod summoned the Magi back before him.

"What was the exact time the star appeared?"

When they told him, he beseeched them to go to Bethlehem and conduct a diligent search for the young child. "When you have found him, bring me word again that I may come and worship him also."[41]

As the Magi were leaving the Palace grounds, they saw the star still shining brightly. The three wise men gathered their belongings, before leaving. They marveled at the splendor before them.

Balthazar asked his companions, "Is it your opinion that this King Herod intends to pay homage to the Messiah? I think not!" The others agreed and they continued on the journey to Bethlehem and the Messiah following the star.

---

[39]   Micah 5:2
[40]   Matthew 2:6
[41]   Matthew 2:6

CHAPTER FIFTEEN

WHEN THE MAGI came to the house wherein the star had led them, Joseph and Mary were astonished at the sight of royalty. The Magi dismounted from their camels to be before the Messiah and present him with the gifts they had brought, their gifts of acceptance; gold as a sign of acceptance, frankincense as a sign accepting him as high priest, and myrrh accepting him as the Messiah.

If there had been any lingering doubts, Joseph and Mary might have had about the majesty of their child, at the sight Magi paying homage to the child, they no longer had any misgiving; their infant Jesus was the Messiah, the visit of the Magi made it abundantly clear.

The Magi made camp while their entourage prepared the evening meal. They asked Joseph and Mary to break bread with them. The eunuchs spread a blanket beside the fire, placed a large bowl of food in the center, and all sat around the bowl dipping their hands. A sweet wine mixed with water was served with the meal and when it was finished eunuchs provided warm moist towels to wash their hands and face. With the meal ended, the Magi spoke to them about Herod and how he had frightened them while seeking to find news of their son.

"From whence have you come," Mary inquired?

Balthazar responded, "We have come from Persia, a far off land. We three kings are also astronomers, and it is because of that we saw the star and followed it here to our Messiah."

"You say that you have been to see King Herod," Joseph said. "How did he receive your news?"

"He presented a smiling face, but in my opinion he was almost fanatical," Melchior was saying. "His eyes looked fierce when he asked us to bring him news. For myself, I was frightened by his intensity."

The others agreed.

When it was time for the Magi to leave, Gaspar told the Holy Family once again how upset Herod appeared to be at hearing of the child's birth and they warned them to be careful. "He had the look of a man possessed," Gaspar said, "rather than an interested regent. You would be well advised to avoid contact with him if possible."

Then, prior to their leaving to return to their homes, an angel of the Lord appeared to them saying: "Do not return to Herod. They departed into their own country by another way."[42]

After several days, the shepherds and Magi packed their camels, gathered their sheep and said goodbye to Joseph, Mary and their child. Joseph and Mary watched as the Magi made their way east toward the Mediterranean Sea and the caravan routes, also going toward the Jordan River such as to avoid Jerusalem and Jericho.

"Joseph," Mary asked aloud, "do you believe in their dreams?"

"We have both had dreams, Mary. I see no reason why Persians or princes, or even kings could not have dreams as well. In answer to your question, however, yes I believe they had a dream and that is why they are taking another route home other than the one they followed coming here. They should be wary lest the King had them followed. If such an event were to happen, the King might have them slain."

Joseph and Mary, speaking about the recent events, were astonished at what had taken place. They believed that the Lord had once again sent a guardian angel to watch over them. That night they knelt in prayer of thanksgiving.

"Lord God Jehovah you have placed your son in our care. You have given us your wisdom and guidance in these very difficult times. All praise and honor be yours."

As they prepared for bed, Mary said, "Your children have told me that you are a well known story teller. Is that true?"

"When they were small, I told them a story every night to give them pleasant dreams."

"May I have one of your stories tonight?"

"Tonight I will tell you about King Solomon, the richest and wisest man who ever lived. He came from the house of David..."

"Just as you come from the House of David.," Mary interrupted?

"Yes, but almost a thousand years ago. His parents were King David and Queen Bathsheba. Their first child was Solomon.

"Now, King David had three other sons from a previous family, Adonijah, Ammon, and Absalom. As the years went by, Ammon and Absalom leaving Adonijah as the heir apparent to King David's throne at his passing.

"King David continued in his reign and while he held the throne, Adonijah began taking steps to have himself declared king. He prepared him chariots and horsemen, and fifty men to run before him."

---

[42]   Matthew 2:12

"Even before his father was departed," Mary questioned?

"In those days, I would imagine, that was how things were done. However, Bathsheba found out about this and together with the prophet Nathan convinced King David to proclaim Solomon as king. It seems that King David had promised Bathsheba that Solomon would resign after him. He kept his word. When this proclamation was made, Adonijah fled and took refuge at the altar. As a result, he received a pardon for his conduct from Solomon with one condition he had to prove himself as a worthy man, there shall not a hair on him fall to earth."[43]

"Solomon loved the Lord and walked in the statutes of David offering burnt incense in high places. Well, one day he went to Gibeon, a high place to make a thousand burnt offerings. The Lord appeared to Solomon in a dream saying, "Ask what I shall give thee."

"Solomon replied, "Thou has shewed unto thy servant David my father great mercy as he walked before thee in truth, and in righteousness and in unrighteousness of heart to thee. Thou hast given him a son to sit on his throne.

"Now, O Lord my God, You have made Your servant king instead of my father, but I am a little child; I do not know how to go out and come in. Therefore give Your servant an understanding heart to judge Your people, that I might discern between good and evil, Solomon's speech pleased the Lord then He said to him, "Behold, since you have not asked for great wealth or a long life, nor the death of your enemies, I have done according to your words given you a wise and understanding heart so that there has not been anyone before you, nor anyone after you. And I have given you what you did not ask; both riches and honor. So if you walk in My ways, to keep My statutes then I shall lengthen your days."[44]

"And that Mary, is how Solomon got his great wisdom and wealth. How he put them to use is for another night. And so to bed.

---

[43] 1 Kings 1:5-52

[44] 1 Kings 3:3-14

CHAPTER SIXTEEN

"And when the days of her purification according to the Lord Moses were accomplished, they brought *him* to Jerusalem to be presented to the Lord; and to offer a sacrifice according to that which is said in the law of the Lord. . ."[45]

● ●

ACCORDING TO JEWISH law, handed down by Moses, and the Lord spake unto Moses saying, "the children of Israel saying, if a woman has conceived seed, and born a male child: she shall be clean; according to the days of the separation for her infirmity shall she be unclean. And in the eighth day of flesh of his foreskin shall be circumcised. And she shall then continue in the blood of her purifying three and thirty days; she shall touch the hallowed thing, nor come into the sanctuary, to the days of her purifying be fulfilled.

But if she bear a maid child, then she shall be unclean two weeks, as in a separation: and she shall continue in the blood of her purifying threescore and six days."[46]

After the birth of Jesus, Mary remained at home denying herself the freedom to enter the temple, nor did she take part in anything rituals. Exactly on the fortieth day after she had given birth, the Holy Family traveled five miles north to Jerusalem for the rites of purification and sacrifice at the temple. There, Jesus, the firstborn, was to be presented before God, in accordance with the law that the firstborn son must be redeemed in memory of God's sparing the firstborn of the Israelites when he threw the first born to the Egyptians at the time of the Exodus.

Mary holding the infant Jesus, and Joseph made their way to the temple. On this occasion, Mary did not ride upon the donkey she had made her way on

---

45   Luke 2-22
46   Leviticus 12: 1-5

foot. At the gate to the temple, she waited for the priest to make her offerings of thanksgiving and expiation.

She was met at the temple by the priests, and together with Jesus and Joseph, made her way inside and the ritual cleansing began.

She cleansed herself and her clothing she made the final offering and gave it to the priest. He took the offering presented there before the Lord to make atonement for her.

After the offerings to the Almighty God of the priest, the woman was cleansed legal impurity, and reinstated in her former privileges.

The blessed mother, having been conceived by the Holy Ghost, and she was always a spotless virgin, she was under no obligation to participate in these rituals.

Although she was within the letter of the law, in the eyes of her community, who were ignorant of the miraculous conception, and she was desirous of concealing her privileges and dignity, she submitted herself with great punctuality and exactness to every couple of circumstance the law required.

At the end of the ceremony, the priest declared Mary to be clean.

Mary went to Joseph who was waiting at the gate.

"Have you finished what needs to be done?"

"The rabbi has pronounced me clean Joseph. We can go home."

As they made their way homeward, Joseph went to the side of the road and stopped in the shade of the Mediterranean Cyprus. Mary dismounted and asked: "There's something on your mind that is giving you pause. Pray tell me what it is."

"This is a continuation of the talk that we had some time ago as regards to your chastity. We know that what we have had was a blessed and sacred virgin birth and our child is the Messiah."

Mary responded, "We both agreed that I would go through the post-childbirth purification ceremony for the same reason we had Jesus go through the post-childbirth circumcision ceremony: out of obedience to the Mosaic Law. Both rites—purification (ritual cleansing of the mother) and circumcision (removing the foreskin of the child)—symbolized being freed from sin. We underwent them not because we needed to be freed from sin but because they are Jews who follow the Mosaic Law. That is why Jesus was baptized: not because he needed it himself but to set the pattern for others to follow. As the fullness of grace will flow from Jesus on to his Mother, so it was becoming that the Mother should be like her Son in humility: for "God giveth grace to the humble."[47]

Joseph gave Mary her son, put his arm around her, assisting her to mount the donkey and the Holy Family returned home.

---

[47] James 4:6 (Theologiae III:37:4)

CHAPTER SEVENTEEN

HEROD WAS INFURIATED at not hearing back from the Magi for more than a week. He had asked them to find the location of the so-called Messiah and to report back to him the Messiah's location. He summoned his priests and advisors to learn what happened.

"These eastern Kings," he began, "left our presence seven days ago. Has anything been learned about them or from them?"

The high priest stepped forward. "We have heard nothing Majesty." Then Asa informed him, "We have even sent out runners in an attempt to get further information. So far, we have heard nothing."

Herod got to his feet shouting, "Nothing?! Have we been taken advantage of? Have we been duped by those foreign devils? Asa," he called out, "what have you heard? First it was the shepherds, and now these foreign kings bring word about this Messiah. I must know who it is, and I must know now!"

"It is too early to tell Majesty. We will know more, I am sure, in several days."

Herod seated himself somewhat mollified.

"By week's end," he seethed, "if we still do not have any word from these foreign kings, I want you back here, along with the Captain of the Praetorian guard, to discuss our next course of action." He rose quickly from his throne shouting, "I must have an answer! If there is a usurper, he must be found and done away with! I alone will reign in Jerusalem! Alert the troops already in Nazareth to be watchful for new male infants and to alert us if one should appear."

"A wise precaution," Asa commented, "O sovereign."

Several days later a company of the Centurion guards marched the five miles into Bethlehem increasing the complement already there. A proclamation was posted in the town square as Herod had directed. The following day, the mothers and about twenty children gathered in the town hall.

When they gathered in the town hall, the women noticed that no tables had been set for a feast. They looked around with concern replacing delight. When all were present the doors were fastened, closed shut. Centurions went to the mothers, took their children away from them. The children were slaughtered before their eyes. While these executions were taking place some mothers went to their children and were grievously wounded. Amidst the streams of innocent blood, and the piercing shrieks of the dying, the mothers realize what a calamity had befallen them.[48]

With a population of about one thousand in Bethlehem, the Centurions knew they had to work quickly. After the slaughter at the town hall, they broke into houses and removed every male child two years of age and younger, as they had been directed, and slew them. It is estimated that twenty children perished.

While Centurions were at the town Hall, Joseph and Mary heard the screams of anguish and terror. They were pondering what was taking place people had been running helter-skelter throughout the city telling their neighbors to flee with their infant children. Then what was said through the prophet Jeremiah was fulfilled:

> "A voice is heard in Ramah,
> weeping and great mourning,
> Rachel weeping for her children,
> and refusing to be comforted,
> because they are no more."[49]

Suddenly an angel of the Lord appeared to Joseph in a dream saying, "Arise and take the young child and his mother and flee into Egypt, and be thou there until I bring you word: for Herod will seek the young child to destroy him.[50]

It was his second dream where an angel of the Lord spoke to him. In the first dream he was instructed to have faith, fear not but take Mary unto himself as his wife. He obeyed the angel then because he could think of no other course of action. In this, his second dream, however, he was being instructed to take the child and his mother into Egypt because Herod was seeking to destroy the child. Just as he had done in the past, so he must do now, obey the angel. He knew that Egypt had long been a place of refuge for the Jewish people which added to his obedience.

---

[48]   Hosea 11:1

[49]   Jeremiah 31:15

[50]   Matthew 2:20 Numbers 24:8 "That it might be fulfilled which was spoken of the Lord by the prophet, saying out of Egypt have I called my son." The main reason he is taken to Egypt is that he may relive the Exodus experience of Israel.

He woke Mary to tell her of the dream. Before doing so, however, a moan escaped his lips.

When Joseph decided to flee it was not the decision of a desperate or timid man. However, remaining in Bethlehem and trying to elude Herod's soldiers would have been foolhardy.

"Lord," Mary said as she woke, "art thou having a nightmare?"

He told her of his dream. He reviewed with her it's content and ramifications. Joseph was well aware of his visible temporal authority over Mary and Jesus. He had come to the realization that it is he who must make the heavy decision to leave as quickly as they can. He must protect Mary's safety and Jesus' life by avoiding Herod's insane wrath! His decision must be in obedience to what the angel of the Lord had instructed him. He knows that Mary will obey this decision with love and docility since this decision is an imperative and it concerns the life of their child.

However, their hasty departure was less than a joyful exodus. Innocent blood was being shed and Joseph and Mary were completely powerless to do anything about it. They were forced to bear witness to the suffering together and this unites them further. At the same time they give thanks to God for sparing their child and saving him from Herod's wrath.

They decided to leave the house to his children, along with the workshop and flee Nazareth as quickly as they could. They had to get away from Herod's rampage and in compliance with the instructions of the angel. What a change of fate had befallen them. One day they were visited by royalty and here they were, fleeing in the middle of the night, hunted as though they were brigands.

As they ate the final meal before leaving Mary asked "How will we get to Egypt, Joseph? It is so far away and we know so little about the country."

"This is not the first time Jews have taken flight into Egypt. I have not plotted our entire course, but at each stop that we make I will make further inquiries. Thus far from what I have learned, if we were to travel in a direct line from Bethlehem to the border of Egypt it would be a journey of about 161 kilometers. Add another 161 kilometers would bring us to the banks of the Nile River.

What I have planned so far is that we will go to Hebron, that ancient and historical city, then to Ashkelon on the Mediterranean coast. I feel quite certain that we can pick up a caravan traveling south. We will join with them."

Mary said, "Let us send word to Elizabeth and Zachariah so they may take action to protect their son."

In point of fact, Elizabeth and Zachariah had already received word of the infant slaughter. Zachariah sent Elizabeth and John to the hill country for their protection. Zachariah would later be called before Herod to tell him the location of his son. Zachariah refused, he was executed.

For two days the Holy Family made their way across burning deserts and stinging sand storms. The trek had to be endured; they had to put distance between themselves and Herod. At night Joseph placed them beside a small hillock and covered everyone, including the donkey's head with cloaks as protection. Food was eaten raw and water consumed sparingly.

As they plodded wearily along, Mary questioned Joseph. "In the temple we heard about the Jews during their flight from Egypt, went into the land of Goshen where they would remain for over 400 years until Moses led them out of their Wilderness Journey to the promise land. Do you think that as we go into Egypt, we too will enter the land of Goshen?"

Joseph replied, "The stories you have heard, if I am not mistaken, involve Joseph who told pharaoh, "My father and my brothers, with their flocks and herds and all that they possess, have come from the land of Canaan; they are now in the land of Goshen."[51]

"So, let me tell you about the land of Goshen. The region known as Goshen, is located in northeastern Egypt, in the delta of the Nile River, where it empties into the Mediterranean Sea. The Sinai Peninsula is just to the east. To the south are the famous Pyramids, and the Valley of the Kings, where many Mummies have been discovered, and we, by the grace of God, will be seeing, is a vast area that includes many cities. The entire complex is known as the land of Goshen."

"So in answer to your question Mary, yes we will be entering that fabled land."

---

[51]   Genesis 46:31-47:1 RSV

CHAPTER EIGHTEEN

JOSEPH AND MARY asked their children to come to the house where they could tell them what was happening. Joseph's sons were: Judas, Justus, James, and Simon, were the first to arrive. Shortly thereafter, daughters: Assia and Lydia joined with them. All of the children sat at the table bewildered by this call for them to gather.

When all were present, Joseph began, "Mary was told in a dream, by an angel of the Lord, that she would deliver a male child and she was to call him Jesus." He turned to Mary who sat with the infant in her arms. "At first I had grave misgivings about going through with our marriage. I had serious doubts until I too had a dream wherein I was told by an angel to fear not, and to proceed with the marriage since the child she was carrying was the Messiah and will come into the world to save mankind."

Justus spoke, "Surely this cannot be true. You have told us all our lives about the coming of the Messiah, but not like this."

Joseph spread his arms as if to embrace his children. "My children what we tell you is true and there is so much more that you should know."

"Does this have anything to do with those royally dressed foreign men on camels who came into Nazareth," Assia wanted to know?

"It has everything to do with them but by no means all. Those men you speak of came from far away Persia following a star. They followed it to Jerusalem seeking the Messiah that had been promised and to whom they might pay homage. They sought information from the King and he instructed them to come to Bethlehem and if they found the Messiah to report back to him. However they were told in a dream that Herod meant to do harm, unto the one they were seeking."

Simon interrupted, "How did those foreign strangers, you called Magi get involved in all this? This sounds like sheer and utter nonsense."

"As I have told you, they had come to Jerusalem seeking the Messiah. They thought the Palace would be the proper place to look, and when they told the

King what it was they were seeking, he asked them to return and tell him where the child could be found so he could pay homage. They came as you know, paid homage to Jesus and instead of returning to Herod, returned to their homes by a different route."

"King Herod wanted to pay homage to my little brother," Lydia asked, a smile covering her face, disbelief in her tone?

"Isaac, a kinsman of mine, works in the king's palace. He came to see Mary and me earlier today. He said that he overheard the King giving instructions to his Praetorian guards, to go into Nazareth and to kill every male child two years of age and younger before the infant should grow and usurp him as Regent.

"Now for the reason we have asked you here tonight. I also had a dream, and an angel of the Lord instructed me to take Mary and Jesus and flee into Egypt, because Herod was seeking to harm him. With so much information coming to us from so many sources, and complete faith, we have no choice but to obey the instructions given us."

"But father," Simon observed, "you would have to leave everything behind. I think you are over reacting."

Mary, who had given no voice until this time said, "Everything that we have," she began, "will be left to you and your brothers, relying on you to take care of your sisters. Your father and I have discussed this and it is our thought that this is the best course of action. What are your thoughts?"

Judas spoke, "It shall be as you have said, father. Do you know when or if you and Mary and Jesus will return?"

Again Mary spoke to signify her agreement with their father.

"The angel said we should go into Egypt and stay there until we are told to return. It is our opinion that we shall not return until after the death of King Herod."

The rest of the evening was spent in making arrangements for the handling of the workload in the shop, the journey they were about to take, and what needed to be packed. Farewells were said as they bade the children good night. It was shortly after midnight when Joseph took the donkey carrying Mary and their infant son on their dissent of the hills outside of Nazareth, and into the plains below. The Holy Family began their odyssey over rough terrain heading for Hebron.

The clothes they were wearing were seasonal: a long gamis, a robe that extended from their necks to their ankles with loose fitting sleeves, a tunica, capulae, that is a kuffingah or head covering was worn over their robes to their waist and a leather girdle called an ugal, and sandals covered their feet.

Joseph purchased a pack animal from a neighbor along with foodstuffs with some of the gold the Magi had given them. He also purchased wine and water skins. These items they would need in the arid lands in which they would be traveling.

Mary prepared Jesus for the journey by wrapping Jesus in clothes and a cloak to keep him warm. She also bundled their belongings for the trip while Joseph packed the donkey. Spices were placed in saddle bags along with the food stuffs, but the gold Joseph placed in a pouch secured around his waist.

As he packed, he thought about another Joseph a thousand years ago, who had been sold into slavery by his jealous brothers. He too went into Egypt and eventually save his brothers, his father and many others as well. He saved them from seven years of famine. Now, he too was on his way to Egypt, into an unknown fate, yet unafraid.

As they sat at their meal, Joseph decided to tell them what was in store. "We are going into Egypt and eventually to Alexandria. To reach this land will require a lengthy journey across sun-baked desert wastes where water will be scarce and the sun burning hot. It will take some time and try our spirits. We have placed our faith in the Lord God Jehovah and he will see us through these times to come."

This was a story he had to tell his son, in a year or so, when he was old enough to understand. He silently prayed that he was right in taking his family into a foreign land according to God's command. Together Joseph and Mary knelt in prayer, besieging the Lord to guide their footsteps on this journey about to begin.

Before their departure from the city, Joseph had purchased a second donkey on which he packed their belongings. As they walked along the road, Mary sat astride the first donkey called Phyllis, with the infant at her breast; both were wrapped in a warm cloak. When Joseph saw Mary shiver, he covered both, mother and child with a blanket over her shoulders.

When dawn came the sun brought little warmth with it. Mary, astride Phyllis their donkey, held Jesus close to her breast to share her body heat. In addition, Joseph again put a blanket over both of them; the animal's body also gave off some heat. Joseph did not fare as well. He wrapped cloth around his hands and shoulders, his feet were bare.

As the day wore on, the wind began to blow up taking the two émigrés colder still. It was so bad and so cold that Joseph was compelled to make a stop in a knoll and making a small fire to warm everyone. The fire was soon ablaze sending off sparks in relieving warmth.

"Is the infant warm, Mary," Joseph asked?

"Yes, bless his heart. While we are by the fire, I will take the opportunity to feed him."

"Try to keep yourselves covered as best you can and close to the fire. That way you have the blanket you have wrapped around you. You can move yourselves closer to the fire."

"What are you going to do with your blanket Joseph," Mary asked concerned?

"I want to heat the blanket and my cloak by draping them over the tree branch near the fire. Also putting warm stones into the saddle bags to give you and the baby more heat. It will not last long but while it lasts, you both will benefit."

"Thank you Joseph. Will we be camping here for the night?"

"No Mary we will not, I'm sorry. If it is not too much for you and the child, we need to move on and place as much distance between us and anyone looking to pursue us. Just let me know when you want to make another stop."

Joseph wanted to avoid the obvious routes south, the usual route to Egypt, those between Jerusalem and Bethlehem. He decided, to take the less frequented way only during the daylight hours. As the animals plod on, all nature was quite.

For several days, they traveled the dry desert floor, camping in caves at night or in wadis. One very cold evening, they came upon a cave already occupied by a group of people. The apparent leader of the group greeted them outside the cave. Upon seeing the footsore and weary travelers with and a young mother and her child, he was moved to invite them to stay the night with the group.

After all had been nourished, one of the women showed Mary where she could bathe the child and where they might sleep for the night. After the children had been washed and fed, the others sat around the campfire preparing themselves for sleep. Mary asked Joseph to tell them a story.

"Well it seems that Joshua," he began, "the son of Nun, began life in Egypt as a slave however, he rose to be the leader of the people of Israel through faithful Holy obedience to God. He became an assistant to Moses and before the Israelites entered Canaan, Moses died and Joshua became his successor. Joshua took over as leader taking the Israelites to the Promised Land. God gave him a command to cross the Jordan River, along with the Ark of the Covenant, and move on to Jericho.

"On a plain outside the city," Joseph continued, "the Israelites made camp. Joshua visited the city he wanted to get a look at the great walls that surrounded the city. He wondered how he could attack the city and win. On his return to camp, Joshua sent two men across the river to find out what they could about the city and its qualifications. When the two spies came to the city they found the gates were opened. They entered and came to a house that belonged to a woman named Rahab. As they spoke with her someone, a citizen of Jericho, ran to tell the King that two men from the Israeli camp were in the city.

"The King could not let these men returned to their camp. He sent soldiers to Rahab's house to capture the spies. At the house they told her to surrender the men but she did not obey. The soldiers searched the house but found no spies. She had hidden them in the stalks of flax on her roof. When the soldiers had gone, she showed the men how to escape, but before leaving she said, 'Promise me that when you return you will save me and my family.' The men told her to hang a red cord in her window and she and her family would be saved.

As Joshua walked about the city wondering what to do, he saw a strange man was dressed like a soldier and who carried a bright sword. Joseph asked who he was and he replied, "I am the Captain in the Army of the Lord."

"What does the Lord want me to do?"

"Take off your shoes, the place where you stand is on holy ground." The soldier told Joshua how he might capture the city if he obeyed the Lord's commands. Joshua relayed the information to his people and they were ready to obey.

They marched around the great city on the first day. On the next day they did the same, for God had commanded them to march around the great stone walls. As they marched the Israelites shouted or talked loudly. The only other sound was the tread of feet, and the noise of the army's trumpets.

On the seventh day the Israelites arose and prepared for a long march, they knew the day of victory had come. This time they walked around the walls of Jericho not once but seven times. Then the Israeli priests loudly blew on the trumpets and at that signal, all of the people began to shout, because they knew the Lord had given them the day. At that very moment the stone wall began to crumble until it fell flat. Joshua told the two men who had spied on Jericho, "Go to Rahab's house and bring her and her family to safety as you have promised."

"The Israelites burned Jericho after that, and only Rahab and her family were saved."

"You mean to tell me," the group's leader asked, "that by calling on trumpets, marching around and shouting caused the walls of Jericho to crumple?"

"There was one other important factor," Joseph said, "they were doing what God had told them to do and that was enough."

The leader, whose name was Micah, stared at Joseph, a puzzled look on his face. "Are you telling me that this God of yours is so powerful that he can have an entire city destroyed by stamping feet, blaring trumpets, and people shouting?"

Joseph respond, "with our God nothing is impossible!"

Micah then instructed Joseph on the path he should take into Hebron. His wife gave Mary additional food for the journey and goats milk for their infant son.

Before retiring to bed, Joseph and Mary knelt in prayer.

"Oh Lord God we thank you for being with us today, for guiding our path and for leading us to these good people who have given us shelter and shared their food. Be with them Lord we pray and stay with us as we continue our journey."

CHAPTER NINETEEN

ONCE MORE ON the rocky, uneven road, the Holy Family doggedly continued walking southeast. The tortuous trails caused them delays and exhaustion almost daily. Joseph continually kept in mind that Mary was a fifteen-year-old with an infant. He carefully picked their way into wadis and alleys and across burning desert. Frequent stops were called for to preserve Mary's strength and stamina. Joseph was ever fearful of wild animals and brigands who were known to inhabit the land. That and the all too human fears of pursuit were allayed by their faith in the Lord .

"Joseph," Mary called softly, "I understand we must avoid the usual tracks to Egypt, but why have you chosen to go this way? It certainly is out of the way."

"Very perceptive Mary, it is out of the way and not a path our pursuers would think to use. Our stop will be in Hebron, a city in the south and of the Valley of Gehcol. It is one of the oldest cities in the world. It has a long history of the Jewish community. We learn from the book of Genesis that it was the favorite home of Abraham. When we camp tonight I will tell you the Genesis story about the history of Hebron."

Later that night he began: "To begin with, the city is quite significant. It was the dwelling place of Solomon and it was where David ruled for seven years as king. And Sarah was a 10 and 20 years old. And Sarah died in Kirjatharba; the name is Hebron in the land of Canaan: and Abraham came to mourn for Sarah, and to weep for her.

"And Abraham stood up, and bowed himself to the people of the land, even to the children of Heth saying, I am a stranger and a sojourner with you: give me a possession of a burying place with you, that I bury my dead out of my sight. The children of Heth answered Abraham saying unto him, hear us, my Lord: thou art a mighty prince among us: in the choice of our sepulchers bury thy dead.

"And Abraham stood up, and bowed himself to the people - - - if it be your mind to bury my dead out of my sight; hear me, and entreat for me to Ephron son of Zohar, that he may give me the cave of Machpelah, which he hath, which is in the end of his field; for as much money as it is worth shall give it to me for possession for a burying place amongst you - - - name my Lord hear me: the field which I give thee, the cave that is therein, I give it to thee; the presence of the sons of my people I give it to thee; bury thy dead."

When he had finished his recitation, Mary said, "I still do not understand why you have selected Hebron. There are many other ways that we could travel."

"Being from the House of David, and due to the fact that David was King and resided in Hebron, and because of the fact that you and your family have a history in the city, I felt safe coming here with you and the child you are carrying.

"I recall, as a child, the story of my father Jacob, about King David and how he became king.

"King Ish-bosheth of Israel, was waging war against the Philistines. His general, Abner, deserted the army[52] after which Ish-bosheth was assassinated.[53] All the tribes of Israel sent representatives to Hebron, the capital, to recognize his kingship over all of Israel."[54]

"So you see wife, I have a good feeling about this place."

By mid-afternoon, outside the city limits, they made camp by a clump of trees and an oasis. The night was cold and a large fire was called for. They were met at the campsite by Salomé, a distant cousin of Mary. She had been in Hebron and when she had word there were travelers on the road, she thought it might be her cousin. She asked Joseph if she might join with them, assist her cousin, and be a wet nurse to the infant. Although it meant there was another mouth to feed, she could be of great help to Mary and the baby. Joseph agreed.

That night Salomé nursed the babe, Mary prepared the evening meal, while Joseph made camp. Joseph set aside extra wood for the fire to keep them warm during the night, as well as discouraging animals from invading their camp. After the infant had been washed and put to bed, the three of them ate their meal.

"Mary tells me," Salomé began, "that you tell a nightly story. What is it to be tonight? Will it be about Moses, Jacob or someone else?"

As they made themselves comfortable around the campfire, Joseph began his story. "Tonight I am going to tell you about Moses. Jacob will be another story. Moses changed his name to Israel and his children called Israelites. They lived in the land of Goshen for more than 400 years.

"Another pharaoh had taken the Egyptians throne and he was afraid of the Israelites. He thought that they would one day rise up against him. One

---

[52]   2 Samuel 3:20

[53]   2 Samuel 4:7

[54]   cf Samuel 5:1-5

morning he sent a message to the Israelites: "Every baby born among your people must be thrown into the Nile River."

"How much his mother loved the child Moses! For three months she hid him from the soldiers. Then the baby grew too old to hide. She gathered bulrushes that grew along the river and wove them into a basket. She decided to keep the water out of the basket with caulking and then she made a bed in the bottom soft and placed the basket into the river.

"The infant's sister, Miriam, played along the river bank and watched the basket float away. Soon the group of richly dresses Christian ladies came to the river to bathe. One of these young ladies was pharaoh's daughter. She saw the basket and sent forth her maids to fetch it. She knew about the command of her father, but how could she let this little baby be killed? She said, "I will take him as my own."

Miriam who had been standing close by, overheard the comment, ran to the Princess saying, "Shall I get an Israelite woman to nurse the baby for you?" Of course the baby would need a nurse, and the Princess would be pleased to hire an Israelite woman.

"Miriam went home and brought back her mother, who was quite pleased to have her baby back. No longer would she be afraid of the soldiers, for everyone knew the baby had been adopted by the pharaoh's daughter.

"When the baby grew old enough to leave his mother, he was taken to live with the Princess in the Palace. The Princess called him Moses, which means 'drawn out,' because she had drawn him out of the water. Moses was given a good education and later, as a Prince, and later he would be the leader in the government."

"Thank you Joseph," Mary said.

"So that we all know," Joseph continued, "why we had started off at Hebron, I will tell you of my thinking. I know so little about Ashkelon, where, I'm told, we must go in order to join with a trading caravan going into Egypt. And Mary, we must first stop in Hebron where your parents lived for a time.

"It is also a Palestinian city, the second largest city on the West Bank, next to Jerusalem. We have traveled far to get here, making our way through the Judean mountains but most importantly, it has a large Jewish population and it is plentiful in grapes and figs. Here too, we will find safe refuge among our people. I will also be able to learn what limestone, pottery and various workshops are in the city. It is also famous for its glassblowing factories. We need to know about Ashkelon, and I think this is the place to find out what we need to know.

On the outskirts of Hebron with Joachim and Anne he would tell them what was happening.

"We have heard what has been taking place. He had been terrified at the prospect might have happened. All Praise to God for His protection!"

When they had settled the night Joseph said, "Joachim, Mary is a very young mother and she is in need of a wet nurse. Angel of the Lord as instructed us to flee into Egypt, and to remain there until we are told to return. How long that will take, we have no idea.

"I have been instructed by the angel to care and protect both your daughter and grandson, and I will do that the best I can. However, I do need help and a wet nurse will help and measurably. Can you think of anyone that can fill that gap?"

Anne spoke up," in the temple we learned of a young woman who is just whom you are looking for. Her name is Salomé. Would you like us to send for her so that you might speak with her?"

"Yes mother," Mary said, "please do so."

And so it came to pass that Salomé joined the band of travelers as they travel south.

* * * * *

"I have been told Salomé," Joseph said, "by a nomad in the desert that our people will be found in Otnid, a small settlement on the outskirts of the city, where we can rest before moving on."

"Yes. Joseph that is so," Salomé said. "You are well advised."

After the morning meal, Joseph and his family entered Otnid. They made their way to the synagogue at the market square. Mary dismounted and they made their way into the synagogue where they were met by one of the priests.

"*Shalom* travelers," he said. "What brings you to our city?"

Shalom. I am Joseph of Nazareth and this is my family and we are seeking temporary refuge. The woman with the infant is my wife Mary and our wet nurse Salomé. Our child is called Yeshua."

"Yeshua? Do you know what that name means?"

"Jehovah saves."

"Do you ridicule that thought? Or have you named your child in hopes of a brighter future?"

"It is a very long story rabbi and one that I would like to tell you when we have time. For now though, we need a place to stay and replenish our supplies."

"I am sorry Joseph. I meant no offense. I am rabbi Saul Ryukin. You and your family are welcome. There is an excellent camp location in the woods west of here. You may also replenish your needs in the village. Are you from Jerusalem?"

"No, we are from Bethlehem, as I said. We are fleeing from Herod's hordes who have instructions to slaughter all young male children."

"I have had word of this disaster. Come, you and your family have some refreshments with me and rest yourselves.

"Where are you going, you have a destination?"

"We are looking for a caravan going South into Egypt. We've also been told that caravans leave from Ashkelon and safe passage can be found there."

"And so you can. Ashkelon and Gaza are equidistant but you are more likely to join with a caravan in Ashkelon. I will prepare a map for you to follow. It is about three days travel. So rest here, and when you are ready to leave, let me know.

"You should know however, you must cross a desert and then a great forest before you reach Ashkelon."

"May I ask a question rabbi?"

"Of course you may. What would you like to know?"

"There is a large enclosure that is visible throughout the city. What is in that enclosure?"

"That my friend is the tomb of the matriarchs and patriarchs. There are also cenotaphs, those are empty tombs, honoring Abraham, Isaac, Jacob, Sarah, Rebecca, and Leah."

"I have heard of them but never thought to see them."

"Abraham was married to Sarah. She died here in Hebron while he was off elsewhere. He returned to mourn her. He spoke to the sons of Heth, requesting a burial place for Sarah. He was offered a choice of sepulchers, but he requested of Ephron the Hittite, the cave of Machpelah in the end of his field. Then, later, he requested the field as well.

"Abraham paid 400 shekels in silver for the cave, the field, all the trees in the field and borders round about. It was here he buried Sarah. The deed was passed on to his son Isaac who would bury his father there. Isaac's sons Esau and Jacob, Isaac did their father well. He was buried along with his wife Rebekah. Jacob's wife Leah would also be buried there.

"Much later, Herod the Great would build the structure you now see. It is a rectangular enclosure over the caves. The entrance, if there ever was one, it has not been found."

"Thank you rabbi," Joseph said. "That is a fascinating story and clears up many things from our past."

Joseph and Mary, along with Jesus, and Salomé, decided to rest for some time in Otnid before moving to the next destination. They spent the next four months refreshing themselves and the animals, and then decided it was time to leave.

That night after the evening meal, Joseph and Mary were talking about Zachariah and her cousin Elizabeth. "Should we visit them," Mary asked?

"I think it best that we do not. We can however, ask Saul to send them word that we are on our way into Egypt."

As they had been told, on the outskirts they found a beautiful campsite by a flowing stream with plentiful grazing for the animals. At dusk the Holy Family stopped and set up camp. Mary made the infant Jesus comfortable as he slept, and she turned to prepare the meal. Salomé was putting their camp in order. Joseph tethered the animals, gathered firewood and started a small fire. The women bathed the infant Jesus, then themselves, and washed their clothes. Afterward, Joseph also washed before he set up a shelter such that it was in the lee of the small hillock affording them shelter and protection from the wind.

Well rested after four months, the Holy Family went to the temple for a Sabbath celebration, after which they went to Saul to say goodbye.

"*L'hitrot* Saul. Thank you for your kindness."

"Go with God Joseph of Nazareth," Saul replied. "In Ashkelon, seek out my cousin Lev Ryukin. He is a merchant and will take care of your needs at his cost." I have already sent word to Zachariah and Elizabeth that you are on your way to Egypt.

Tzeth beshalom.

The men shook hands in parting.

CHAPTER TWENTY

The story of the Holy Family's journey from Bethlehem into Egypt will be divided into four areas: using Via Maris, the coastal road linking Palestine to Egypt, the Nile Delta, the vicinity of Cairo, and the Nile Valley. Our story continues at the head of the Coastal Road in Ashkelon.

• •

ON THE FIRST night out of Hebron, there was a biting chill in the air. It was dark and bleak, and the road is equally treacherous. Joseph led the donkey with Mary riding astride, the baby Jesus wrapped in a sling over her shoulder. Salomé walked on the other side of the donkey. Ashkelon, Joseph had been told, was quite well known since early times. It lay inland on the banks of the Mediterranean Sea and the headland of the caravan route southward, first they had to enter into the desert country, and they were told that it was infested with robbers.

As they made their way along the road they came across a band of brigands asleep on the side of the road. A number of others were also off to the side of the road, apparently confederates of theirs, and they too were asleep. The two men on the side of the road were Dismas and Dumachus. Dismas wanted to rob them of their belongings, but Dumachus talked him out of it, beseeching his friend to allow them to pass unmolested.

"Why should we do that? These people," Dismas said scornfully, "are easy pickings, a man two women. Nothing could be simpler."

"You are right. Dismas took a look at them Dumachus, these are simple travelers with a donkey, small bag of coins, and the clothing on their backs. They are not worth the effort. I say let them pass."

"Let us save energy to more prosperous sojourners. Come," he turned his attention to Joseph and his party, "join us. We were about to eat and from the looks of you, a warm meal would be welcomed."

Hesitantly they dismounted and joined the men by their fire.

"Take a small frond and help yourself to some food," Dumachus said. "Your people look as though you're running away from something or someone. Where are you going?"

"We are coming from Nazareth and are going into Egypt," Joseph said. "And you are right we are fleeing from people who do not want to rob us but want to take our lives. In point of fact, helping us like this could possibly put you in danger."

"We have been in danger before," Dismas said boastfully. "People are pursuing us too, so we know how you feel."

Dumachus interrupted their chatter. "Have something to eat, bed down by the fire, and in the morning we will part company."

After they had eaten and were sitting around the fire, Joseph asked the men if they knew anything about the road they were taking to Egypt.

"If you're heading into Egypt," Dismas began, "you will be traveling mostly on Via Maris, an ancient trade route and the name means 'way of the sea.' It is a historic road running along the Palestine coast. Together with the Kings Highway, Via Maris was one of the major trade routes connecting Egypt and the Levant with Anatolia and Mesopotamia."

Dumachus added, "You would be well advised to join up with a caravan at Ashkelon heading south. People that you will be traveling with will give you better information than we possess. Joseph thanked the men bade them a good night.

After a warm, comfortable night, the Holy Family were back on the road heading for Ashkelon.

As they went on by, Mary said to them, "The Lord God will receive you to his right hand and grant you pardon of your sins." *

Sometime later Mary asked, "Lord, do you know anything about the city to which we are going?"

"Saul told me that Ashkelon was one of five cities of the Philistines, twelve miles north of Gaza. At one point in its history, it fell into the hands of Judah; but soon thereafter, it was retaken by the Philistines,[55] who were deposed by Alexander the Great. He also said that Samson went down to Ashkelon from Tininath and slew thirty men taking their spoils.[56]

"Besides that, he said that King Herod had decorated the seaport city with fountains and beautiful buildings. It's hard to believe that a man who would kill children could also build beautiful cities."

---

[55]   2 Samuel 1:20

[56]   Judges 14:19

*   Thirty years later, as Jesus hung on the cross, Dismas was on the cross to his right, Dumachus on his left

When they left the Hebron, the Holy Family and Salomé were wearing Arab dress at the time, to ward off the biting winds and the stinging sand. Their garb consisted of the gamis, long white shirt, the 'abayah, the top robe. a kuffeyah, the scarf and the 'uqal, a dress. Specifically, the clothes they were wearing were the same for men and women, consisted of a linea, long robe reaching the neck to the feet with close fitting sleeves, a tunica, reaching to their knees with long sleeves, the palenta or casula, a large round material with a hole in the center for air to pass through, and fell with folds on the shoulder and arms to envelope the entire body down to their knees. It provided them with much-needed warmth and protection against wind, rain, and blowing sand, on such occasions. In addition, they wore girdles or belts along with a pair of sandals. The men wore kippahs on their heads.

In Ashkelon, a city also known as 'the fire of infamy.' Joseph immediately sought out Lev Ryukin. Lev greeted them warmly. Joseph told him that his cousin Saul had said to meet with him and to have Lev provide all that was needed for their flight into Egypt.

"I don't suppose," Lev asked, "you are wealthy people with a great deal of money to lavish on goods and supplies."

"No," Joseph responded, "we are poor and humble people from Nazareth. I am a Carpenter with few coins."

"Since it was my cousin who sent you, I have an empty shelter two doors away. There is a small stable, a hearth for cooking and warmth. Stay the night and in the morning we will discuss what you need and I will get you listed with the caravan Kelmar. He is the boss or leader and his name is Kelmar Isaac. Go now and rest the night."

"Thank you Lev. God bless you and yours."

Joseph and his family went to the building, unpacked what they needed and settled in for the night. As had become their custom, after dinner had ended and the infant put to bed, Mary asked Joseph to tell them of their past.

"I will tell you a story from our past about Esau and Jacob. Isaac, the father, live in Beer-Sheba. When he became old and blind, he wanted to give the birthright to his son Esau. He told Esau to go out and hunt deer, cook it and to feed him its meat. When he had eaten it would give Esau his blessing. Esau went off to hunt and do as his father had directed.

Rebecca, their mother, wanted her son Jacob to receive the birthright. She told Jacob that she would cook a meal of goat meat, and season is as Esau would. She told him to dress in Esau's clothing and serve the meat to his father. He will think you are Esau. Jacob hesitated. Rebecca said, 'Let the sin be mine.'

"When Jacob brought the food to his father, Isaac said, "You found the deer quickly. How was it so?"

Jacob replied, "God helped me."

Suspicious, Isaac ate the meal but thought the voice was not that of Esau. "Come near that I might feel you and know you are Esau."

Rebecca had covered Jacobs's arms and neck with goat hair. When Isaac touched his hands, he said, "These are Esau's hands." He finished eating and gave Jacob the blessing of his father Abraham.

When Esau returned home to claim his birthright, Isaac told him that he had given it to another.

Esau said, "Give me a blessing too!"

"How can I when I have given it to another." Finally, Isaac blessed him with the lesser promise of greatness. Esau came to hate his mother and brother and plotted to kill them after his father had died."

"That is all for tonight, go to bed and get some rest."

"No," Salomé pleaded, "please do not stop there. Did Esau kill his brother?"

"That is for another time. Now it's time for us to thank the Lord for being with us this day."

The next morning, Lev brought the Holy Family to meet the caravan leader, Kalmar Isaac, who entered their names in the caravan rolls. They were assigned to a position in a caravan and told that they would be leaving in the morning.

After the midday meal, Salomé asked, "What sort of city is this Ashkelon?"

"From the priest histories," Joseph began, "from Saul and what Lev has told me, Ashkelon is a sandy coastal strip of land, famous because of its trading with Cyprus and Egypt. It is enclosed by great walls. Is one of three cities established by the Philistines along the coastline of the Mediterranean Sea. It is part of the multinational roadway from Jerusalem to Egypt. The city has no springs, but abundant wells so there's no problem getting water for cooking and bathing. They also tell me that this is the city where Samson killed eleven Philistines, and allegedly, many biblical people of folklore have passed through this city.

"It is said, that it is the probable birthplace of Herod the great who had the city rebuilt after it had been destroyed. It covers fifteen acres and is surrounded by semicircular walls. It is also, however, the starting place for many trading caravans. It is also at the apex of the Via Maris, the ancient trade route that parallels the Mediterranean Sea into Egypt.

The Holy Family spent the rest of the day packing their belongings and food stuffs. Toward evening Joseph asked, "What do you have planned for the evening meal?"

"Since we are uncertain when our next good meal will be," Mary said, "I am making a vegetable stew that you like so well. We have vegetables and I will add lentils, onions, celery, and garlic. I will add dumplings to thicken it.

They had eaten the evening meal, Salomé had a question for Joseph. "Why do you call the donkey Phyllis," she asked?

"It is short for Philistine," Joseph responded. "She is stubborn, ornery, and a nonbeliever. What other name could we give her?"

The next morning, before joining with a caravan, they stopped at one of the shops to make some extra purchases. They met with a shopkeeper named Alisa.

"*Yom Marcus*," Joseph said in greeting.

"And a good morning to you as well," Alisa replied. "What a beautiful baby! What is the name of your child," she said referring to the infant in Mary's arms?

"Our son is called Yeshua," Mary replied, "and it is said, he is the Messiah come to save his people. Would you like to hold him?"

"Most certainly," she replied disbelief apparent in her voice. "And who are His people He will save," she asked?

"We are all His children."

Handing the baby back to Mary, Alisa said, "let me give you some milk and porridge for the child on your journey." She hurried off but returned shortly with earthen jars filled. As Mary packed the jars, she allowed Alisa to feed Jesus. A smile brightened the woman's face.

They thanked the woman and went off to see Lev to join the caravan.

Joseph settled accounts with Lev, thanked him for his generosity and shook hands in friendship.

CHAPTER TWENTY-ONE

Traveling the caravan highway, Via Maris, the Holy Family's journey, will be divided into four separate geographic groups consisting of the central coastal road linking Palestine to Egypt, the Nile Delta, the vicinity of Cairo, and the Nile Valley.

• •

ON THE FIRST night after leaving Ashkelon the caravan made a stop at an oasis. The Holy Family shared a communal meal with another family heading south. It was bitterly cold causing the group to move closer together to benefit not only from the fire before them but from their body heat as well. The toddler Jesus was held close, warm in Mary's arms, and wrapped in her cloak.

"Do you know anything about Gaza," asked Aziz a wizened fellow traveler?

"Very little," replied Joseph. "Our knowledge of the world outside Nazareth is very limited. My knowledge of all the places comes from what I have heard."

"I know some things," Aziz said. "Would you like me to share that with you, what little I know?"

"Yes," Mary replied eagerly displaying her lack of years.

"To begin with," he began, "Gaza is one of the oldest Canaanite strongholds and cities in the world and it is mentioned early in the Bible. It is also known as Azzah, which in Hebrew means strong. After God directed the Israelites to enter the Promised Land, Gaza was allotted to the tribe of Judah.[57] Gaza is an important settlement on the Via Maris, three miles off the Mediterranean coast, marking the southern border of the ancient, biblical Canaan. It intersects with the Incense Road coming from Petra and the Dead Sea. It was later captured by the Philistines and played an important part in the story of Samson and Delilah. It was Delilah who betrayed Samson by having him blinded and taken prisoner

---

[57]   Deuteronomy 29:4

by the Philistines and taken to Gaza[58] and it was here that Samson died when he pulled down the temple pillars and the walls piled down upon him, killing not only him but some 3000 Philistines as well.[59]

Also the prophet Jeremiah spoke of Gaza's devastation by the Egyptians."[60]

"For a man who knows a little about Gaza," Joseph observed, "you seem to have a great deal of knowledge. I remember my father Jacob telling me many of these stories but they had little meaning until now. I thank you."

"I am a merchant who has traveled these roads frequently. In my travels some knowledge has been gained. From my own observations however, I find that Gaza is a fertile plain, rich in fruits, wheat and vineyards. It is also a popular trading post for people like me."

The next day the caravan continued its journey south. The Holy Family stopped for the midday meal, all the caravan moved forward, but Joseph and the others remain behind to have their meal. At dusk they rejoined with the caravan.

Joseph started to regale them with a story as had become the custom after the evening meal. They sat around the fire while Joseph told them another story.

"Lord," Mary asked eagerly, "please tell us about King David."

Joseph banked the fire then sat holding the infant Jesus to his chest. "As you know, King David was born in the same city as my father, the same city where I was born, and the same city where our son Jesus was born."

The ladies leaned back smiling. Mary, who had taken the child from Joseph, held him close to keep him warm as Joseph spoke.

"David was the second King of the United Kingdom of Israel and Judah. He was a righteous King, although not without his faults. He was an acclaimed warrior, he killed the Philistine giant Goliath, was also a musician and poet, credited traditionally with writing many of the Psalms contained in the Book of Psalms.

"Before that however, the prophet Samuel was seeking a new King that should come from the sons of Jesse of Bethlehem. Samuel examined six of Jesse's sons, but after the examination Samuel said to Jessie, 'The Lord has chosen none of these.' Samuel inquired if Jesse had other sons?

"There is still the youngest," Jesse answered referring to his son David. Samuel said, "Send for him." When this was accomplished, the Lord said, "Rise and anoint him; this is the one." So Samuel took the horn of oil and anointed David.

---

[58] Judges 16:18,21

[59] Judges 16:25-30

[60] Jeremiah 4:1-5

"Later, King Saul was seeking someone who played the harp before he did battle with the Philistines. Jesse sent David, now grown, who was asked to bring wine and food and bread, for his brothers. He went into Saul's camp. Saul instantly made him an armor bearer. He asked Jesse saying, allow David stand before him saying that he found favor in his sight.[61]

"Now the Army of Israel went out against the Philistines to do battle, and encamped beside Eben-ezer: and the Philistines encamped in Aphek. The Philistines sent their champion, Goliath, who stood before his Army taunting the Israelites.

"Come," he shouted, "send out your champion and we will do battle."

"None in the Israel army came forward, except Saul's armor bearer, one of their own, David, the shepherd boy. He was dressed in his shepherds clothing and on his way out to meet Goliath, picked up three smooth stones and a leather sling. Goliath raised his sword taunting the Israelites. David inserted one of the stones in his sling, and threw it at the giant striking him between the eyes. He collapsed to the ground quite dead. David picked up the Giant's sword, cut off Goliath's head, and holding it up by his hair, showed it to the Philistine Army who fled in panic realizing that God was on the side of Israel.

"When the men of the Army were returning home, the women came out from all the towns to meet King Saul. They were singing and dancing with joyful songs and with tambourines and lutes. As they danced they sang: 'Saul has slain thousands, and David has slain tens of thousands.'

"Hearing this, Saul became jealous and angry; the words of the song galled him. A feeling of hatred overtook the King and, thereafter, he sought David's death."

"And now my dear family," Joseph said kneeling before them, "it is time for our thanks to the Lord before calling it a day." Raising his hands to heaven said, "Oh Lord our God we give thee thanks and praise for the blessings thou hast bestowed upon us. You have guided our footsteps and we pray that you remain with us throughout."

The next several days were spent crossing blistering desert. Never before had the Holy Family experienced such intense heat. When they looked forward the sands appeared to be shimmering. Walking in the sand was almost unbearable. Perspiration poured from their bodies causing them to drink precious quantities of water. Jesus was kept, frequently washed down with a wet rag to cool his body.

They stopped at a small oasis after sundown. The infant Jesus was washed down completely and his clothing changed. After which Mary fed him. When he had been cooled, his parents did likewise. Merely changing their garments lowered their body heat.

---

[61] 1 Samuel 16:20-23

The following day, although the temperatures did not reach the same levels, a sand storm developed that slowed their forward movement considerably. Jesus was covered with the cloak over his mother's shoulder and Joseph had devised a facial screen that was put to good use. Joseph covered both women with blankets and cloaks to protect them from the biting sand and wind. He covered his face and the donkeys' with his scarf.

They had to keep plodding on.

CHAPTER TWENTY-TWO

JOSEPH WAS WATERING their animals when Mary asked, "Joseph do you know where we will be stopping next?"

"I think that Aziz has the answer to that," Joseph responded.

In response Aziz said, "Caravans usually stop at a small village called Salqah. It is three to four days from Gaza to Salqah. But in order to protect caravans such as ours, pilgrims and travelers, a vast khan, you probably know it better as a caravansary, was constructed by Emir Yunus al-Nûrûzi. The khan and the quickly growing surrounding area were given the name of Khan Yunis after him. In the center of the town there is a large square that the Emir had constructed for caravans to refresh themselves. It became quickly a popular trading center and marketplace. Our stop should be for about an hour or so perhaps longer judging by the size of our group."

After Khan Yunis their next stopover was in Rafah Pelusium, the gateway to Egypt, which was very important since it was on the caravan route from Africa to Asia, also because its harbor joined the sea to the branch of the Nile called Pelusiac. The Pharaohs, when they ruled the area, put it in a good state of defense lines from Pelusium to Heliopolis.

Joseph would enjoy walking the streets of Pelusium, the city that was once a resting place for caravans. It also meant they had traveled about one-third of the way he had projected.

Because of the blazing sun once more at their backs, and the scorching heat beneath their feet, they put Jesus on the donkey's back, while the others walked and made their weary way toward Pelusium. Tired and exhausted, they made their stop to rest. After the evening meal outside the city, the evening before they were to enter Egypt, Joseph, Mary and Salomé sat by the fireside reminiscing on the journey. Jesus has been bathed, fed and put to bed.

"The trade routes had been busy," Joseph was saying, "with scarce means of replacing our immediate needs. We will have to make some purchases from our fellow travelers."

After a lull when he was pondering what had taken place during the day, Mary said, "The ancients tell us there are communities of Hebrews who had been led into this foreign land by Moses. It is exciting to be able to get in touch with our roots. Was it not your kin Joseph of the many colored coat who was sold into slavery?"

"Yes, I believe it was wife. Do you remember the story I had told you? We should be meeting some of those ancestors. We must tell our son those stories; Moses delivering the Israelites from slavery by his brothers which made them, later on, belong to him through a fiat. The story of the exodus tells of the enslavement of the Israelites in Egypt following the death of our ancestors, and their departure under the leadership of Moses, the revelations at Sinai, and their wanderings in the wilderness up to the borders of Canaan."

Mary observed, "The boy is barely three years old and has so much he has to learn."

"I just spoke to the caravan master," Joseph informed his group, "he said that we will be making a mid-morning stop at Tel Basta, the city we must pass through before entering Egypt."

"That's good news Joseph," Mary said smiling. "Is there any available water, I would like to bathe Jesus and myself? I am sure that Salomé would like to bathe as well."

Salomé added, "We need to clean some clothing as well."

"Let us hope," Joseph said, "that you find what you need."

At Tel Basta they did in fact find a small stream suitable to their needs. Joseph left the women there, with the infant, while he entered the ancient city in ruins. Joseph once again sought out their caravan traveling mate, the merchant traveler.

"*Shalom,*" he said in greeting. "*Ma nish-mah?*"

"I am well Joseph. Where is your family?"

"They are bathing and washing clothes. I never did learn your name."

"An oversight Joseph. My name is Rafael Kahn."

"Rafael," Joseph inquired, "do you know anything about the city Tel Basta?"

"Not much, I'm afraid. I know that it is 80 kilometers northeast of Cairo in the eastern Nile Delta region. It is as you may have guessed on the route between Memphis and the Sinai. Ages ago, when it was the capital city, the capital was moved to Tanis. The ruins that you see about you are the remains of the Round temple at Bastet. The temple is dedicated to a cat god that they worshiped and there are steles with engravings of cats. Some pharaohs, on their death, had as many as 1000 cats mummified and placed in the pyramid with them."

"I am continually disappointed at your lack of knowledge," Joseph said smiling. "Let me ask you this, if I may, with the vast need for felines, a wise merchant could make a fortune breeding cats and mummifying them. Do you, in your vast lack of knowledge, know if that were so?"

"And many did! They too had many cats buried and mummified with them to pay them homage."

The small caravan began moving over the ground where their ancestors trod and the significance was not lost to them. It was a land of green that lined the Nile River as far as their eyes could see. They marveled at their arid surroundings yet people settled and prospered here in the green fields. The Holy Family made their way to the delta city of Tanis (Zoan), the former capital of Egypt. Along the way they were able to speak with Jews already settled there. They were told of Stone Age farming villages that grew over the years into cities, then provinces until they became separate Kingdoms of Upper and Lower Egypt.

Making sure that his family was safe, and as they prepared the evening meal, Joseph sought out the synagogue and anyone who could help them. One of the elders told them that if Egyptian scribes had recorded the Hebrew's escape on papyrus, the scrolls did not survive, at least none had ever been found.

"Tell me, rabbi," Joseph asked, "were the pharaohs identified who reigned during the oppression and Exodus of the Jews while in Egypt?"

The rabbi thought for several moments gathering his thoughts, "The simple answer is no. Tradition has said that Rameses II, who was the ruler twelve hundred years earlier, was the oppressor. However, his son, Merneptah, was the pharaoh during the time of the Exodus. As a matter of fact, one of the inscriptions on his stele boasts of a campaign in which 'Israel is laid waste' and that, as far as I know is the only reference to Israel in ancient Egyptian literature."

Off in the distance there was a gathering of people from the city. They were approaching the small group demanding that they leave Tel Basta immediately. They expressed no reason for their demands.

Joseph inquired, "What have we done to offend them?"

The rabbi thought for awhile and said, "sometimes they behave in this fashion for no apparent reason. I apologize for the rudeness. Go with God Joseph and you and your family as well."

"*Toda,* rabbi," Joseph said bowing.

"*Bevakasha,*" the old man said as he turned to leave.

As the Holy Family went their way south, they were pelted by stinging, blowing sand that got in their eyes and teeth, behind their ears and in their undergarments. Mary covered the baby's head and face and held him close to protect him from being hurt. The heat, winds and pelting sand lasted for several days.

Along their route they saw pagan pyramids rising from the sand. Joseph marveled at the engineering, mechanics and suffering involved. Mary was almost overcome by the sorrow she felt for the brutality and suffering it took to make these edifices. "It had to have taken thousands of slave's labor to build those things in this blistering heat and pelting sand storms. Those poor souls."

That night, after camp had been laid out, the meal prepared and eaten, Mary coaxed, "Tell us, Lord, the story of Moses and how he was able to take the oppressed slaves out of Egypt and away from their hardships."

As the women made themselves comfortable, Joseph began, now comfortable in his role as storyteller, began: "We are near the Nile River and its deltas. It was in the river marshes of this river that Moses' mother placed him in a small barque.

"Let me begin at the beginning. Some of the stories you have heard before.

"Now a man of the tribe of Levi married a Levite woman named Jochebed and she became pregnant and gave birth to a son. When she saw that he was a fine child, she hid him from her husband for three months. But when she could hide him no longer, she got a papyrus basket for him and coated it with tar and pitch. Then she placed the child in it and put it among the reeds along the bank of the Nile River. A servant stood at a distance to see what would happen to him.

Then pharaoh's daughter, Midash, went down to the Nile to bathe, and her attendants were walking along the riverbank. She saw the basket among the reeds and sent her female slave to get the basket. The slave opened it and saw the baby. He was crying, and she felt sorry for him.

"This is one of the Hebrew babies," she said to herself.

Then the attendant asked pharaoh's daughter, "Shall I go and get one of the Hebrew women to nurse the baby for you?"

"Yes, go," Midash answered. So the girl went and got Jochebed, the baby's mother.

Pharaoh's daughter said to her, "Take this baby and nurse him for me, and I will pay you." So the woman took the baby and nursed him. When the child grew older, she took him to Midash and he became her son. She named him Moses, saying, "I drew him out of the water."

Moses was raised amidst all the splendor of the Egyptian empire and had lived the life as a prince among riches. In spite of that, he felt a deep depression at the plight of his people laboring under such harsh, cruel brutality to produce such splendor. He received a divine commission to confront the pharaoh, which he did. He beseeched the pharaoh to release his people and was denied.

The pharaoh asked, 'Who is this Yahweh of yours that I should obey his voice to let Israel go?' Joseph's request was denied.

"Moses then called down ten plagues on Egypt, one of the last took the life of the pharaoh's son. The pharaoh received God's words and was moved."

"I could have stretched forth my hand," Joseph replied, "and stricken you and your people with pestilence and thou would have been effaced from the earth. Nevertheless I have spared thou for this purpose: in order to show thou My power and in order that My fame may resound throughout the world."[62]

Salomé asked, "Joseph, I know thou have learned these stories from your teachers in the temple, but you have such vivid memory all these years after. How is it?"

"Throughout my life my father, Jacob had repeated them often to me and I have told them to my children. So it is through the generations."

---

[62] Exodus 9:15 -16 JPS

CHAPTER TWENTY-THREE

THE EVENING BEFORE they left Tanis, Joseph spoke with Mary and Salomé. "I think it best that you should know why we are leaving. Tanis is too close to the border, Herod's jurisdiction and on the caravan route as well. We would be too easy to locate. I think it best that we go to Alexandria where there are large enclaves of Jewish settlers; some say more than 100,000 Jews. We could mingle among them, making ourselves more difficult to find."

Mary asked, "Will we be traveling through desert country as we did on the way down here?"

"I know you have a reason for concern that was a most difficult journey we made getting here. It is my belief that we will be traveling to the delta lands of the Nile. It should be cooler there, should be more cities to go through, and means for replenishing our supplies. I have given this move great thought, and I think it best. We will leave at sunrise."

Joseph clasped his hands, bowed his head and closed his eyes saying, "Lord God we ask for your presence and guidance on our journey to Alexandria."

At the river's levee, Joseph left his family in the shade of several palm trees. He went to seek out a boat captain going to Alexandria. It was fortunate in that he found one by the rivers' edge. Passage was arranged, the sale of Phyllis, their donkey, covering their fares and meals. As they boarded the boat, Joseph noted its construction. The boat at the front and back had a half-moon configuration. In the rear was a steersman on a platform, in the center was a tall mast with a sail attached a raised platform in front, and in between decking for cargo and passengers. Once on board, they made themselves comfortable. Jesus was excited and wanted to examine everything.

As the boat went into the mainstream, the sail was raised and the Captain steered to the center of the river. The wind billowed the sail and they were on their way. Meals were taken from a large cauldron in the center of the lower deck atop a kiln that kept it warm. With the setting of the sun, Mary asked

Joseph to tell the story. When he began, crew members gathered around them to listen to the tale.

"The story I will tell you is about a young man who listened to the word of God. Unlike his grandfather Rehobo'am and his father, Abijah, Asa was a good king who followed after God and ruled his people wisely. He commanded the people of Judah, seek the Lord God of your fathers, keep his laws and commandments. He ordered the people to take away the idols and smashed them. "He then said, build cities and around them put up walls and towers, plant dates, figs. Because we have sought the Lord, he has given us rest from Moore's from the war." And the country prospered. The Ethiopian, King, Zerah saw how prosperous Judah was, he started to make war on that country. They marched upon Judah with a great Army. Asa gathered up his small army of 300,000 but they were no match for the Ethiopians. Asa prayed to the Lord, 'Lord, can you give power to a few just as easily as you gave to a great country. Help us, Oh Lord, our God. We rest on you, thou art our God.'

"When the men of Judah met the mighty warriors of Ethiopia in battle, the Ethiopians turned and ran. They did not even stop to pick up their belongings. After the victory, the men of Judah found many valuable things their enemy left behind." One of the crewmen asked, "You are telling us, the men of Judah defeated a large Ethiopian army because they believe in God?"

"Belief in the Lord our God and great things can happen!" The crewmen went back to their duties and Joseph and his family said their evening prayers. On the morning of the third day, the boat pulled ashore and was made fast. The Holy Family debarked and found themselves a secluded location to get organized for their further journey. They were settled when Joseph said, "I will seek out the synagogue to find out how far we need to travel to reach Alexandria."

In a small section of the city Joseph spoke to the rabbi who identified himself as rabbi Nahor Haran.

"*Shalom* my son. How may I be of help," the rabbi asked?

"We, my family and I," Joseph was saying," just come ashore and we wondered where we were, and how far we need to travel before reaching Alexandria?"

"You are in Sais, about 100 kilometers west of Alexandria. Would you be going further overland or continue going by water?"

"We are uncertain. What would you recommend?"

"If you are to travel overland, you will need a pack animal for the trip. Such an animal can be purchased at the Ferrier, and other such beasts."

"Thank you for that information rabbi. Just to be clear, you are saying that we are at least ten days from our destination, traveling overland."

"Yes my son. May I ask why you are going to Alexandria? Your manner of speech indicates that you are from Judea. What brings you so far away from your home?"

"You are correct, we are from Judea and I am Joseph, son of Jacob, the woman with the young child is my wife Mary, our companion Salomé and our infant son Jesus. We are from Nazareth fleeing from King Herod's wrath. He seeks to kill our infant son."

"Why on earth would he want to do that?"

"Well in Jerusalem and the surrounding areas, he had all male children two years of age and younger, fearing that one of them was the newborn Messiah. We moved our son from that threat."

"Fear not, in Alexandria there is a large Jewish population. Go among men, live and be well. However, before you leave, might I suggest that you continue your travels by barge going east along the tributary of the Nile. You will reach your destination far faster than if you traveled overland."

"That sounds like a much better way to go. Where can we book passage?"

"Where your other boat docked earlier today. The barge that you want should be leaving this afternoon. See Captain Abram Siemens and tell him that I sent you."

"Thank you rabbi." Joseph left with his family and together they sought out Captain Siemens. Joseph, with his inquisitive eye, determined that this craft is smaller than the one they had come in on. Captain Siemens came forward to greet them. He told them that he would be quite pleased to have them come along with him. On board, Joseph asked, "This boat is smaller than the one we traveled here on. How was it constructed?" "The whole of the craft is made from reinforced papyri form, or bonded papyrus caulked and made water resistant. We have used this sort of craft for more years than I can remember."

Once the craft was in midstream, Captain Siemens visited them. "I apologize for the crude accommodations, but we are limited by the size of the ships that ply these waters. If I may be so bold to ask, what is your purpose in visiting Alexandria?"

Joseph answered, "To join with other Jewish exiles and make a new home. We are escaping a tyrant who wants to take our lives."

"No wonder you are escaping. I think you'll find a safe harbor in Alexandria. Do you know anything about the city?"

"I must confess," Joseph admitted, "that our information is quite scarce."

"If you allow me, perhaps I can fill in some of the blank spots for you."

Mary spoke out trying to relieve the tension she felt. "Please, do share the information you have. We are anxious to learn all we can about this new land we are entering."

"Alexandria is anything but a new land. It is hundreds of years old and takes its name from Alexander the Great. The city became one of the greatest of the ancient cities. It is located on the Mediterranean Sea, on the western side of the Nile Delta. It was built to become the major Egyptian seaport. It has a lighthouse that is a tall structure with a rotating light that can be seen 57 kilometers out to sea. "In its day, Alexandria was a great center of ancient knowledge and learning. It is said that the famous Alexandrian library held 700,000 volumes that were destroyed when Arab forces burned down the library. It is unknown the amount of knowledge that was lost and may never be regained.

"Before I forget," Captain continued, "water on board is plentiful. We eat only one meal a day and that is at the midday. Your child can run about freely and safely on the lower deck."

"Thank you Captain," Joseph said.

The Holy Family gathered at the ship's deck railing to watch the sun set beyond the river. The sounds and smells of things that had never been experienced by them before. White birds flew out of trees to travel downstream. Every once in a while some sort of animal could be seen slithering its way into the stream and disappear from view.

Salomé observed, "This is also wondrous."

Salomé asked, "How could Our Blessed Lord create such beauty?"

Mary affirmed, "This is all so wondrous!"

"Mary asked, "How could Our Blessed Lord create such beauty?"

"We must keep in mind," Joseph said, "that with God, all things are possible." Joseph clasped their hands with his, raised his eyes to heaven saying, "We thank thee Lord, God Almighty for being with us and watching over us."

CHAPTER TWENTY-FOUR

A CHILLY MIST covered the tributary, fog lying close to the water. It was a long journey. The Holy Family huddled together cold and hungry. Captain Siemens came by to tell them that they would soon be entering Lake Mareotis, later in the day they would be landing on a spit of land called Alexandria.

"We will be having a meal," he said, "in about an hour. The rest of the time will be taken up in preparation for landing and getting you ashore."

As promised, they were called to the meal which they hungrily devoured. The food was warm as was the honeyed wine. Their bodies began to warm up. Jesus must have sensed landing was near. He ran here and there, climbed freight bundles and asked dozens of questions; when will the land, will it get warmer, will we get some more to eat? The meal was completed when Captain Siemens joined them.

"Let me tell you about the city called Alexandria," he began. "It is a long island almost split in half by an inlet. To the right of the endless land you see, that would be west, is a virtually undeveloped land called the Jewish quarter. To the east, and still part of the Jewish quarter, is the developed city itself. Offshore is the Isle of Pharos. On that Isle is the lighthouse guiding ships into the harbor.

"The city of Alexandria is walled in on three sides, and is connected to Pharos by a causeway. The people in Alexandria, mostly Jews, are accommodating and will welcome you warmly. Before you ask Joseph, I will give you some of the history of Alexandria. The city was founded by Alexander the Great. It is the second largest city after Cairo, and it was the capital city of Egypt around 330 BC but fate did not allow Alexander who wanted to see the completed city. That was done by Ptolemy I after Alexander's death. His keen vision however, enabled him to see the importance of Alexandria's location and harbor which would serve her for eons. The city would become the magnet attracting the ambitious, the seeker of glory, just as she would attract the seeker of knowledge and scholarship. The Alexandrian library, consisting of some 700,000 volumes

---

were destroyed by Arab invaders 42 BC, had become the beacon of light with all the treasures she was able to amass from every part of the world.

"The ancient Egyptians had a settlement on the Mediterranean, for Alexander named the city "Alexandria". To them, it was Ra-aa-qedet (Rakhotis), which meant the city which Ra blesses and presides over, or "place of building." It was known by that name until the end of the Byzantine era. It is said that Rakhotis was found 700 years before Alexander renamed it and it became a city comprised of twelve villages. It has since become the largest Jewish community in the world, along with the once famous Alexandrian library.

"The city is on the strip of land sandwiched between the Mediterranean to the north and Lake Mareotis to the south. The city's topography is characterized by a series of elevations consisting of limestone hills that stretch along the seacoasts. The Jewish quarter of the city can be located in the northwest quadrant, and you will note that the city is almost completely surrounded by the canal of Alexandria. On the North Shore, inside the great harbor, you will find Cleopatra's Needles, what is left of Alexander's library and museum.

Offshore there is the island of Pharos that can be reached by a causeway. On the island there is an ancient and well-known lighthouse called Pharos Lighthouse. It was built in three distinct structures. The first is a square base, the second is an octangular tower with the cylinder extending into a cupola where there was a fire platform which provided the light that burned. A spherical ramp allowed mules to carry the carts of firewood. Topping this off as the statue of Poseidon, 134 meters above the ground. A large mirror, it is said, rejects the light for 48 kilometers.

By that causeway you will find the Agora, the city's center of athletic, artistic, spiritual and political life.

That gives you some background, Joseph. Once you are on shore and through the city gates, and to the marketplace where you should find what you need. Good luck and Godspeed."

"Before you leave us Captain, I am a *tektôn* by trade," Joseph informed him, "will there be work for me here in Alexandria?"

"Joseph, let me put your mind at ease. Alexandria is an ever-growing city, with the skills you have and if you develop maritime skills, your work may soon become overwhelming.

"One thing you should know, there are synagogues in the city and work has begun on a temple. Let me remind you, when next you go to the temple you'll find that people of similar occupations, crafts and skills seat themselves together. They do this I am sure because they speak the same language, have similar interests, and help one another out. If there is anyone seeing a particular craftsman, these people know about it."

As they were debarking, Jesus crinkled his nose and made a noise. "What," Mary asked no one in particular, "is that terrible smell?"

Captain Siemens chuckled, "I am so used to the smells here that I hardly realize how bad it is. We are on Lake Mareotis and on the other side of Alexandria's Mediterranean Sea. Both are at low tide, which brings about the smell. Inland you will not notice the smell at all."

On shore Joseph took his family into the city. The smell of the waterfront was replaced by a multitude of smells of different origins. They made their way to the marketplace where they beheld a bustling city. Merchants were everywhere and off in the distance they saw a synagogue. They made their way to it. There was a small courtyard before the synagogue that they entered. A robed priest approached them saying, "*Shalom* travelers. *Ani yakhol laazor lekha*," he asked?

"Yes you can help," Joseph responded. "We have just come into your city and are seeking a place to stay and find work for me to do."

"*Ma shimka*," the priest asked?

"*Hashem*. . . I am Joseph, son of Jacob. This," he said placing his arm around Mary, "this is my wife Mary, the little one with a firm grip on my fingers is our son, Yehoshua, and our companion Salomé."

"Yehoshua? Isn't that a sacrilegious name for a small child?"

"There is a long story about that. We are fleeing from a tyrannical king in Nazareth who seeks to have us put to death."

The priest looked at them quizzically, reached a decision then spoke.

"What do you do for a living Joseph?"

"I am an experienced *tektôn*. We need someplace to make a home and for me to open a carpentry business."

With a smile on his face, the priest said, "You do not seek much do you? No matter. I am Ezrah Pincus and I can help you get started. To begin with, let me get you and your family something to eat then, we'll talk further."

After they had eaten and refreshed themselves, Ezrah sat with them and spoke. "I have made some inquiries and I have found that you have come at an opportune time. There is a recently vacant house by the hippodrome, with a stall attached by the hippodrome. The former occupant left to return to camp Judea. The place is empty, and you and your family can rent it. I will speak to the owner then you can deal with him.

"I will let it be known in the community that we have a skilled craftsman in need of work. Let me ask you, when your son will be coming to school here?"

"You are overwhelming us Ezrah! Thank you for locating us a home so quickly and yes, Jesus will be schooled here."

"Jesus? I thought his name was Yehoshua?" Joseph smiled.

"Both names have the same meaning, as you know, but Jesus is easier to say."

"Well then my friends let us get you settled."

Ezra escorted them to the Jewish quarters of the city to introduce them into the temple. The Holy Family was made welcome and living quarters were provided. That evening there was to be a community dinner they were invited. When dinner had ended the rabbi introduced Joseph and his family and they were made welcome.

"Joseph," the rabbi called out, "Mary tells us that you are a storyteller of some renown. Would you share one of your stories with us?"

"We usually close our evenings with a story. I see no reason why we should not do so tonight. Jesus is the one with the inquisitive mind so with your permission, I would ask him to select a story for tonight."

Jesus, pleased to be the center of attraction, called out, "Tell us a story about the garden of Eden. You mentioned once before Rivers flowed from there, but not much else. What else do you know about the rivers in the garden?"

"As usual Jesus, you have selected a story that is rather difficult to tell." After a pause Joseph continued. "Any discussion regarding the four rivers is shrouded in mystery. The descriptions given in the Torah are rather vague, and there has been much debate throughout the ages regarding their exact identity.

According to legend, river water flowed out of Eden to water the garden, and from there it separated and became four heads.

"What can be clearly deduced from a brief reading of this is that there exist four rivers, Pishon, Gichon, Chidekel and Perat, which all seemingly flow from the same source, the Garden of Eden.

"Let's begin with the second two, since their identification is agreed upon almost unanimously.

"The name of the third river is *Chidekel;* that is the one that flows to the east of Ashur. It is otherwise known as the Tigris River which flows from southeastern Turkey through Iraq, and eventually spills into the Persian Gulf.

And the fourth river, that is *Perat,* identified as the Euphrates River, which runs almost parallel to the Tigris. Together, these two rivers defined a large part of the Fertile Crescent, the cradle of civilization in ancient times.

The Euphrates River is mentioned as God's promise to Abraham regarding the Land of Israel, and is used as one of the defining borders of the Promised Land.[63]

"While these two rivers are easily identifiable and their location is readily agreed upon, the identification of the other two proves more difficult and is the subject of much debate.

---

63   Genesis 15:18

"The name of first one is *Pishon*; that is the one that encompasses all the land of Havilah, where there is gold. And the gold of that land is good; there is the crystal and the onyx stone. The name *Pishon* is associated with the Hebrew word *pishtan*, or flax, a reference to the ancient Egyptian flax industry, which was watered by the Nile River. From what I have been able to learn, the area called Havilah refers to some area along the Nile region, perhaps Egypt or Sudan.

"The name of the second river is *Gichon*; that is the one that encompasses all the land of Cush. The land of Cush, according to Marcus Yekem back in Memphis, is associated with Ethiopia, and the *Gichon* is therefore understood to refer to what is known as the Blue Nile. The Blue Nile begins in Ethiopia and meets the White Nile in Khartoum, Sudan, where together they form one river that flows all the way to Egypt."

A man sitting in the audience, one Marcus Meyer, commented, "the rabbi promised a good night story but failed to mention that the story would teach us some of the history from our past. For this we thank you Joseph."

CHAPTER TWENTY-FIVE

EZRAH WENT WITH them to the vacant building that was to be their home. On entering, Joseph observed that the building was completely empty, there was straw on the floor in the front room, but nothing else. There was a smell about the building but that was caused by the building being unoccupied. That could easily be remedied. There were two rooms in the rear, one appeared to be the kitchen area, complete with a small oven, and second in larger room for eating or family room, climbing the stairs on the outside of the building, they found three additional rooms which could be used for bedrooms. Fortunately, there was sufficient lighting throughout. At the rear was a small courtyard with an arbor.

Ezrah pointed out, "On the roof there is a stove and an oven I think you will find useful. It was put on the roof so that the kitchen would not become too hot."

Jesus ran from room to room exploring every nook and cranny. In every room he called out, "Look at this!" He also negotiated the back stairs rapidly and frequently. At last Salomé slowed him down to change his clothes.

"Can this work for you Joseph," Ezrah asked?

"We have been living out in the open, in caves, and an occasional tent. To answer your question, yes we can make this work nicely. Thank you for your help."

"Yes," Mary joined with Joseph, "thank you for your thoughtfulness."

"We are here my friends, to help one another. *Shalom.*"

The women unpacked their belongings, then set about cleaning the house. Jesus went with his father to locate a supply of wood. At the mill Joseph showed his son the different types of wood, their uses and durability. Between them they purchased the wood needed for their immediate use. Payment arrangements were made along with their delivery to get their new business going.

They returned home to join the others in unpacking and deciding which rooms would be used for what purpose. It was general consensus about their use. Downstairs the kitchen area was obvious because of the stone flour grinder, mortar and pestle left behind. That room and the dining area would be the domain of Mary and Salomé. The front room would be the workshop of Joseph and Jesus. The rooms on the second floor would be used for sleeping and storage.

When they had unpacked, Joseph sat with everyone in the arbor. He began by saying, "Let us make a list of those things that need to be made immediately."

"We will need," Mary began, "a cupboard for storing dishes and earthen pots, tables and chairs, and you will need a work table and cupboard."

"Yes, Jesus and I will begin work on those items as soon as the wood arrives. We will also need to have some money coming in, our money is almost gone."

And so it was that the Holy Family went to work, Joseph and Jesus handling the woodwork, Mary and Salomé putting the house in order. By the third day their first client came to the shop.

"*Shalom*," he said. "I am in need of latticework for the windows in my house. Can you do this," he asked Joseph?

"We, my son and I, will have to go to your house to take the measurements of the windows. Then, you have to decide what type of latticework you want. We can go back with you now if you want."

"I am Yaakov Eisenberg, and I live close by."

Joseph stooped to pick up Jesus saying, "I am Joseph and this young man is my helper, Jesus. Let us go to your house and take those measurements."

At the completion of this work, other work followed. Jesus was being schooled at home by Mary and Salomé and he was also being schooled in the temple with other boys of his age. Rosh Hashanahs, Yom Kippurs, Hanukkahs and Passovers, came and went. One evening before returning home after the Passover feast, Ezra asked Joseph to stay behind.

"Joseph," Ezrah began, "people of the community like you and your family and the work that you do."

"But," Joseph interjected.

After a pause Ezrah continued, "But you and your family have people pursuing you and they are quite fearful. They know you are fleeing from King Herod's wrath and because of that, they fear he may send troops seeking you and in so doing, caused them trouble that they neither need or want."

"What is it you want us to do," he asked him what was the answer?

After a long pause during which time Ezrah could not make eye contact he said, "Can you take your family to another city to live?"

By way of reply Joseph said, "We have become established here, we have begun to take root. What is being asked is cruel and unkind! Is there no other way this can be handled? No other option?"

"No Joseph, the delegation that came to me was adamant. I am sorry."

"Sadly and with a heavy heart, we will move on."

When they had returned home, Joseph told the others what was being asked.

"That is so unfair," Salomé wailed! "We have worked so hard to become one of them and now they turn on us."

"These people," he said by way of explanation, "are all exiles as we are, fleeing from one persecution or another. They want to be left in peace."

"I do not think we have to leave immediately. Let us gather together what we will need in the morning, I will return to the temple to find out where to go and the best way to get there."

The packing was well begun when Joseph returned with news. "I learned from merchants who had traveled westward, that we can sail to Salána. From there we go to Heliopolis, which is a much larger city. Once there, we can decide where to go next."

"How much of our belongings can we take," Salomé asked?

"As we have done in the past, only pack essentials. However, I have learned that we can ferry a donkey with us. That will allow us to take additional items. Mary, if you will come with me we will book passage to Salána and also see if we can find a donkey we can afford."

In the city proper they arranged for passage. Then, in a stable recommended to them, they found a gentle, strong donkey that came to put his muzzle against Mary. "This one Joseph," she exclaimed! "I will call her Portia."

Two days later the Holy Family left Alexandria and three days after that, they went ashore at Salána located on the west bank of the Nile River. The city to be spread over a low terrace that has been given over to agriculture.

They were informed that they would be stopping here overnight. Ashore they found a small oasis. The city, they found, and a dank smell was quite humid. After the evening meal Salomé asked Joseph to tell the story as they sat about the campfire. Joseph agreed. As they set about the fire Joseph began.

"Solomon was the second son of King David and the wisest man who ever lived.

"In Gibeon the Lord appeared to Solomon in a dream by night; and God said, "Ask what I shall give thee. And Solomon said, Thou hast shewed unto thy servant David my father great mercy, according as he walked before thee in truth, and in righteousness, and in uprightness of heart with thee; and thou hast kept for him this great kindness, that thou hast given him a son to sit on his throne, as it is this day. And now, O Lord my God, thou hast made thy servant king instead of David my father: and I am but a little child: I know not how to go out or come in. And thy servant is in the midst of thy people, which thou hast chosen, a great people, that cannot be numbered nor counted for multitude. Give therefore thy servant an understanding heart to judge thy people that I may discern between good and bad: for who is able to judge this thy so great a people?

"Solomon was the builder of the First temple in Jerusalem. It portrays him as a king whose sins, including idolatry and turning away from Yahweh, led to the kingdom's being torn in two during the reign of his son Rehoboam.

"Solomon had 700 wives and 300 concubines. The wives are described as foreign princesses, including pharaoh's daughter and women of Moab, Ammon, Sidon and of the Hittites. These foreign wives have been depicted as leading Solomon away from Yahweh toward idolatry because they worshiped gods other than Yahweh[64].

"The only wife mentioned by name is Naamah, who is described as the Ammonite. She was the mother of Solomon's successor, Rehoboam.

And it was obvious that Joseph was with his storytelling, Mary and Salomé began putting things away for the evening. Mary said, "It would appear that your father spent many hours such as this telling you stories ever told to him by his father."

"Alas Mary, that is true. It is also how legends are made, told by his father, and so on down the ages. Is there anything else?"

"Your nagging wife would like to hear the end of the story that he began some time ago."

"And what story was that?"

"The story about the Garden of Eden and the four rivers that ran from it. You said it was something else may we hear it now?"

Joseph sat down his back against the tree his feet toward the fire.

"If these four rivers, that I have mentioned, all flow forth from the Garden of Eden, their identification should give us some clue as to the location of the Garden. The major problem is, however, that there is no central location from which all of these four rivers flow. The Euphrates and the Tigris are in the northeast region, whereas the two Nile's rivers are in the southwest.

"While the exact location of the Garden of Eden cannot be identified, I do not believe, we can infer that it is somewhere within this region, between the Nile River and the Euphrates.[65] Some sources go so far as to identify the location of the Garden as being exactly 32 degrees south of Jerusalem. The fact that the Garden itself cannot be detected in our world does not mean that it does not take up physical space; it exists perhaps on a higher plane of reality and is therefore not detectable by our human senses.

"While discussions seemingly indicate that the rivers all flow from the same source, this is clearly not the case. It has been suggested that the Hebrew word

---

[64] 1 Kings 3: 4-9

[65] Genesis 3:22

for "separated," *badal,* can also be understood as "lost or missing."[66] According to this interpretation, the river sunk into the ground at the exit of the Garden of Eden, and later reappeared at four distinct locations. The interpretation reads, "A river flowed out of Eden to water the garden, and from there it was lost (sunk into the ground) and (later reemerged and) became four heads."

"It has further been pointed out by Marcus Yekem that the four rivers are referred to as four heads and not four branches, which may imply that they are not four branches of the same river, but rather four distinct riverheads.[67]

"I would conclude with this piece of information you can think on and discuss at future meetings. The Hebrew word *eden* means "delight and pleasure," and is symbolic of the ultimate source of all delight and pleasure: God. This Godly delight is then channeled into our world by way of the *"river that flows from Eden,"* and becomes the source for all worldly pleasures. The river splits into four heads, symbolizing the four spiritual worlds through which the river must travel before reaching this physical world."

---

[66]   Psalms 92:10 and Job 4:11.
[67]   Genesis 2:20

CHAPTER TWENTY-SIX

JOSEPH PACKED THE donkey for the three-day trip to Heliopolis. As he was packing, Jesus pointed out several mud uncovered oval houses, silos and granaries that look to be abandoned. Once the animal was packed, Joseph took the lead with Jesus at his side. Mary and Salomé were on either side of the animal.

Their meals were prepared and eaten out-of-doors and they slept at night on the ground. On the second night before reaching the destination, Mary asked Joseph to tell the story.

"Tonight I will tell you," he said, "of the second Passover.

"Many years ago while the Israelites were near Mount Sinai, God reminded Moses that a year had passed since they left Egypt. 'The time has come,' He said, "to have another Passover supper because I want you to remember how the death angel passed over your house in Goshen. Moses told the Israelites what God had said.

"Moses instructed the people saying, "Every family should prepare a meal of unleavened bread and bitter herbs." He told them that God said, "Do not leave any of it." The people obeyed. Several days later, the Israelites saw the cloud that had been covering the Tabernacle, float away to the north. The people knew that this was the sign for them to move on.

"How pleased they must have been to be on their way to Canaan."

Joseph knelt, clasped his hands together saying, "Oh Lord our God you have seen us safely on our journey. Be with us still as we have to travel on. All praise to you!"

The Holy Family made camp the night in an abandoned shepherd's cave on the outskirts of Heliopolis. The evening meal had been consumed and Jesus was given his bath and put to bed. It had been a hard day of travel from Goshen. They relaxed by the campfire, exhaustion putting a damper on conversation.

"I will leave after the morning meal," Joseph replied.

The morning air was chilled but as he walked along, he began to feel warmer. At the temple door he was met by one of the priests.

"*Boka Marcus*, good morning," the priest said in greeting. "You are a stranger to our community. I have not seen you before. Welcome."

Joseph made a slight bow. "*Bokya Marcus*. I am Joseph, son of Jacob and we are from Nazareth."

"The ancient home of King David," the priest noted.

"Yes, I am of the tribe of David, but without distinction. *Aich korim lachca*? May I ask your name," Joseph asked?

"Yes, yes please forgive me my name is David Hirsch and I am a priest here in the synagogue. Is there anything you need?"

"Yes, I am a carpenter by trade, rather a *tektôn* and I'm seeking work."

"Is it your intention to stay with us a while," David asked?"

"Yes, we have been traveling for some time and for a great distance. We need rest. It is our intention to stay at least one year, possibly longer."

"There are many in our community, that are in need of your services. I will start referring people to you. The rest will be up to you. Is there anything else?"

"Yes. I need to purchase some supplies and I wonder is there anyone in the community that has knowledge on pyramids and how they were made."

"With regard to your question about the market, I will take you there. About the pyramids, what sort of information is it you are seeking about our ancient neighbors?"

"In learning of my trade, I have gained some knowledge about architecture such that I have an unquenchable thirst to learn more. I would like to know how they were built, who built them, how long they are...?"

"Yes, yes," David said interrupting, "I see that you are on the journey, a quest for very specific information. We have an older man, who has such knowledge. The man you seek is rabbi Yo'ash Pensak. He has devoted many years in studying Egyptology and pyramids. I will give you his address and tell you how to get there. After you have spoken to him, return and we will go to the marketplace."

"You are most kind David."

Joseph followed the directions given him and before long found himself at the gate of a large house fronted by a wide courtyard.

"*Boker Marcus*, welcome to my home," an elderly man called out. They sat beneath an Olive tree. "*Cos tay*, come in and sit down."

"*Toda* rabbi. I am a pilgrim seeking knowledge."

"We are all pilgrims my son. Come, sit down and have a glass of tea. Without fear, you can tell people who you are and where you are from."

"I am Joseph son of Jacob and my home was in Bethlehem. We left our home fleeing from the wrath of King Herod. If this knowledge makes you uncomfortable, I shall leave."

"Nonsense! Tell me how I can be of service to you. Oh, by the way, I am Yo' ash Pensak. Drink your tea."

Joseph explained why he had come to Yo' ash's house and who had sent him.

"I will be pleased to share what I have learned about the pyramids. It allows me to put on my hat as the teacher, a calling I have always wanted to be part of. Do you want the long version of the construction or the short version?"

"I do not want to impose on your generosity. Just a general overview, if you please."

"Where to begin? Let me start by saying that Egyptians believe in the Sun God Ra, who is believed to be the father of all pharaohs and it was he who created the pyramid shaped mound symbolizing the sun's rays.

"Many years ago the Nile Delta served many settlements, and most of that is now submerged in water. A point of fact, over the years the Nile River has been redirected west eight miles to its present course. That reason, although the pyramids appear to have been built inland, they were actually built along the banks of the river.

"The first area selected for pyramid construction was in Saqqara then, from north to south, but not in any particular order, pyramids were built in Abu Rawash, Giza, Abu Garah, Abusir, and Dashur. The northernmost pyramid, Abu Rawash, is unique in that it is an open-air pyramid, now mostly demolished. It is eight kilometers to the North of Giza, it is the site of Egypt's most northerly pyramid, also known as the lost pyramid — the mostly ruined Pyramid of Djedefre, the son and successor of Khufu. Originally, it was thought that this pyramid when completed would be about the same size as the Pyramid of Menkaure – the third largest of the Giza pyramids.

"The first pyramid built was in Saqqara, was called Step Pyramid was built by King Djoser, or rather his Chancellor Imhotep, during Egypt's third dynasty. This Chancellor build a stepped pyramid by stacking a mastabas-those are rectangular squares of decreasing schematic view of a mastabas Step Pyramid size, once placed upon the other, into which Kings and pharaohs were entombed. The site selected by Imhotep was in Saqqara overlooking Memphis.

"The best-known and the largest pyramid is the Great Pyramid in Giza. That is the largest pyramid you see off in the distance. It was designed by King Khufer. That one, so the story is told, had to be built using 20 to 30,000 conscripted laborers, not slaves, and it was completed in less than twenty-three years.

"The pyramid that I will tell you about is the great pyramid. Imhotep and his planners, selected a site on flat bedrock in the western desert. They made star sightings keeping five basic requirements in mind. For religious reasons, it would have to be built west of the Nile, in the region of the setting sun. For safety reasons, it would have to be located higher than the Niles floodplain. For logistical reasons, since many materials to be used must be transported by rail, would have to be built as near as possible to the Nile's bank. For political and social reasons, it would have to be reasonably close to Memphis, the Egyptian capital. Finally, for architectural and geological reasons, it would have to be based on solid bedrock with no apparent cracks or weaknesses.

"When the location was found the pharaoh visited the site and with the aid of his priests, Chancellor and counselors, the alignment was fixed and true North marked in the stone bedrock known as the Giza Plateau. Then, came the task of leveling the ground. Laborers built shallow walls of Nile mud all around the construction zone. Water was poured into the shallow basin until it reached an appropriate level. Laborers cut a series of trenches beneath this shallow pool, ensuring first at the bottom of each trench was exactly and precisely the same distance beneath the water surface. The water was drained off and the space between the trenches was meticulously carved out until the rock was perfectly smooth and even.

"There was then needed a labor force. From the surrounding villages, the pharaoh's foremen selected one man out of every ten to work on the pharaoh's tomb. Gangs of conscripted laborers were sent to work in the quarries near at hand and at Aswan. Others were sent to the location where the pyramids were to be built.

"King Khufer had previously approved Imhotep's plan for his final resting place. In the plan, the largest structure would be the pyramid covering his tomb. To the east, the plan called for a mortuary temple in which the pharaoh's Ka, (soul) would dwell. Extending from both sides of mortuary temple and enclosing the area around the base of the pyramid, the plan called for a wall called the temenos wall. Further eastward on the banks of the river Imhotep showed a valley temple to which the pharaoh's party would be brought. The temples, mortuary and valley temple, would be connected by an enclosed passage called the causeway. The plan also indicated where the pharaoh's funerary boats were to be buried.

"According to the plan, the pyramid would have three main parts. The innermost section was shown to have a step like central core. Only the facing blocks of each sloping band of the core were carefully finished. Second were the packing blocks, which rested on the steps around the core. They were carefully placed and fitted. Third were the outer facing blocks laid against the packing stones. These were of the highest quality and cut with the greatest care and precision. All three parts were constructed simultaneously, one course or layer at a time.

"As an added attraction, Imhotep also indicated in his plans, and well below ground level, shafts that would include tunnels, vaults, galleries, stairways and passages for a subterranean, palace and outfitted with gold and other essential paraphernalia.

"At Aswan, and other quarries, work gangs began cutting limestone blocks to be transported down river to the site. These great stones, were cut and put on barges or boats for the trip where they were off-loaded, then placed on wooden skeds, with ropes attached, then manhandled over wooden parallel staves that had been set into the ground, and coated with alluvial mud that were kept wet by gangs of water bearers slopping the water over the staves.

"At the construction site teams consisting of eight men went to work on the blocks. Four men using wooden levers, two men using brute strength moved the stone and make adjustments, the last two men were trained stone masons to do the finishing. Using the same hauling methods, the stones would be moved up a stone and mud ramp to the next location where they were levered into place, where foremen arranged for the placement of galleries and the sarcophagus as they went, fitting joints with copper chisels. An upper crypt was built with stress relieving chambers, and two air vents awaited the pharaoh's mummy.

"Work crews at the top of the 206 layer pyramid, place a gilded capstone. Once in place they began removing the ramps as they worked their way down. They cased the core's stepped sides with smooth limestone. When completed," he said referring to a tablet," as you see this structure is 146 meters high, the capstone is nine and three-quarter meters, each side of the base is 230 meters in length, 2,300,000 blocks of stone, each weighing two and one half tons, the interior blocks of stone between forty tons, and the casing stones weigh ten tons each.

"I should also tell you that alongside his pyramid, there are three boat pits, for Kings and Pharaohs to travel on the Nile in their own boats. The reason these boat pits have boats in them, they are to be use the afterlife.

"For another time we will speak of how the conscripts lived, where they lived, what they ate, where those that died are buried."

Joseph sat quietly, trying to absorb all he had been told. Finally, he broke the silence.

"What you have told me rabbi, is unbelievable! The people who made all this happen, have a wisdom and intellect beyond anything I have ever heard or even imagined. Where did this knowledge comes from?"

"Yes Joseph, even today we cannot fathom how they accomplished many facets of the construction. We have not yet spoken of the astrology that was used in pyramid construction."

"Astrology," Joseph asked bewildered?

"Yes, the alignment of the planets in conjunction with the position of the stars, were all used in the calculations of the builders.

"If you are interested in learning more, come by anytime, something to keep in mind Joseph. Every spring I go to Giza to show travelers around the complex and tell them the history of its construction. If you are there during the springtime, seek me out and I will be glad to share what knowledge I have with you."

"*Rav todot* rabbi. Go with God."

"*Eyn davar*, you are welcome."

Joseph returned to the encampment. When he had greeted his family, he told them all that he had learned during his visit. The women sat fascinated listening to his account.

"It would appear," Mary observed, "that you had an important day. I can tell a smile on your face. Salomé and I have news for you too."

"I had a wonderful day and now I am anxious to hear of your news. What happened?"

"Salomé and I were grinding flour and preparing the lentils, when Jesus could not be found. We looked around and found our son up on the hill tending the goats. It gave us such a warm feeling."

"Our son, Mary, is growing so fast. Soon I will have an actual helper with my workshop." Joseph picked up Jesus, held him above his head saying, "I can see Jesus that my work is cut out for me. No longer can we consider you a babe, you are entering another phase of your life. Praise be to God!"

Later when they were preparing themselves to retire, Joseph sat at the table with Mary and Salomé.

CHAPTER TWENTY-SEVEN

AT SUNRISE THE following day, the Holy Family was on the road to Memphis. It soon became very warm, a sandstorm developed with stinging winds. Their progress was slow with frequent stops to rest. It was nightfall before they found a place to make camp. Joseph tethered the donkey, built a small shelter on the lee side of a dune where they rested for the night.

Later, when they were at the table with the meal, and Jesus had been put to bed, Joseph addressed the women. He began, "we are too close to the border for my liking." Joseph observed "there is word circulating the city about a troop of soldiers in the area who was seeking someone. I could not find out who it was, but it seems quite certain that they were seeking someone. It may not be related to us but I don't think we should take any chances. Tomorrow we will go to Memphis according to the rabbi, it is a rather large city, with a large Jewish population and perhaps we can get lost in their midst. He also said that it was the city where we could rest for a time and perhaps resupply.

"Once we get there," he continued, "I will buy the necessary materials for our encampment. I will also buy another donkey, since we had to sell the last one. We will need such a beast to assist us in transporting our belongings whenever we make a move.

"What a relief," Mary observed, "from the muggy heat and weather we have been having. Do you think there will be enough work for you in this new location we are going to?"

"I do not have an answer for you Mary. rabbi failed to tell me and I neglected to ask. For now, let us finish our meal, prepare ourselves for bed and go to the Lord in prayer. Let me thank him for his protection and guidance for the journey that follows."

"Mother," Jesus asked, "what caused the sand to blow around as it did?"

"I do not know my son. Perhaps your father may know the answer. Let us ask him. Joseph," Mary called out, "your son wants to know what causes a sandstorm."

"You do not ask easy questions. To the best of my knowledge I believe that heavy winds are developed in the atmosphere and as they blow around they pick up loose particles of sand and dirt. Then, when the winds are as strong as they were today, they make it difficult to see. I do not think there is anything that can determine how long a storm will last.

"For now though, let us have our meal before we call it a night. We will go to the Lord in prayer seeking his guidance and protection for the journey."

"Lord," Mary asked as she ladled out the food, "why not tell us one of your stories?"

"I told you in another story that Solomon asked the Lord for wisdom in order that he rules people wisely. He was unlike his brothers, Absalom and Adonijah, who were proud, selfish and ambitious. Solomon had recalled that the Lord had come to the aid of his father David. He knew that he too needed God's help.

"Solomon took one thousand burnt offerings to Gibeon and sacrificed them on the altar. For an entire day he watched them as they burned and as the smoke drifted skyward, he prayed earnestly asking the Lord to provide help. When night came he lay down to rest.

"While he slept, Solomon had a wonderful dream. In the dream God was standing nearby and he said, "I will give you anything you ask for."

"Immediately Solomon thought how much a good ruler needed to know. Because he thought he was not wise enough nor understanding, he answered, "Oh Lord my God you were with my father. You taught him how to follow your ways. You gave him a son to be king in his place. You have let me follow my father as king, but I do not know how to be king. Give me an understanding heart. Then I shall be able to judge the people. I shall be able to tell what is good and what is bad.

"God was pleased with Solomon's request," he said "because you have asked for wisdom instead of a long life or riches or power over your enemies, I will give you what you ask for. No king in the land shall be as wise as you and as honorable as you.

"That is my story for tonight. You should notice my son that the stories I am telling all of you focus on obedience to the love of Yahweh."

CHAPTER TWENTY-EIGHT

UPON REACHING THE city of Memphis, the search began for a good campsite with water and grazing. They were fortunate to find just what they had been looking for on the outside of the city; it was in a small pasture, with a well, and a running stream. Joseph built, with black goat's hair, a shelter tent to keep the women and infant from direct sunlight, and blowing sand storms that were a frequent occurrence.

While Mary and Salomé made the young child comfortable, they also unpacked their belongings. Joseph walked into Memphis to make the necessary purchases. Here too he stopped an elder in the temple to ask for help.

"*Shalom*," he called out, "*Ata yakol laazor li?*"

"*Meayin ata*," the man asked?

"*Shmee* Joseph, son of Jacob, from Nazareth and I have only arrived with my wife and young son and his wet nurse, Salomé. We have camped outside the city. *Ma scheemcha?*"

"*Hashem sheli* Marcus Yekem. I am a shopkeeper here in Memphis. You must be the Jews, we have heard about fleeing from Nazareth."

"Has word also been received," Joseph asked, "as to the reason we are fleeing Nazareth?"

"Alas, no. We only learned that you are fleeing but fleeing from what, is unknown."

"By my telling you this story, I am placing our lives in your hands.

"King Herod went on a murderous rampage killing all children two years of age and younger. Our child falls into that age group. We could not stay and have him imperiled! Will we be safe here?"

"Here you will find there are many who have also fled their homes, seeking asylum for various reasons. We did hear about these events in Jerusalem. But to answer your question, you will be safe."

"That is a relief, thank you for the information. I need to purchase materials for a family tent, food stuffs . . ."

"Say no more. Today you can get everything you need from me. While you and I are doing business, it would give me great pleasure to have you and your family take the evening meal with me and mine. Shall we say at sunset?"

Joseph returned to camp to tell of their good fortune. He then set about making a temporary covered latrine, a small hole into which their garbage would go before burial and a tethering post for the donkey. Then, as the sun began to set, they made their way to Marcus' home, Lydia, Marcus' wife greeted them at the portal.

"*Shalom,*" she said. Immediately she held out her arms to hold their son who was now four years of age. Jesus was given over for Lydia to cuddle him, which brought a broad smile to her face. The child returned her smile. She laid the sleeping child on a padded mat and covered him with a robe.

"Come," she said, "you can help me with the meal."

Turning her attention to Mary, she asked, "What are your names?"

Mary replied, "I am Mary, daughter of Joachim and Anne, wife to Joseph. We are from Nazareth in Judea. This woman is Salomé and she travels with us." They nodded to one another as they set to work.

Marcus greeted Joseph as they walked to the small corral.

"Let us begin supplying you with an animal." This," he said petting a large tan colored donkey with a black snout, hooves, and the black tail. The animal walked over to be fed. We will call her Rebecca. As you can see, she is friendly, strong and loving. She is a female and can be bred."

The men discussed her price and when a price had been agreed, Marcus jotted down the sale on papyrus. He then led Joseph to a large tent and upon entering Joseph could see a treasure trove of goods.

Marcus began his litany of those items he felt were necessary for their camp and any future journey; a large woven floor covering, blankets, pottery and finely woven mattresses. Again pricing was discussed and agreed.

"What about a table, chairs, a bench . . ." Before he finished, Joseph interrupted.

"Pardon me, you are a generous benefactor, but I am a *tektôn* by trade and I will make those items myself."

"Are you so," Marcus inquired? "We have great need for a craftsman with many skills. Are you such a person?"

"I am well trained in metals, wood, masonry, mortar, alabaster and crafting, and building construction. Once we are settled in, I will open my workspace outside the city limits."

"Regarding your woodworking skills, can you make yokes, cabinets, dishes, eating utensils and the like?"

"Yes, all that is possible. I will need to find a source of available woods. I also do carving in wood and metals."

"Those things too I can furnish for you. Before that, however, let us discuss your method of payment. You have available funds?"

"We still carry a quantity of frankincense and myrrh which I intend to sell as needed. I also have a few gold coins."

"Excellent! Let us settle accounts and go have our meal. Where, by all is good and holy, did you come by frankincense and myrrh? It has been many years since we have seen those commodities used in the marketplace?"

Marcus noticed that Joseph was reluctant to speak openly.

"We can save that story for another time. You and your family should be tired and anxious to make camp.

"That is a very interesting story," Joseph replied, "and you're quite right, and one of you might have trouble believing. Several days after the birth of our son, three princes from a foreign land came riding camels with their entourages to our village, and to our home to pay homage to our son. They presented him and us with these gifts. I must also tell you, the shepherds tending their flocks, saw a star and followed it to our home. They also paid homage to our son."

"Three princes from a foreign land, and shepherds following a star came to pay homage to your son. Is that what you are saying?"

"Marcus. I told you that you might have a problem relating to the story, but those events did take place."

"There is more to this than you are telling, but that is for another time."

On entering the house, Joseph touched a mezuzah attached to the door frame, commented on the table and chairs they were to eat on.

"In my old age," Marcus said, "I find it more and more difficult to get up from the ground for whatever reason. Therefore, I spoil myself and my family with these items," he said spreading his hands.

"Lord," Mary called to him, "what do you think of the aroma that greeted us? Is it not wonderful?"

"Today has been most blessed! Marcus has been very kind and understanding of our plight, such that we are now the owners of a donkey named Rebecca and we have all that is required at a fair and equitable price!"

The women clapped their hands in delight and all thanked God for His love.

Marcus stood. "Now may I hold Jesus?"

"Yes you may, we also ask that you remain with us while we continue our nightly ritual. Joseph sends us to bed with a story from our past. Would you like to stay and listen?"

Marcus replied, "With great pleasure."

Lydia said "Oh yes!"

All sat around the table, a look of eager anticipation lighting their faces.

"Tonight I think," Joseph said, "I will tell you the story of Moses when he left the pharaoh's Palace. He went from a place where shepherds tending his father-in-law, Jethro's sheep. His clothing now consisted of a course mantle usually worn by shepherds, cinched at the waist by a leather belt. He stood on a hillside watching the sheep graze with his staff in his right hand. He was still tall but his skin was tanned by the sun, wind, and rain. His hair had grown white with age.

"He had the flock feeding in green pastures at the base of Mount Horeb. As he looked on the hillside, he had to take a second look. Flames blazed from the bush. Strangely, the flames were having no effect on the bush. He moved closer to find out why.

"Moses! Moses!" A voice called out from the flames.

"Here I am," he replied.

"Take off your sandals you are standing on holy ground."

Moses realized that the voice coming from the flames was the voice of God. He removed his sandals and covered his face, afraid to look into the flames again.

God told him how miserable the Israelites were living as slaves in Egypt. "Now," the voice said, "I have come to deliver them from the Egyptians and bring them into the land I have promised their father. I have chosen you to carry out that task."

Moses was terrified on hearing this. "I am incapable of the assignment you have given me."

"I will be with you," God said.

"What if the Israelites have forgotten you? If they asked, who is this God? What shall I say?"

"Tell the Israelites that my name is I AM WHO I AM,[68] who sent you to help them."

Joseph looked around the table saying,

"That is the story for tonight, but before you leave I ask that you raise your eyes to heaven while I praise the Lord for this wonderful company, the excellent meal we had, and ask that He bless our days."

"Thank you Joseph," Marcus said as he rose to leave. "This has been a most memorable story. And now since it is apparent that you will be staying with us for some time. I would like to tell you something about Memphis I think you will find interesting.

"One thousand or more years ago, Memphis was the ancient capital of Egypt. But first, there is something I must explain. Northern Egypt is considered and called Lower Egypt because the waters of the Nile River flow into the Delta and out into the Mediterranean Sea, and not from the Mediterranean inland.

---

[68] Exodus 3:1

"The city is located on the western side of the Nile and is twelve miles south of Cairo. It is believed that the founder of the city was Pharaoh Menes during the first dynasty, and it was the principal city for about three hundred years before being supplanted by Thebes and later Alexandria.

"Memphis at the height of its grandeur marked the boundary between upper and lower Egypt. There is an alabaster statue of Pharaoh Ptah in the city that I will show you later. It serves as a memorial to the city's power and prestige.

"The city is so important to Egyptian culture that every pyramid built had to face Memphis. Its history however, is closely linked to the country itself. Its downfall, so it is said, was due to the loss of economic significance in late antiquity, following the rise of Alexandria and its coastal location.

"At the peak of its prestige, Memphis was the center for education of royal princes and sons of the nobility.

"For another time I will take you on a tour of the city and show you our statuary and monuments if that would please you."

Joseph was quick to respond, "It would please me greatly. Mary and I want to thank you for sharing this meal with us. It is good to be reminded, every now and again, of family and friends, and you fit into both categories. *Shalom* my friends."

CHAPTER TWENTY-NINE

MARY AND SALOME met with Lydia, the next day, in the city to do some shopping. Joseph was left behind to put the finishing touches to their tent home. He had the help of four men from the town. They had been sent by Marcus. Joseph met with them to outline what he wanted to accomplish. Their names were Amir, an apprentice stable hand, Chai, Eran and Zach, all day laborers. They began work with the tent which had been woven from black goat hair.

They placed the tent on the ground then placed two stout center poles inside the cloth. The poles had strong ropes attached. As two of the men, Joseph and Eran lifted the poles inside the tent, the others, Amir and Chai pulled on the ropes pulling the poles upright and the tent with them. Heavy stakes had been driven into the ground and the ropes tied to them, once secure, the rest of the tent was rolled to the ground. To further secure the tent, eight more lines were tied to stakes and pegged down; four on the east and west sides and two on the north and south. The tent opening faced the east.

Joseph began work on his workshop; he had Chai and Eran work on stoves and he assigned Amir and Zack the task of building a more permanent stable for the animals.

The workshop would be a portion outside of the tent facing north. The overhead and east and west sides were also made of woven goat's hair held upright by two small tent poles pegged into the ground and tied down. The rear opened into the tent but could be closed off; the front was left open. When it was completed it measured ten feet by ten feet. He turned to making a work table, a cupboard for storing his equipment and wood that had been delivered. He would use the outdoor stove as a kiln if and when needed.

With the help of the workers, floor mats were later put in place, mattresses laid on the ground and curtains attached to the walls of the tent to enclose heat in cold weather and keep cool in the heat. Joseph sought their advice on the placement of the Tanakh.

"Is there a special place you would like us to place it, "Amir asked?

"Yes there is," Joseph instructed. "We must be guided by some early Old Testament toilet guidance that instructs the Jewish people to have a place outside the camp and go out there, and you shall have a spade among your tools, and it shall be when you sit down outside, you shall dig with it and shall turn to cover up your excrement.[69] Over there, away from the camp is where we shall place it." Joseph would later build a seat with a hole in it for their comfort.

The men advised that it be over the hill with a tent covering for privacy, "As thou have," Amir interjected," with your temporary structure."

Following the midmorning meal Mary and Salomé had prepared, the men went to Joseph for further instructions. He asked Chai and Amir to build the structure they thought best for the Tanakh. While he, Zach and Eran built a corral and stable shelter. They separated and began work.

The donkey, Portia was tethered to a tree in the shade, watched with interest as first the corral and then the stable began to take shape. While they worked, Joseph walked to the hill to fill the goatskin and observe their progress. The Tanakh was much like those found in Bethlehem or Jerusalem. The timing was perfect. Just as the men gathered, their work done, Mary, Salomé and Jesus returned on Phyllis from their outing in Memphis. The men went to meet them.

"Look wife what these men have accomplished. We have a home that is ready for furnishing, a corral and stable for our animals and," he said pointing to the Tanakh, "a private place of comfort. Life is good wife."

"The Lord is good and we are most fortunate to have such talented men to take care of us. Wash yourselves while Salomé and I prepare our meal."

The men did as instructed and when cleaned they sat around the fire that had been started. He paid the men their agreed wages.

"Tomorrow," Joseph said, "I would like you to go and see Marcus. He is preparing further wood and other materials I have ordered. If you could see to its delivery, using one of the donkeys, I will continue your wages and I have work for you on some other projects I have in mind."

"Yes, Master," Eran replied, "we will do as you ask."

"There is no servant and Master here, Eran. I am Joseph." They were called to meal. When they entered the tent, Joseph saw two most apparent changes. The women had lighted lamps in the four corners of the tent and they had stored the household supplies and baggage along the cloth wall covering. He was interrupted from his musings by the exclamations of the men about the sumptuous meal they saw before them.

"The worker," Salomé said smiling, "is worth the meal he is served. Sit and eat!"

Before sitting, however, Joseph went to his son, took him in his arms and held him close. Mary joined him at the table.

---

[69] Deuteronomy 23:12,13

"Oh Lord God," Joseph said in prayer, "we thank you for the labors of these men, the blessings you have bestowed on our family, and the food we are about to eat."

"Jesus," Mary said, "was given warmed goat's milk by Lydia as she held him. Both of them enjoyed the encounter. "He is a good child, Lord. We have been blessed."

The meal was devoured by hungry men. The women removed the remaining food and dishes. When done, Mary and Salomé joined the men to talk.

"Lord," Mary implored, "tell us the story of Daniel please."

"Each night after the evening meal," Joseph explained, "I tell the story to my family, as my father told me. That way, it is passed down from generation to generation. Let me see what should tonight's story should be? You want to hear about Daniel do you?" They all nodded and settled back.

"Daniel," Joseph began as he picked up his son and held him close, "was one of four children, Shadrach, Meshach, and Abednego, who were taken into captivity by the Babylonians. The children were educated in Chaldean but not Daniel, however, never converted to Babylonian ways. He was given the name Balthazar.

"He was supposed to be an advisor to the court because of his skill at interpreting dreams but, it was through instruction from 'the God of Heaven,' he interpreted these dreams and visions of kings. In so doing, he was becoming a prominent figure in the court of Babylon.

"Eventually, Daniel became an official in the Persian empire under King Darius. Darius, at the urging of his other jealous officials, made a decree that no one was to offer prayer to any god or man except him for a period of thirty days. Daniel continued to pray as was his habit, knowing that praying could have him killed.

"For this action, Darius had Daniel and his companions arrested and thrown into a lions' den over night. However, they were unharmed, and after Daniel was released the following morning, the officials who had cajoled the king into making the decree for the sole purpose of getting at Daniel, were thrown into the lions' den themselves. They did not make out as well as Daniel and the others."

The men had been fed, sat to listen to a story, then rose to leave. Joseph asked that they stay a moment.

"Tomorrow when you pick up my order from Marcus, please tell him that I will be in to see him later in the day to make additional purchases and buy foodstuffs."

The men said they would do as he asked and thanked him and his family for sharing the evening meal with them and for his telling them such an interesting story. They said, "lailah Marcus", good night and left.

CHAPTER THIRTY

THE DAY AFTER his materials had been delivered, Joseph rode Phyllis into Memphis. He wanted to visit Marcus and thank him for his assistance. He had also come into the city to purchase supplies for Passover. "Shalom, Joseph. All is well?"

"*Shalom*, Marcus my friend. Yes, all is well, praise God, because of your generosity, guidance and help. Is Lydia and your family in good health?"

"Quite well, thank you. Is there something I can do for thou, Joseph"?

"Would you show me where I might purchase Passover supplies. And while we are talking about that, Mary and I would be pleased if you and Lydia would share the Passover meal with us in our new home. We are also inviting the four young men you sent our way. They are marvelous workers!"

"I have known them since they were young men running to the synagogue for their lessons. I knew they would work hard for you. I have spoken to them since and they have nothing but praise for you and your craftsmanship. With regard to your kind invitation, Lydia and I would be most pleased to join with you. What may we bring to the Seder?"

"If it would be no problem, it would be helpful if you could bring the appropriate wines." "An excellent suggestion! It would also give us another opportunity to be with your young son once again. Lydia so loves that child." Marcus indicated which shops could fill his table. Joseph left. Later that night, their guests began arriving on this, the first night of Passover. Joseph and Mary greeted them as they entered their home, Marcus handing Joseph six bottles of wine. He looked around at the progress the family had made in converting a humble tent into a warm welcoming home. The walls were covered with white linen curtains, the floors covered with several mats and the table covered with delicious foods. The oil lamps scatter about the tent added light and lent a warm atmosphere to the room. Lydia went immediately to Mary and Salomé to be with the child. She held Jesus, cuddled him and gushed over him. Mary and Salomé stood by seeing broad smiles lighting their faces. Lydia spoke

---

first. "Your child grows every day. He is bigger and heavier and sturdier," she exclaimed!

"I had trouble initially," Mary said, "weaning him to goats milk but as you can see, he has overcome his reluctance. Just today he took his first steps. Soon he will be running around yelling like a banshee. Salomé has been his wet nurse but her job has changed."

Looking around the tent, Lydia observed, "You two have done wonders with putting everything in order. I can see a good deal of hard work has been done here. It is truly a home!" Salomé added, "We have had to scrimp and save where we could to make our money serve us well. We are not wealthy after all."

Mary said, "Joseph has made the furniture you see about you; the table, chairs - which are new to us, and the cupboards. It has been a family effort."

Joseph called them to table. Once seated, he gave each of them a plate and a glass of wine. At the head of the table he placed a Seder plate Mary had filled with various symbolic foods. Nearby was another plate with enough matzo and dishes of salt water for everyone for dipping.

Joseph stood to say: "As you can see on the table, there is the Seder plate. My good wife and Salomé have placed Maror and Chazeret which are types of bitter herbs. Charoset a sweet paste of figs and nuts, Karpas that are celery and potatoes, Zeroa that is a roasted lamb and finally, Beitzah and there are enough hard boiled eggs for all. Let us begin with Kadeish," Joseph asked. The group stood as Joseph offered the blessing and they drank the first cup of wine. Once the wine was consumed, they turned to a side table where there were six bowls of water and towels for them to wash their hands. The Urchattz phase of the meal completed. Again, as a group, they went to the table and took Karpas to dip into salt water.

"At our table," Joseph began, "when everyone has eaten their afiknman I ask that each of us take turns reading parts of the Haggadah including the Magid's four questions. We can discuss various parts as they are read."

Marcus stood to refill the wine glasses for this portion of the ritual. Then Marcus, his wife and the four men raised their Seder plates over their heads and chanted: *"Bivhilu yatzanu minitzrayim, halahma Anya b'nel horin."*

Joseph translated for those unfamiliar with the chant to the others. They chanted, "In haste we went out of Egypt with our bread of affliction, now we are free people."[70]

"Yes," Marcus added, "We Jews in this land have adopted this custom."

"Thank you Joseph for your explanation of the chant. Let us wash our hands before going further." When they returned to the table, a second glass of wine was consumed. "I will begin with the first question," Joseph announced.

---

[70]   Deuteronomy 26:5-8

He closed his eyes saying, "Why is it that on all other nights during the year we eat either leavened bread or matzo, but on this night we eat only matzo?"

Eran spoke up, "Because our ancestors could not wait for their breads to rise when they were fleeing slavery in Egypt so the dough was flat when they came out of the oven."

He seated himself and the others joined him. After a brief wait Marcus rose to ask:

"*Hebb'khol hallelot anu okh'lin sh'ar y'rakot, vehallayla hazze maror?* We eat only Maror," Marcus continued, "a bitter herb, to remind us of the bitterness of slavery that our ancestors endured while in Egypt." And so the ceremony went throughout the evening with songs of praise, two more glasses of wine drunk, a short prayer asking the night's service be accepted.

The service is ended with Joseph saying, "*L'shanah haba'ah b'Yeruchalayim*" Next year in Jerusalem!" When Joseph and Mary bade goodnight to their guests, Marcus took Joseph aside. "That was a wonderful celebration, Joseph. You have done this before? Your good wife and Salomé set a fine table for your family."

"Thank you my friend. Your family is always welcome at our table."

"I need to have you make some items for me. The items will serve two purposes. First, I need them and second I can show others the quality of your workmanship."

"Do you really need the items, Marcus? Or are you promoting my business?"

"Yes! The items I need are a six shelved cabinet and a small low table for Lydia to put her laundry. I will want them finished as best you can." Joseph made his calculations and quoted Marcus his price. They agreed. Their guests rode into the night while Joseph, Mary and Salomé cleaned up the tent. Everyone was quite content and went about the work cheerfully. Joseph put Jesus to bed, made sure he was warm enough, then went about closing the tent for the night. As he went about doing this, he recalled the Passovers' they had celebrated recently, but none were as nice as this. It was truly blessed. He joined Salomé and Mary in prayer and all retired.

CHAPTER THIRTY-ONE

THE FOLLOWING DAY the family sat together discussing the previous evening. Mary noted how quickly Lydia had pitched in helping with the meal.

"Of course," she quickly added, "she had to frequently cuddle Jesus, little knowing who it truly was she was cuddling."

Salomé commented, "it is probably just as well." Changing the subject she continued, "how pleasant your guests were last night and, so well behaved."

Joseph listened quietly as the women chatted. He was pleased at how well they had adapted to the hard times they had been through.

"Lord," Mary began, "Salomé and I have been discussing planting a garden. She has seeds with her, at least enough to start a garden. We thought we would begin planting close to the stream so that water would be readily available. Could you make us a small plow and hoe for tiling the soil?"

Joseph sat looking at them trying to give the impression that he was undecided at their suggestion. As he continued to look at them, saw their resolve, he smiled.

"You will be undertaking hard work but I will make the tools that you require. While I am busy at that task, you and Salomé take Jesus into Memphis, and ask Marcus where we can purchase a harness for the donkeys. We have almost used all of our spices. Those too can be reordered. I must tell you though, before I can work on the plow and hoe, I must first finish another contract. It should not take long. Is that acceptable?"

"Yes," Mary replied excitedly. "Salomé," she called out, "please get and harness Phyllis while I make Jesus ready for the journey."

Joseph went with their workers to unload the lumber they had just delivered. That done he got his tools from the tent, put the final touches to his workshop, and began work on Marcus's cupboard.

Matters began moving quickly once these initial steps had been taken. Joseph's workshop was set up and in use. Mary, Salomé and the young Jesus had their garden planted. Jesus who had been crawling between the rows of planted vegetables, now joined his father in his workshop where work began on learning his trade. Then, once Jesus had reached the age of five, Salomé took him into Memphis where, in the temple, he began his religious education.

Joseph put Jesus with him to finish work on a corral for the animals. From a nearby tree, Joseph constructed the goatskin seat into which he placed the child. To this he attached ropes that allowed him to put the seat on a tree limb allowing Jesus to swing back and forth. He had fashioned openings for his legs, and made it high enough to keep Jesus within the swing, his arms free to flail about. The child sat there in the shade, laughing and out of harms way.

As the child watched, Joseph began work on a storage silo for animal feed. After he had worked for a time, checking the infant in the swing, when he looked at him the next, Jesus was sound asleep.

Mary and Salomé went about grinding flour for bread, baking it and storing it on a shelf in the tent. The next task was to finish turning the tent into a home they could live in. Linen drapes were hung on the walls, a wider rug was put on the floor, sleeping pallets were laid out, and a grand salon set aside where they could eat their meals and spend the evenings. The kitchen was outside the tent and under the overhang where Joseph would also have his workshop. Shelves were placed by the grinding mill and an area for the Marcus and oven lay out.

Salomé turned to Mary saying, "I wonder why Joseph has not brought Jesus back for us to watch over?"

"Joseph oftentimes surprises you. He is very capable at handling many things. Besides, it is a good chance for father and son to get to know one another."

When people in Memphis learned that there had been a *tektôn* in their midst, Joseph's workload began to accelerate. Yokes were ordered, cupboards, tables, chairs and lattice work was ordered and some of which was installed. Joseph had no idea how quickly word had gotten around. Evidently Marcus had been beating his drum.

In addition to enjoying the increased workload, he also enjoyed having his son at his side. He recalled his first time. Joseph could also tell that his son enjoyed being with his mother helping her at her labors, tending the garden. In addition to crawling around between the rows, he also weeded and plucked worms as they stuck their heads out of the soil. These, his father would later use when they went fishing.

Mary and Salomé had prepared for the midday meal and decided to take it out to Joseph and the men working. They set aside an area under a shade tree and called them in to eat. Mary went, called Jesus from his swing, and brought him to be with the others. As Salomé served the food, Jesus called for one man then the other as if by way of greeting, "come and eat."

As they rested after the meal, Mary told Joseph that she had laid out an area under the overhang to be used for kitchen.

"What we need you and the men to do is build us an oven."

"An oven would be a good thing, if we are to continue eating cooked foods. I will have one of the men begin working on it, while the others finish up some odd jobs."

Amir spoke up, "I can handle that Joseph," he said. "I have built others and know what needs to be done. Do you mind if I do it?"

"The job is yours, Amir. Mary will tell you where to do it, and if I am not mistaken, she will also tell you how to do it. Chai, you will work with me setting up the workshop, Eran and Zach, I would like you to finish the corral, animal shelter, and feed storage bin."

"Salomé and I," Mary said, "will clean up, put Jesus down for his nap, and finish the work we have begun."

CHAPTER THIRTY-TWO

EVERYONE WAS BUSY about the encampment when, over the knoll someone emerged. As Joseph and Amir worked in the shop, a stranger seated on the donkey came over the rise.

"Hello, *ata yakhol laazos li*," the stranger called out as he rode up?

"*Shalom* neighbor," Joseph replied. "I certainly will try to help you. Please dismount and let us talk."

As the man dismounted, Mary and Salomé brought up two benches for them to sit on.

"*Hashem sheli*, excuse me my name is Cleopas and I have a farm not far from here." Joseph brought the two benches closer together, he sat on one and motioned to Cleopas to sit on the other. Salomé came from the tent with two glasses of tea and handed it to the men.

"Thank you Salomé. My name is Joseph, the woman who just served you is Salomé, and the other woman, with the child, is my wife Mary. How can I help you?"

"I was in town getting some things, and I spoke with Marcus Yekem, the shopkeeper. As we spoke together, I told him that I was in need of some carpentry work and he highly recommended you. He told me where to find you, and said that you did good work."

"That was very kind, and yes, I am a *tektôn*, skilled in many forms of wood, iron, stone and the like. What is it you need?"

"I need you to make at least one yoke, perhaps two. A yoke is the wooden crosspiece that is fastened over the necks of two animals and attached to the plow or cart that they are to pull.

"One of the yokes I use for my oxen cracked down the center. I tried making repairs but every time pressure was put on the yolk, it would crack again. I believe it's time for a replacement. Do you do that sort of work?"

"Oh yes, and I am quite versatile in making that sort of item and I make the yoke to fit the oxen that will be using it. How many teams do the work?"

"Often two teams at the same time."

"Do you want me to make two yolks or just the one? I recommend making two since the yoke to fit the oxen that will be using it. How many teams do you work?"

"I have had these yolks and harness for many years. Perhaps it is time for them to be replaced. Can you make the harness as well, if it is not too expensive?"

"I will have to come to your farm take the measurements of both teams, so that I can make them to fit the animals. Tell me how to get to your farm and I will meet you there tomorrow morning. As to the cost involved, that will depend on my measurements, and the kind of wood you want me to use to make the yolks. I will also make the harness for you. I'm sure that I can work within your budget."

"Will you do the work on my farm or do it in your workshop?"

"The work will have to be done in my workshop. The tools and equipment needed are not easily transported, the final fittings will be done on your farm with the animals."

"Marcus speaks highly of you and tells me that you will be doing some work for him."

"Yes, mostly furniture, tables, chairs, cabinets, and some small benches."

"Will you have time to do the work that I want?"

"Oh yes, I have since very good help recommended to me by Marcus."

"Very well then, I will see you tomorrow morning. I've taken the liberty of writing directions." He handed Joseph a small piece of parchment saying, "*Shalom* Joseph."

"*Shalom* Cleopas. Go with God."

CHAPTER THIRTY-THREE

IN MIDWEEK, THE Holy Family traveled to Memphis to do some shopping for various items, now that they had some money from recent contracts that allows them to purchase additional materials and household items. Jesus had been left with Salomé, who had to begin Jesus' lessons. Once inside the city, they made their way to Marcus Yekem, the merchant's shop and home. Marcus and Lydia made them welcome, and invited them into their living quarters.

Lydia asked, "To what do we owe the pleasure of your visit?"

Before he had an opportunity to answer, Lydia asked, "Where is my angel?"

Mary responded, "Salomé was in the midst of her lessons with Jesus, and after that he needed a nap. As a result, we thought it is best that Joseph and I went forward with our shopping plans, leaving him with our dear Salomé."

Joseph spoke up, "We have satisfactorily completed some work for Cleopas, and he has paid handsomely. Thank you Marcus, for sending work our way. Because of that, we can do some shopping and I promised Mary I would buy her lunch at one of the shops."

"No you will not," Lydia called out! "Would you insult us? You will take your meal in our home. I will hear no more about it."

"Do you have some time to spare," Marcus asked? "Must you return immediately after your shopping?"

Joseph looked at Mary who smiled at him. She knew of his insatiable interest in how differently things were made, what tools were used and the materials. She was equally certain, that Marcus would take delight in quenching his interest.

Marcus observed the exchange between Lord and wife he turned to Lydia saying, "we will be back for the evening meal." He too was rewarded with a smile.

Joseph opened his mouth to say something, but Lydia held up her hand.

"Come Mary to the kitchen where we can share a glass of tea and you can tell me all about your son."

With Joseph and Marcus on either side of the donkey and with the sun over their heads, they made their way into Memphis. Joseph stared wide-eyed at the number of statuary that could be seen.

"There is so much to see" in this historic city," Marcus began "Is there anything that you would like to see," Marcus asked?

"Anything and everything you would care to tell me. Please, do not forget that I am a stranger in your homeland."

"Well then, my friend, I will tell you something about our city. Memphis is an ancient city, equal in years to Jerusalem. At one time it was the capital of the Old Kingdom. That is, three millennia ago when there was a continuous peak in population.

"The city is at the apex of the Nile Delta, and twelve miles south of Cairo.

"The scholars in the temple and in the synagogue pass on that information."

"Please go on."

"The first god in Memphis was Ptah, the city administrator and vizier, otherwise known as a minister. He is credited with writing, 'Wisdom literature,' that was used to instruct young men in their appropriate behavior.

"Regarding the city of Memphis, it was the capital of ancient Lower Egypt. I must explain that northern Egypt, is considered lower based on the northward flow of the Nile River, through the Nile Delta and emptying into the Mediterranean Sea.

"It is believed to have been founded by Pharaoh Menes during the First Dynasty and was a principal city for more than 300 years before being supplanted by Thebes and Alexandria."

"Marcus, you never cease to amaze me. Where have you learned all of these things?"

"Everyone starts someplace, Joseph. Earlier on, I fitted myself out as a city guide to all those interested in paying a fee. There were many people who travel here having heard of Memphis and what it held. It was unusual, I will grant you but it put bread on the table."

Joseph interrupted, "What is that statute that looks like a crouching lion or a dog? Did the ancients worship animals?"

"Yes, they did in fact worship animals, but that sculpture you see is in fact a sphinx guarding the ancient Pharaoh Rameses. But I was speaking of Ptah. His body lies in a mastabas in the city of Saqqara, but his temple is here in Memphis."

"I'm afraid I must plead ignorance, Marcus, but I do not know what a mastabas is," Joseph said.

"There are none visible, but there are burial plots called the mastabas or eternal house. They are made in the form of a tomb, they are flat roofed, rectangular in its structure with downward slopes of stone or bricks.

"Ptah's temple is here in Memphis, in fact, there it is just ahead of us. At one time there were three colossal statues, one of Sekhmet, Rameses II and Ptah; all first century pharaohs. There is an alabaster sphinx standing in front of the Ptah's temple that serves as a memorial to the power and prestige of the city. Memphis is believed to have been under the protection of pharaoh Ptah.

"The goddess Sekhmet, the statue on Ptah's right, is the warrior goddess as well as goddess of healing for Upper Egypt, when the kingdom of Egypt was divided. She is depicted as a lioness, the fiercest hunter known to the Egyptians. It was said that her breath formed the desert. She was seen as the protector of the pharaohs and led them in warfare.

"Pharaoh Ramses II is someone quite different. Wherever you go throughout Egypt, you will see statuary dedicated to this pharaoh, so great was his impact. He is regarded as the greatest, most celebrated and most powerful pharaoh in the Egyptian Empire. I will give you a brief history so that you may better understand.

"As a teenager, he was appointed Prince Regent and he later ruled Egypt for sixty-six years. On his death he was buried in the Valley of the Kings, his body however was later removed and placed in a royal cache. He gained fame as an unparalleled, famous warrior, and his victorious battles, but even more so because of his building projects. He was dearly beloved.

As the sun began to set on the horizon, the two men made their way toward Marcus' home, weary but each content; Marcus because he enjoyed telling Joseph about the city, and what it held. Joseph, because his thirst had been partially sated.

"One less piece of gossip Joseph."

"From the past," Joseph asked?

"Yes, it seems that there was a great Queen called Nefertiti, she was the Great Royal Wife of Akhenaten, Egyptian pharaoh of some renown. Lord and wife believed in one god, Aten the sun God and they started a religion of sun worshipers. At his passing, Nefertiti took his place and role before the ascension of Tutankhamen.

"It was her reign when she and Rameses had their affair." It was at this last statement that Marcus leaned toward Joseph and whispers, "Who knows whether or not this gossip is true or not. However, Rameses had a limestone statue created in her image."

At the house the wanderers were warmly greeted. Mary spoke with Joseph. "It is too late Lord for us to go shopping and return by nightfall. Lydia has graciously invited us to stay here."

"But what about Jesus. . ." Before he could finish, Lydia spoke up saying,

"We have sent a runner, Amir one of your workers, to see Salomé and tell her that you would return in the morning."

Mary frowned, "Joseph, you look upset. Forgive my impertinence, but it seemed best, and Salomé is quite capable of watching our child."

"Yes, of course dear heart," he said as he smiled.

CHAPTER THIRTY-FOUR

AS THE HOLY Family lay around the fire after the evening meal, Salomé asked Joseph to tell once again the origin of the Passover feast. As soon as they heard the request for the nighttime story, Amir, Evan and Zack took places by the fire. They made themselves comfortable.

"Salomé, how many times do you want to hear it? The story is part of our tradition. Surely you must know it by heart."

"I would like to hear it again Lord," Mary said.

Smiling Joseph picked up the babe and put him onto his breast, gently rocking him. He began, "For many years the Israelites were slaves in the land of Egypt. Time after time Moses beseeched the pharaoh to let his people go, but the pharaoh hardened his heart at each request. Moses, with the help of God, brought down many plagues one after another. Each time the pharaoh was unmoved. Finally, Moses stretched out his hands above his head toward heaven and darkness overcame everything. For three days there was no sunlight and no starlight. pharaoh called for Moses to come before him.

"Get out of my sight," the pharaoh yelled at him. "And if I ever see you again I will kill you!" God had told Moses before this meeting that the pharaoh would send the Israelites out of the land and the time had come for them to leave.

Moses told his people, "Tonight at midnight God will send an angel through the land who will enter every house that does not have blood on the door. The oldest child in that house will die.

"He told them to slaughter a lamb for each family and sprinkle the lamb's blood on the door frame. They were to roast the lamb and eat it with vegetables for a midnight supper. When the death angel passed through the land, they were to be dressed and ready for the journey.

"The children gathered the flocks and herds, a lamb was slaughtered and its blood sprinkled on the door frame, while the women prepared the evening meal. The midnight meal was called "Passover" because the death angel passed over every house who obeyed God's command. To remind them of this night

---

when God had saved them from death, God commanded the Israelites to eat such a supper each year at this time.

"The Egyptians did not sprinkle lamb's blood on the door frames or prepare a midnight meal, went to bed expecting a good night's sleep. However, at midnight they were awakened, even the pharaoh, who hurried to his oldest son's bedside and found him dead.

"The pharaoh sent a messenger to Moses telling him, "The pharaoh wants all of you to leave Goshen at once and leave nothing behind!"

"The Israelites, 600,000 of them, including men, women, and children together with their flocks and herds, began a journey.

"The women mixed dough bread but had not put leaven or yeast in it. The dough was baked over coals and is called unleavened bread. Now every year we eat bread but without leaven in it."

"Lord, that story must be told to our son," Mary insisted.

"Mary, we will tell him all the stories about our people along with our traditions."

Joseph had everyone hold hands as he said the nightly prayer.

"Lord God Jehovah we thank you for what you have blessed us with today, a good day's labor, a fine meal, and meeting in your presence. Be with these young men as they make their way home and be with my family as we sing praises to you."

"Joseph, before we leave your company, I have a question that I need to ask you."

"You can ask me anything you like to and if it is within my power I will answer you wisely."

"You have a flourishing business, you have made roots in the community, and those that know you respect you. It would appear that you will be with us for a while. For that reason, I would ask you to become an elder in the synagogue. We need someone who is stable, reliable, and trustworthy. You have all those qualifications, would you consider it?"

"You honor me. Under different circumstances I would gladly accept. As you know my family's safety is a day-to-day concern. At any time we may have to pack and leave. At this point in time we lack stability. Please do not be offended but I must say no."

CHAPTER THIRTY-FIVE

THE FAMILY HAD come in from their encampment for the celebration of the Passover. Before the service began, rabbi Solomon Arkin asked to speak with Joseph. He invited Joseph into his office and told him to be seated.

"I have heard nothing but good things about you and your family. It is a pleasure to have you among us. Our lead merchant, Marcus Yekem also tells me that you do very fine wood carvings and wood panels. Is this true?"

"Yes it is true. I take delight in the wood carving and wood panels. Why do you ask?"

"I would like to rekindle the religious zeal that seems to be waning. I thought some wood carvings of the temple, or on the front door, to reawaken that zeal."

"And you would like me to do the wood panels for you?"

"Yes, that is what I had in mind. What are your thoughts?"

"This is the land of Moses after all, so as I envision it, Moses should be in the central panel with four of the Major Prophets surrounding him."

"I like that thought rabbi. With perhaps, a central theme of worship to Jehovah."

"Can you do some renderings for me so that I might see beforehand, what it will look like."

"That of course, I will do. In order to do it properly rabbi, you need to decide on where you want the panels to be placed, inside or on the outer doors. Also, the size of the panels that you want. Then I must take measurements."

After a brief survey of the interior and exterior of the temple was conducted, it was decided that the panels would be placed on the outer doors.

"Is there anything else we need to discuss Joseph?"

"For now though we need to speak of the commission and the down payment. That will allow me to buy the wood for the panels so that I might get started."

Negotiations were gotten into, the fee for the panels and installation were agreed to and Joseph left to begin the work.

When he reached home, Joseph told the others of the commission he had just agreed to.

"That's wonderful Joseph," Mary exclaimed. "Our purse was getting a little light. This commission will help."

They sat around the fire that evening, talking about the days of thanks and the commission they had just received. There was a quirk about Mary that Joseph found most endearing. When she displayed such quirks, Joseph would often smile. When Mary wanted something built, or something to be purchased in Memphis, she frequently prefaced her request with a question.

"Would it not be nice," she would say, "if we had a shed where we could store clothing and other items that clutter up the tent? Would it not be nice if we had another table?"

Whenever she began that way, he knew he could not nor would not refuse her. Thinking of the routine they had begun forming, Joseph felt it was part of the education of their son. Each morning Mary would sit with him teaching him the beginnings of writing, reading, or answering the thousand questions he would ask. Then, later in the day Mary would return with him from the temple attempting to answer one of the questions he posed about the days' teaching.

One night after the evening meal, as they lay beside the fire, Mary said to Jesus, "Would it not be nice if your father would tell a story about Noah and the big boat he built?"

"Wife," he replied, "sometimes you are as subtle as a hammer's peen. Well," his audience sat back ready to hear his words, "this is a long story and you will have to be told over several evenings.

"It seems that God beheld the wickedness of the people he had put on earth, and he regretted what he had done, and it grieved him. He was so upset that he decided to destroy every living thing on earth.

"However, there was one man, whose name was Noah. Noah was a just man and who walked with God. Noah had three sons, Shem, Ham, and Japheth. One day God was talking with Noah saying, "The way of all flesh has come to my attention, and the earth is filled with violence through man. Behold," he thundered, "I will destroy them and all the earth!"

"Because he found favor in God's eyes, he told Noah to build a large boat called an Ark for him and his family in preparation for a huge flood that would destroy every living thing on earth.

"God also told Noah to bring into the Ark two of all living creatures, both male and female, and seven pairs of clean animals. In addition to that he was told to bring every kind of food to be stored for the animals and for his family while they were in the Ark.

"Now," Joseph said, "let us raise our hands to heaven in Thanksgiving for everything the Lord has given us this day."

Early the next morning Joseph met with his laborers, to pay them off for work already completed. Each was given his wages promised. Before they left, however, Joseph asked Amir to stay behind, explaining to the others that he needed one helper to continue working with him in the shop. He told them he had selected the most experienced and the one with a family.

When the others had left he sat with Amir to discuss his interest in continuing to work, what was expected of him, what he would be paid, and where he would live. It was decided that Amir, rather than travel back and forth each day, would bring his own tent, and place it down by the corral, he would work from sun up to sun down, meals would be provided to him, and his weekends would be free. The men shook hands and their work relationship would begin the following day.

Jesus was pleased with the addition to the workforce, with this new fellow Amir. His father's work had backed up and he could use the help. The quality of the work that was turned out soon became apparent.

With each passing day, Jesus grew from a toddler to a curious young boy. Mary saw to it that his education, both at home and in the temple, continued uninterrupted. Joseph saw to it that his education, as a carpenter, and honest and righteous young man also continue to grow.

At Mary's request, Joseph purchased a loom and yarn. It was not long thereafter, that either she or Salomé were busy weaving. Their skill also became apparent such that some of the items they wove were also offered for sale.

CHAPTER THIRTY-SIX

HEROD WAS IN the Palace throne room, screaming for his chief attendant to come to him at once. A groveling Asa, his robe flowing and his sandals clapping on the marble floor, hurried to his presence.

"I am here your Majesty," Asa said groveling. "How may I be of service?"

"Dolt! Wastrel! I rely on you to bring the information that is vital to me, and you have failed and failed miserably. Why do we keep you in our presence?"

"I have never failed you most August Herod!"

Herod leaned forward from his throne, pointed his right index finger at his terrified attendant.

"Then why have I heard from household servants that the family I have been seeking, for more than two years, is in Egypt? Why did you not bring me this information?"

"How reliable is this source of information your Majesty? If it were from a truly reliable source, then I am certain that I would have heard it. Since I have not, I have great doubt about its reliability."

"The servant heard of the location in the marketplace outside the palace from the caravan master. We have had no word but, when we do, it is from a palace servant and not from my attendant! Go! You are a fool! And tell the Captain of the Centurion guards that he is to report to me at once!"

Captain Alpheus responded quickly to his King's summons.

"Ah Captain, so good to see a reliable face come before me."

"At your service Majesty," said as he struck his breast with his gloved fist.

"Good, good. I have a charge for you and I want you to carry out at once."

"At your command," he said again striking his breast.

"This is the information we have been able to put together, there are three fugitives in the city of Tanis in Egypt. These are the same three fugitives we have been seeking for years. My advisers tell me that Tanis is on the caravan route. Take as many men as you may need and go there at once. Once you have found them, you are to kill them where they are found and you are to bring their heads back to me."

"Who is it we are seeking Majesty?"

"You are looking for a carpenter whose name is Joseph of Bethlehem, son of Jacob, his wife Mary and their son. They have eluded me for two years. I want them found and put to death. Can you handle that Captain?"

"It shall be done Lord!"

A food bearer in the Palace, Isaac by name and a kinsman of Joseph, overheard the outburst of Herod and became terrified for his kinsman. He knew of his kinsman's whereabouts and he was not in Tanis. Joseph had sent word to him earlier, by way of a merchant coming to Jerusalem, about twelve months ago. On his return trip the merchant told him that Joseph had gone to Memphis, and as far as the merchant knew he was there still.

When his work ended he went to his supervisor, the chief cook, telling him that he must leave on family business and would be gone for a month or more. The cook granted him permission to leave.

At his home Isaac told his wife, Esther, what had taken place and what he had to do.

"Today in the palace Esther, I heard King Herod screaming at his chancellor, abrading him for his failure to locate my kinsman Joseph and his family. He sent for the Captain of the Centurion guards, and gave them the assignment of going into Egypt, specifically Tanis, locate my kinsman and kill them on the spot. The Captain will leave today."

"What can we do Isaac? We must warn them!"

"Tell my brother, Paito, what has happened and that it is my intent to warn Joseph. He will watch over you while I am gone."

That night, Ester helped him get ready for his journey. At sunrise he left.

CHAPTER THIRTY-SEVEN

JOSEPH, TOGETHER WITH his family, Amir, Marcus and his wife Lydia, were having a midday meal in the shade of a tree by the stream. As usual, Joseph was telling a story.

"Joseph who had been sold into slavery," he began, "was sold to Potiphar the Captain of the pharaoh's guard. While he was in Potiphar's service, he prospered in everything that he did. As a result, he was appointed his personal servant. Then, later on he was appointed as Potiphar's household superintendent. Later still, Potiphar's wife. . .

"But the rest of the story will have to wait until next time. We have a visitor approaching our camp."

They all rose to greet the visitor riding over a hillock.

"*Shalom*," Joseph called out as the rider came to a stop. For some reason, chills passed through Joseph's body. Then, he recognized the rider, it was Isaac his kinsman. He must be bringing us news of dread, Joseph thought.

"Shalom Isaac," Joseph said again. "Welcome to our camp. Dismount and tell us all the news from home."

Isaac dismounted, he spread his arms to embrace all in greeting.

"*Sheh-Elohim Yivarech Otcha*, and all here!"

"And may God be with you as well Isaac."

Isaac nodded to the others, waved to Mary and said, "We must talk Joseph."

Marcus and the others saw the look of concern on Isaac's face. They stood, preparing to leave. "Joseph," he said "Lydia and I must leave for home. With your permission, I will have Salomé and Amir help us make ready. Salomé take Jesus since it is time for his nap."

Distractedly Joseph replied, "Yes Marcus, thank you for coming. I think that Mary and I must speak with my kinsman."

Mary served Isaac food and wine to refresh him. When he finished eating he said, "Herod has learned that you are in Egypt."

"Oh God spare us," Mary sobbed.

129

"He has sent the Captain of the Praetorian guards to Egypt with the company's centurions to seek you out and execute you, Mary and the child."

"How did you come by this information kinsman," Joseph asked?

"As you know, I am a food bearer in the palace. King Herod was in a rage and I overheard him giving instructions to the Captain of the praetorian guards. He was told to seek you out in Tanis and when he found you, kill you and your family. I left immediately to warn you of the danger."

Mary and Joseph clung to one another trying to absorb the shock of this devastating news. "Does anyone know you are here?" "When I overheard Herod's orders, he told the guards you were in Tanis."

"Before we came here, we stopped briefly in Tanis, went to Sais, Alexandria, Heliopolis, and then Memphis. We had been without food, without shelter, in sandstorms and freezing cold weather. Through it all we knew that God was with us. When we settled here we thought that our hardships had come to an end. And now you bring the news that we were too prideful. We must accept that. Thank you Isaac for warning us, how much time do you think we have?"

"I would estimate that you have three weeks or more before they arrive in Tanis. Where will you go from here Joseph," Isaac asked?

"We have great faith in you Isaac but I think it's safer for you and for us if we do not tell you. Besides that, I have no idea right now. We have some lead time since the Centurion guards have not reached Tanis as yet. I have some work to complete for a synagogue in Memphis which should take me another week. When that is completed we will leave.

"Stay with us tonight and in the morning, when you and your animal have been well fed, we will give you some things to take back with you since we need to pare down to the bare essentials."

"Yes I will stay the night with you, and I think you're right, I should return as soon as I can and I thank you for whatever you give me."

Mary's calmness had settled over her, said, "Let us return to the others and catch up on the gossip from home."

After the evening meal that night, when they were all gathered about the fire, Salomé asked Joseph to finish the story he had begun earlier that day.

"Where did I leave all this afternoon?"

"You started to say," Salomé replied, "that Potiphar's wanted to do something."

"Oh yes, she wanted to make love to Joseph but he would have none of it. She then went to her Lord and said that he did try to make love to her. Potiphar believed his wife and had Joseph put in prison.

About the same time the pharaoh became angry with his chief butler and baker and they too were sent to prison where Joseph cared for them. These men were having strange dreams but no one could interpret them. Joseph did. He predicted, from his interpretation of the dream, that the chief butler would be back serving the pharaoh in three days. From the baker's dream he predicted that the banker would be hung in three days. The butler had promised to tell the pharaoh about Joseph's interpretation of the dream; he did not. Two years later he did tell the pharaoh when he heard that he had had strange dreams that no one could tell the meaning of.

The Chief Butler told the pharaoh about Joseph, how he interpreted his dream and that it had come true. The pharaoh sent for Joseph who told him what the dreams meant. He said that both dreams had the same meaning. In one dream it meant that there would be seven years of plenty and in the other, there would be seven years of famine. The pharaoh believed him and as a result made him ruler over all land of Egypt.

"What was your reason," Isaac asked, "for telling that story?"

"I don't think I had a particular reason, it just struck me and because Joseph kept faith in the Lord, despite his tribulations, God would see him through. And so it is, I think, if we too keep faith, God will see us through these difficult times."

CHAPTER THIRTY-EIGHT

THEY WATCHED ISAAC leaving with the sun at his back, heading east. Joseph called for a family council to discuss what should happen next. He summarized, "Isaac told us that he was at least three weeks ahead of Herod's Centurion guards and that they were heading toward Tanis seeking us. That will allow us another two or three weeks to finish up the work here, pack up those things that we must take with us and be on the road to where the Lord sends us.

"Amir and I will finish up the work on the temple doors and install them." Jesus was looking at them quizzically. "With of course, the capable assistance of our young apprentice." He reached over and messed with Jesus' hair and was rewarded with a smile.

"While we finish up the contract, the two of you will begin packing our belongings, and harvest whatever vegetables are available for us to take with us. Unfortunately, it has to be the barest essentials."

Mary questioned, "Are we going to take Portia with us?"

"Yes, I think we should. It will allow us to take more of our things even though each of us will have to do more walking." He took Mary aside to continue this conversation.

"This recent news has taught us a lesson we should not forget. With your consent, I think that we should move frequently, not making any location our permanent home. If you recall what I told you back in Bethlehem, the angel told us to go into Egypt until he tells us to return. And I am quite sure that that will happen when Herod is no longer a threat. We must survive until we get that call to return."

"I agree Joseph. This lesson has been a better part one we should heed. What are your thoughts?"

"I think to remove ourselves from Memphis as quickly as possible. We should first go to Saqqara which is only several miles south. From there we can go to Fayum, which is to the north, then to Giza which is further north and then, if enough time has elapsed, we can go to Cairo. That way we will be closer to the caravan routes when the time comes. Not heading out of here in any one direction, it is hoped to confuse our pursuers"

"Let us return to the others," Mary said, "we can plan when we are ready to leave."

Amir approached Joseph. "What will happen to me Joseph?"

"You and I will finish the work we have contracted for. We will install it and be finished with the work we have at hand. I will, of course, be taking my tools with me. Everything else is yours, the shelter, the workbenches, shelving and anvil. If you need to purchase tools, Marcus knows your work and I am sure, he will lend you the money you need. Use all of these things wisely and continue doing quality work at an honest price."

"You can't leave me everything Joseph. It would not be fair!"

"I can Amir, you have done everything asked of you and done it well. Use them wisely. I would ask you though to help us prepare for our departure once we have finished our work."

Turning to the others he said, "Mary and Salomé, I ask that you take charge of making the preparations."

For the next several days, the hours passed quickly as the accumulated work in completion. Early one morning when they had finished eating, Joseph asked, "If you have no objections Mary, I would like to visit Marcus and his wife Lydia to thank them for what they have done. I have a second motive as well.

'Marcus tells me that he has spoken to the rabbi who has knowledge about my ancient kinsman Joseph, the one who was sold into slavery but survived to become a force."

"A good plan Joseph," Mary said. "That will give us an opportunity to thank them properly and thank them whole heartedly."

And so it was that they found themselves at Marcus's house and workshop. They sat at the table following the midday meal talking amicably, allowing Jesus to run about the house and do his usual exploring.

Joseph was saying, "We have given the workshop and all it contains to Amir. It is just impossible to transport everything with us. Everything else, the tent and its furnishings, we give to you and Lydia. The tent can be resold along with the rugs and wall furnishings. Everything. "Let me pay something Joseph," Marcus insisted.

"Please accept this in friendship. I would however, ask you to introduce me to the rabbi who has information about Joseph, I believe is a kinsman of mine."

And so it was later that afternoon, while the woman visited, Marcus introduced Joseph to the rabbi explaining why they had come.

"Joseph, may I introduce our venerable rabbi, Joel Rifkin, and rabbi, this is Joseph new to our community.

"*Shalom Alekhem*, rabbi," Joseph said in greeting.

"We can speak your native tongue Joseph. How may I be of service to you?"

"An ancestor of mine, so I have been told by my family over campfires, is Joseph son of Jacob, was bought in slavery to Egypt and yet was instrumental in Egypt's future in many ways."

"If it is one and the same, he was a driving force during his reign here. I say reign because the Joseph of whom I speak, rose from a captive to the second highest-ranking Egypt. Are you seeking validation of your heritage, my son, or do you have something else in mind?"

As they settled in to speak, Joseph was quiet for a time. As they sat there quietly women of the temple served them tea.

"I do not know rabbi. Right now I am more interested in learning what I can about him."

"Well then, I can give you a brief history and suffering of our Joseph. He became a favorite of the pharaoh, because he was able to interpret dreams the pharaoh was having. His seers could not.

"Joseph's position in the pharaoh's court was on the rise he was able to interpret the claims pharaoh was having."

"I know that part of the story rabbi. In fact, I was telling you and my family only last night. Is there nothing else?"

"Oh yes, the pharaoh made him the head of Egypt with the ability to act on the pharaoh's behalf. In the years of plenty he had canals built to water and fertilize land, when the grain was harvested, silos were built for storage along with many of the pyramids. Then in the years of famine, he returned the grain to the people so that they might live. This elevated his position even higher. The dams, silos and other engineering feats were among the greatest in the world."

"Engineering," Joseph asked astonished?

"Yes Joseph, engineering. The crops not only had to be fertilized but watered. The harvested grain was to be stored where it had never been stored before and kept usable, and then seven years later, it was removed from storage where the grain remained fresh. The watering of the crops required the use of the Nile Delta to a series of canals and sluices never before tried."

"I have some skills but they are nothing compared to this man. It is too bad our lineage cannot be more firmly established."

"Regardless," the rabbi said, "be thankful that the one he choose was in our family."

The men returned home in time for the evening meal. While women cleaned up, Marcus placed a hand on Joseph's shoulder and said, "It would be my belief that you seek to put as many miles between you and your pursuers. It would be my suggestion to them that you make arrangements to take one of the Nile boats heading south. You can travel as far as you wish, but I would recommend that you make a stop in Dashur to get your bearings, and decide when and where you want to go next."

"We went by boat from Sais to Alexandria. At least they called it a boat, but it was more like a barge."

"The boats I am talking about are called feluccas. That is the primary source of transportation on the Nile River. Lydia and I will go with you to see that you are not taken advantage of." The following morning at sunrise the small caravan made their way to the banks of the Nile.

CHAPTER THIRTY-NINE

THE HOLY FAMILY stayed overnight with Marcus and Lydia. With the sunrise they enjoyed the morning together in friendly conversation.

"Where would you go, Joseph," Lydia asked?

Joseph replied, "we will be heading south with no particular destination in mind, going where the Lord leads us."

Marcus asked, "You have no definite destination in mind?"

"We have given it great thought and we think it best that you do not know, my friends. The praetorian's, the centurions, are seeking to kill us. With knowledge of our whereabouts, it would be dangerous knowledge indeed. We are sorry but we think that best."

"You are right, we could be threatened and your family put in peril. Know this, we bless you in God's love and our wishes for safe journey."

With saddened hearts the small caravan took the road south waving goodbye until they were out of sight. As they walked, Joseph informed them, we will look for a place to stay in Saqqara, it is only two miles away. "It is located, according to Marcus, at the entrance of the Nile Delta which means there should be plenty of water and, since it is fertile ground, we should be able to get the food we need. He also told me that Saqqara once served as the city's massive necropolis, or burial ground. There is a pyramid here in the city that I would like to see. It has two meanings, the Step Pyramid and also the Pyramid of Djoser. I am told that it is the world's largest structure."

"Who is Djoser, Joseph," Salomé wanted to know?

"I am afraid I do not have that information. We will have to ask someone in the city."

It was almost midday before they found a plot of ground just north of the city that was covered and provided a good deal of shade. They made a small camp and, for no better reason than curiosity, they entered the city and walked around. Joseph was ever mindful to watch the path they had traveled, looking for pursuers.

"It does not appear that we are the only ones wondering about the city," Mary observed.

All three of them looked about the city. Then Joseph said, "With so many pyramids surrounding the city, would seem that they are an attraction people have come to see.

"Over there," he said indicating a robe clad bearded man with several camels, "that man is, I would guess, a man who escorts people about the pyramids."

The Holy Family had been speaking in Judean dialect, when they were interrupted.

"S'leecha," the stranger said, but, he said continuing in the Judean dialect, "from your speech I would place you as Judeans, somewhere near Bethlehem. Am I correct?" Warily Joseph answered. "We are from that area, yes. How could you tell?"

"From your speech, it gives you away," he observed. Joseph became immediately cautious. They were, of course, fleeing from authority and did not know to whom they should give their trust. "Fear not," the stranger went on, "I am also from that area, Hebron in fact, although I have been here for many years. I just wanted to speak with someone from my home. I apologize if I disturbed you. As the man started to leave, Joseph spoke out. "What is your name, if I might be so bold?"

"My name is Chaim Simeon. I am an elder in the synagogue looking to get some food. And you are?"

"Joseph of Nazareth, the people with me are my family, Mary my wife, Jesus my son and Salomé, his nurse."

"Jesus? Are you aware of what his name means, Jehovah saves?"

"Yes we are," Joseph replied. "We thought it appropriate and nothing more."

Bewildered, Chaim went on. "I know that you are troubled and I will not ask you about it. Your business is after all your business. Instead, may I help you in any way?"

"Please excuse my impertinence. Salomé has just asked me who Djoser was and I have to confess, I did not know."

"If you allow me, King Djoser rests in that large Stepped Pyramid, many of these people have come to see. King Djoser, like all kings and pharaohs, work is begun on their final resting place as soon as they take the throne.

"King Djoser's vizier, Imhotep, who was the head of the royal navy yard and overseer of all state waterworks, was the main architect of the pyramid. His design was a departure from anything done before in that it was made from quarried white limestone rather than mud-brick. It is believed that it started as mastabas, you know what a mastabas is," he asked?

"Yes," Joseph replied. "We were informed about them some months ago when were up north."

"Well then, King Djoser's tomb is really five mastabas piled atop one another, each succeeding mastabas was smaller than its predecessor thus creating the stepped effect. The burial crypt lies in the chamber beneath all.

King Djoser's pyramid was the very first one built and its architecture is quite unique. It comprises the oldest stone building complex known in history. King Djoser's complex is surrounded by a wall of light Tura limestone with inlaid panels that imitate bundles of reeds. There are also false doors only to be used by the pharaoh in the afterlife. There is however, one ordinary door.

"Another interesting point is that the city has been known as the City of Necropoleis because we have at least sixteen pyramids, all of which are ancient. If you are interested and if you have the time each site has its own distinctive addition."

"Thank you Chaim," Joseph said, "for a very interesting lecture on the city and its cemeteries. I think we will make the time to see as much as we can."

"How long do you believe you will be staying in the city?"

"We have only just arrived and have made no long-range plans."

"The reason I ask is that, as you know, Yom Kippur is three days away and I would be pleased if you would be with us during these high holy days."

"That is most generous of you. We would be pleased to be with you. Where should we meet?"

"In the temple at midweek and, in case you do not have the proper clothing, we have a wardrobe in the temple for just such situations."

Mary and Joseph met Chaim outside the synagogue. Joseph was given a *tallet* and a *yarmulke* as they joined the *Kol Nidrei* celebration. Following the Yom Kippur service, they joined Galen and Martha for the evening meal.

As the meal was coming to an end Joseph announced, "As you may be aware we are in constant fear for our lives. King Herod's soldiers who seek us, we have been told are in Tanis. Their sole mission is the death of our child and we along with him."

Martha gasped. "Mary. Joseph. I cannot think of anyone who would do this. Surely you have committed no wrong."

Mary answered, "When Jesus was born, King Herod issued a proclamation stating that all male children two years of age and younger were to be executed."

"That is insane," Chaim exclaimed!

Joseph replied, "Be that as it may, that is the burden that we must live with."

"I do not know what to say I am stunned," Martha moaned. "What do you intend to do?" Joseph answered, "Sadly we will be leaving in the morning seeking shelter elsewhere." "Where. . ." Chaim began.

"Chaim my friend, it is better that you do not know. But know this your friendship and Martha's have been a blessing to us that we shall not forget. The memory of you both will be with us in our travels. Go with God always."

"Mary. . ." Martha said as she embraced her friend."

Chaim and Joseph shook hands and then embraced one another.

"Walk in God's love, friends." Joseph said as they left.

CHAPTER FORTY

SAND AND, GUSTS of windblown sand, wind and heat. Day after day the same hardships, same scenery, palms, trees, more sand and food and water were running low. The sameness day in and day out began gnawing at their resolve. However, they must put distance between them in Memphis. This hardship had to be endured.

Joseph dug a shelter in the side of a dune where they could wearily make camp. Joseph did his best to make the site comfortable, as Mary and Salomé prepared the evening meal.

Mary looked forlornly at her Lord and child. She knew he wanted to do the best for her and for them. The women were making a vegetable stew made from the last few vegetables they had. When it was cooked he doled out portions to everyone. Jesus was given a larger portion since he was a growing child.

"Mother may I have more," he asked?

"That is all that we have Jesus," Mary responded catching her throat.

Salomé asked, "How much further do we have to travel, Joseph? My feet are sore from the hot sand."

"Wrap your feet in cloth Salomé and unwrap them at night so that they might have some fresh air. To answer your question though, what I've been told back in Saqqara, Fayum is sixty miles southeast of that city. We have traveled about ten miles a day and we have been walking for four days."

"Did the people you spoke to tell you anything about Fayum," Salomé asked? "There were many travelers in Saqqara, some of them merchants for caravans. I find that they usually have the most and best information.

"Fayum, they tell me is an oasis in the Libyan Desert. It is in a vast depression below sea level. Hills stand between Fayum and the Nile River. The area is one of the most fertile in all of Egypt and produces flax, cotton, rice, hemp, sugarcane, oranges, peaches, grapes and olives. There is also fishing, raising sheep and chickens. It must be a lush city if only half of that was true.

"Some mention was made that Joseph, the one we have been hearing about, is responsible for rerouting the Nile River to make this area as fertile as it is."

"Jesus," Mary cooed caressing her son, "two more days of this torment and we will be refreshed. Isn't that good news?"

"Two days and two nights," Jesus asked Joseph. "What are they?"

"The sun comes up in the morning and goes down at night; that is one day. Two of those are equal to two days."

"Oh," Jesus responded.

To the others Joseph said, "Yes two days and perhaps two nights. Can we last that long?"

"Yes we can Joseph," Mary answered enthusiastically! "Send us off to our slumbers, Joseph, with one of your stories."

And so he did.

"When I last spoke with you about Moses, he had the Israelites crossing the Red Sea, and leaving the Egyptians behind. Well, for about three days these newly freed slaves wandered the desert between Elim and the mountain where God spoke to Moses from the burning bush. Now they had grown hungry, tired, and thirsty, just as we are now. They had forgotten how God helped them in the past.

"We wish we had never left Egypt," he grumbled. "You have brought us into the wilderness to die," they complained. God heard the complaints and their grumblings. He gave them bread from heaven, they called manna.

"More days passed and the Israelites came to a place called Rephidim. The gray cloud that had been following them, stopped and so did the Israelites only to begin complaining again. "Did you bring us here to die of thirst" he wailed?

Moses turned to God in prayer. God answered his prayer by telling him to take the elders and go to Mount Horeb. "When you get there strike your rod and water will flow from it."

"Moses stayed in the city as he had been instructed. He went to the mount struck a rock with his rod. Immediately water flows from it and they were satisfied.

"Because they had doubted their Lord God, Moses was ashamed and scolded them."

"We like those Israelites, I don't mean grumbling and complaining, I mean hungry and thirsty but in two days we will have food and drink." They joined hands in prayer. Moses said, "Lord God we beseech you to help us through these trying times. We know that you will provide for our needs."

When it was time to sleep Joseph covered everyone with cloaks and robes, including the donkey's head to protect her and the others from the fiercely blowing sandstorm. On the morning of the fifth day, the sun shone through and off in the near distance was the city they had been seeking, Fayum. Bahr Yousef in prehistoric times was a natural offshoot of the Nile River. In this instance it flooded the natural depression and eventually changed the fallow fields into fertile plains and created Lake Moeris; a natural reservoir. This offshoot from the Nile was meant to serve three purposes: control before the Nile, regulate the water level of the Nile during dry seasons, and equally important serve the surrounding area with water for irrigation. pharaoh's Chief Chancellor, Joseph, believing in his dream interpretations, immediately envisioned an area that could be given over to farming and agriculture. He devised a series of canals that would accomplish that end. Canals allowed the water to flow into that depression 140 feet below sea level. Into that area are now overgrown with date palms, open fields of grain, large areas of vegetables, and a vast sea of cotton plants.

When they entered Fayum, they were directed to an area where there was a large population of Jews. They went there and were immediately made welcome. Their first concern was for food and water. It was amply supplied.

One of the elders in the area, Solomon Niemann, pointed out an area where they could set up camp, and once they were settled, he would help them replenish their supplies and asked that they spend the Sabbath with him and his family.

At the location indicated, Joseph and Jesus went about gathering palm fronds, from which they created a temporary shelter. Jesus was born a supervisor rather than a laborer. It was he who directed Joseph in what palm fronds to select and which ones to leave alone. Mary and Salomé, who had unpacked the donkey, tethered it nearby, now what about turning the temporary shelter into a home for the four of them.

Before eating the evening meal, Joseph clasped his hands together saying, "Lord God we thank you for delivering us safely, for providing us with sustenance, and for providing good people to greet us." They gathered around the fire with everyone looking at Joseph to tell them a story. He did not disappoint them.

"For the last two years we have lived in, gone hungry, and prospered in the land that the angel told us to go to; Egypt. Many of the stories of fathers and forefathers told us, also dealt with this plan called Egypt. I will tell you the story of a young man also affected by Egypt.

"On the plains near Ur an elderly man called Terah, who was a shepherd farmer. He had three adult sons: Abram, Nahor, and Haran who died when he was still young. He left a fourth son named Lot. Abram was not a believer in moon-god but believed in the true God. Terah took Abram, his wife and Lot. When they left they took all they owned, tents, their flocks of sheep and their herds of cattle. Day after day they journeyed the great river called Euphrates until they came to Haran, where they settled.

"After the passage of some time, Terah died. Shortly after that Abram heard God calling him saying, "Leave this country, your relatives, and your father's house. Go to the land that I will show you. I will bless you and make you a great blessing. Through you all families of the earth will be blessed.

"As many people came to realize later, this meant that the Savior would be born into the family of David and the son would save the world.

"Abram took his wife Sarai, his nephew Lot, and their servants. Driving their flocks and herds before them, they turned away from the river Euphrates, journeyed southwest toward the land of Canaan. When they reached the land of Moreh, God spoke again to Abram, This is the land that I give to you and your children. Abram built an altar there, and worshiped God.

"Now this land was called Canaan and the people who lived there were called Canaanites. He pastured his flocks of sheep and cattle, prospered and became rich. Later, there was a famine in the land and the water and grass dried up so we moved into Egypt and when the famine was over they returned to Canaan."

"So you see my family," Joseph said and he reached out and embraced all, "Egypt has been with us for a long time and only the good Lord knows how much longer. Our plight is not unlike that of Moses and the Israelites fleeing Egypt."

Joseph raised his arms and eyes to the heavens saying, "Benevolent father, we are being pursued by Herod's centurions. We have been forced to go without food and water and we have walked for many, many miles. We come to you for guidance."

CHAPTER FORTY-ONE

"ABBA," JESUS ASKED, "why have we packed our things and are moving to a new location? Did you not like where we were?" Each time Joseph heard Jesus address him as he did, a warm sensation filled his body.

"It was an excellent location but there is a threat from the Centurions who seek to take our lives because of an irrational command by King Herod. We cannot reason with him so we must flee his minions."

They, the Holy Family, were in fact packed up and on the road once again. "Jesus," Joseph said explaining to his son, "it might be hard for you to understand but soldiers from King Herod are pursuing us."

"Why?"

"They want to take our lives."

"Why, we have done nothing wrong."

"King Herod is afraid of you and what you are destined for. Our job, your mother's and mine, is to see that no harm comes to you so that you can meet your destiny."

"I don't understand."

"No you do not, but there will come a time when you will. Please understand that we are doing this for your protection, and not for any wrong doing, but out of fear."

With the sun at their backs, they began to sweat profusely. The sand beneath their feet made walking difficult, still they plodded on. Their sandals were well worn and did little to protect their feet from the heat. The day after they had left the city and as dusk began to descend. The silhouette of the city could be seen through the haze.

"We have come at this distance more rapidly than I had anticipated. From what I have been told by other travelers, the silhouetted city we see in the distance should be Dashur, the next stop on our journey."

As they neared the city, they came to the encampment of other travelers. From their looks and the borings they carried with them, it seemed apparent that they were tourists who have come to see the attractions that Dashur has to offer. An empty space beside their encampment allowed them to set up camp for themselves. As they unpacked, they heard, "Joseph! Joseph!"

Joseph turned from unpacking the donkey when he heard his name being called. He turned around and recognized the caller.

"Rabbi Pensak," he called back. "It is good to see you. Why are you here," he said as he walked toward the rabbi?

"There is a new temple under construction. It is nearby and I am here to preside at its opening." Joseph returned to the others and called out, "Mary, Salomé, look who's here." The women turned to wave to the rabbi.

As Pensak came near the group he said, "Ladies it is a pleasure to see you again. Oh look, how your boy has grown. As I recall his name is Jesus was it not?"

Salomé replied, "Yes rabbi that is his name and I am Salomé."

Pensak was surprised at Salomé speaking out. Undaunted he shook hands all around, the pleasure at this meeting apparent. When it was done he took Joseph aside.

"Are you and your family still being pursued?"

"Yes rabbi we are. We received word that Herod's troops were in Tanis looking for us."

"How long will it be do you think, before they stop looking and you stop fleeing?"

"We will flee until we receive word that it is safe to return to our home."

"Once you get settled in the city, let us make you welcome. The temple is being built as bait for a great deal of work, and you can help us. We do not have much money to pay for your services, but we can provide you with food and help you establish a shelter."

"I am sure we can work something out. It is good to be among friends again."

The next two days were spent in making their encampment habitable. On the third day Joseph and Jesus went to the temple to see for themselves what work is needed to be done. Father and son sat with the elders to discuss what was needed, its approximate cost, and an appropriate wage for father and son.

The temple was too distant from their encampment and so it was decided that Joseph would have his workshop within the temple.

One day as they were eating the midday meal, Joseph pointed to one of the pyramids saying, "What an odd shape that pyramid has."

An elder, Ezekiel Maas responded, "That is the Bent Pyramid one of the first ever built."

"As a matter of fact," Jonathan Freiberg, another elder amended, "it was built right after the Step Pyramid. You see Dashur is my home and since this temple will be built under my supervision, I have made it my business to learn about the city, its history, and the pyramids you see about you."

"Pray continue," Joseph urged. "Since we came to Egypt my interest in pyramids and their construction, has been aroused. I am anxious to learn more."

Joseph smiled and continued. "I am a teacher by profession and I enjoy showing off my knowledge. Imhotep, the designer and builder of the first pyramid, started things off. Dashur pyramids became an important learning experience for Egyptians who were transitioning from step-sided pyramids to smooth sided.

"It must first be understood that Dashur is a necropolis. So it would appear almost inevitable, that tomb development would follow.

"Two of the pyramids, the bent pyramid and the red pyramid, you see in the distance, was first attempts at smooth siding. I will take you to see them later on.

"There were however, design flaws. One of the major flaws at the Bent Pyramid is that it was built on an unstable base. Another of the flaws was the kind of the stones being used, their weight to push down to the center. This is the main reason the pyramid stands in its present condition."

"But they have lasted so long," Jesus observed.

"Yes they have young man. I said that they were flawed and useless. Pharaohs are happily entombed in the pyramids. The second pyramid, the one I was telling you about, is called the red pyramid. It gets its name from the red coloring it takes on after a good rain. It is also the first smooth-sided pyramid. But that is not all there is yet another, the Black Pyramid. It is now badly eroded so that its name has become Rubble Mound. What makes it important however it was the first to house the deceased pharaoh and his Queens? Since then people have come from far and wide to see and study the structures and their construction. They having the same interests Joseph as you seem to have."

"Thank you, Jonathan. Your study on the subject has been extensive indeed."

Six weeks went by rapidly and the work progressed quickly. One night at dinner Mary observed, "You look as though you are please Joseph. The work on the temple goes well?"

Jesus answered excitedly, "We are making a lot of things for the temple. rabbi Pensak tells us that we are the best carpenters he has ever seen!"

"Are you a big help to your father Jesus?"

"Oh yes, mother. He tells me to get things for him and I go to get them." Joseph rustled Jesus hair, "yes mother we are good team."

"Your father and I are proud of you son. Soon you will be as good a carpenter as your father."

CHAPTER FORTY-TWO

IN THE MEANTIME, back in Jerusalem, Herod was pacing back and forth in the throne room, his hands clasped behind him, mumbling to himself. Asa had entered and stood watching his king's look of concern on his face. Herod turned and saw Asa for the first time.

"What is it you lowlife," he bellowed?

"My King," Asa said his voice quivering as he approached the throne. "I must sadly report that we have had no word about the three Kings of the free people that you seek. Tomorrow I will go to the marketplace, and question the merchants there."

"What did you hear from the Centurions that we sent to Tanis? Surely they must have heard something."

"Nothing Majesty. Nothing. It is almost as if they vanished from the face of the earth."

"That is impossible Asa, you clod. My patience is running thin. I must know something of the so-called Messiah. No one shall take my place on the throne. Be gone from my sight!"

The next morning Asa went to the marketplace where he questioned merchants about newly arrivals from the caravans, drivers, anyone who might have news about the three king's family being sought but no information was available. He dreaded to return to the palace.

He timidly approached the king. Herod got to his feet and roared, "Where are they, you worthless dung heap?"

"Majesty, they are nowhere to be found. I have searched, we have troops searching, and we have questioned the people, without success."

"Get out of my sight!"

CHAPTER FORTY-THREE

RABBI PENSAK APPROACHED the workers as they were having lunch. "*Tzohora'im Tovim*," he greeted them.

"Good afternoon rabbi," Joseph said as he stood. "What brings you to our table? Are you hungry?"

"No Joseph I am not hungry." Please sit. "I have come to bring you news that you may find upsetting. I have just received news that Roman troops are moving south. They also told that there is a search party seeking people that are wanted in Jerusalem. I'm afraid it could be no one other that you. I am sorry."

"You are right rabbi they are seeking us. I am sorry because this means that we must leave you at this community. We must return home, tell our family, and make ready to leave in the morning."

"Joseph my friend, it breaks my heart to say goodbye. You and your family will be sorely missed. I will join you for the evening meal and we will pray together for your safety of the Lord's protection wherever you go."

The Holy Family was on the road early in the morning attempting to cover as many miles as they could before the sun became too hot. It did not take long however, before their perspiration dampened their clothes. Anytime they found a shady place they stopped to rest. Since the last journey in the sand, Mary had seen to it that each of them had new sandals. Only Jesus road the donkey, even with the new sandals, the sand was too hot for his feet. Making matters worse, another sandstorm blew across the desert. The winds were so strong and blowing so fiercely, they had to cover their faces and the face of the donkey for protection. Only Joseph took an occasional glance to be sure they were walking in the right direction. He used the hazy sun and its position in the heavens as his sextant.

The evening meal was taken in Québec and was eaten in a secluded bluff. The sandstorm had blown itself out earlier in the afternoon and was replaced by a chilling wind. Mary made a vegetable stew that they ate with a little while wine. Joseph tethered the animal, fed it and covered its head as protection against the wind and sand.

After dinner they sat around the fire covered by their cloaks. Joseph said, "We have not had a story for some time. Perhaps we should get back into that routine."

Eagerly Salomé said, "Yes, please do!"

"Long ago Moses and the Israelites were having similar difficulties as we're having crossing the desert.

"Even though God had saved them from the cruelty of the pharaoh, when their food became scarce they began complaining to Moses. But God spoke to Moses and told him that he would not let his people die. The next morning when they awoke they found manna, was something like bread, covering the field. The people ate it hungrily.

"Still later when the water began to run out, the Israelites complained to Moses. Again God spoke to him telling him to take the elders to mount Horeb where he was to strike a rock. Again he did as he was instructed, he struck the rock with his staff and the stream of clear water flowed out allowing the Israelites to quench their thirst.

"What we can learn from this is that we must keep faith in the Lord our God and he will provide. He always has, he always will."

At mid-afternoon the following day, the silhouette of the city could be seen through the haze off in the distance. At the same time they came across another party of travelers heading in the same direction.

"*Shalom* friend" Joseph called out.

"*Shalom,*" came a distance reply. "Where are you going," the voice inquired?

"We are seeking water transportation on the Nile River."

Both parties stopped to converse with one another. Jesus ran over to the newcomers to introduce himself. "*Shalom,* I am Jesus of Nazareth."

Joseph caught up to his son saying, "Do you know the name of the city up ahead?"

"Yes I do, it is called Lisht and is at the River."

"I am Joseph, and that little scamp is named Jesus. The women coming our way are my wife Mary and with her is Salomé."

"And I am Ramassu and my wife is Baktre. You and your family looked thirsty. May we offer you some water and perhaps some food?"

"Yes," Mary said quickly. "We are both hungry and thirsty and you are most generous." "Baktre," he called to his wife, "please give these people some water and bread.

"When we get into Lisht, I will show you to the marketplace where you can purchase whatever you need."

"Are you from Lisht?"

"No, we are from Fayum, just north of here, we are going to visit our family, as we do every year. Would you like to know something of the city and its history?"

"I must be wearing a sign about my neck saying that I am interested in the history of the location wherever I am. Yes, I would like to know some of the history of this area. I am a *tektôn* by trade, and in our journey, whenever I speak to someone asking how something was made, and historical background was usually added and was always fascinating. So in answer to your question, please tell us about the city's history."

"Lisht, like many cities along the Nile, is a necropolis. We have two pyramids here surrounded by small ones for members of the Royal Family. There are many mastabas for high officials. It was a key city between Upper and Lower Egypt and when the pyramids were first erected, they had to have others for their queens."

"Perhaps you give me the answer to something that is puzzling me," Joseph asked?

"If at all possible, I would be pleased to."

"All the pyramids that we have seen were built thousands of years ago. It would appear there are none being built presently. Do you know the reason why?"

"You are quite observant Joseph. There are a number of reasons why this is so. Primarily among which were the grave robbers. The Pharaohs believed, after this blight took place, it would be a waste of time since everything would be taken or stolen. Another reason was a failing economy and yet another, the dwindling workforce. Of course there were other reasons but these are most prevalent."

"Thank you Ramassu, I thought you would know."

"Apart from learning the history of our lands, I sense there is a dire meaning behind your tour of Egypt. Is there anything that we can do to assist you and your family?"

"There is much going on Ramassu that we cannot tell you about. To do so, would place you and your family in danger. Briefly, I will tell you that we are being pursued by King Herod's troops seeking to kill us although we are not villains."

"It is evident to me that you and your family represent no danger. Therefore, you cannot be dangerous criminals. If you will follow us we will take you to the marketplace in Lisht that is where we will leave you. Travel in peace and safety."

"*Shalom* Ramassu and thank you."

CHAPTER FORTY-FOUR

SAND, GUSTS OF wind, and unbelievable heat, day after day after day. Food and water were running low the sameness of the day in and day out began gnawing at their resolve.

Joseph dug a four foot trench, three feet deep in opposition to the direction of the wind. He covered three feet of the trench with their cloaks, and then he anchored with more sand. The donkey was tethered with a heavy stone after which he had covered his face. The closure was somewhat cramped up for their protection. He built a small fire at the open-end of the trench in order that the women might prepare the evening meal.

Mary looked forlornly at her Lord and Jesus. She knew that Joseph wanted to do the best he could for them. She prepared a vegetable stew, made from the last of the vegetables that were left. When this was done, she doled out portions to everyone, Jesus getting the largest portion. When that was consumed Jesus asked, "May I have some more, mother?"

"That is all we have Jesus," Mary said with a catch in her voice.

"How much further do you reckon we have to travel Joseph," Salomé asked? "My feet are sore from the burning sand."

"Do you sleep with your feet bare at night," Mary asked? "Wrap them in cloth and put on your sandals. That will afford you some protection. From what I have been told in Dashur, the distance between the two cities is between 80 and 96 kilometers. If we can travel 16 kilometers a day, we can be there in about five days. Today, with the sandstorm, we will be lucky if we can travel 10 kilometers but we covered more than that in the past two days. That gives us about two more days. Our best hope to come across a small village, caravan or an oasis. When we go to prayer tonight asked the Lord to show us the way."

Mary said, "Amen."

To change the subject, and in order that they may think of something else, Salomé asked, "Were you able to find anything about Fayum?"

"What I heard confirms what we have heard before. Fayum is an oasis in the Libyan desert and is below sea level. Hills stand between the city and the Nile River. The land is one of the most fertile in all of Egypt because of that it is a very lush city.

"Some mention was made to Joseph that the pharaoh's vizier, being responsible for rerouting the Nile that make this area as fertile as it is."

"That sounds wonderful Joseph," Mary observed. "Two days and two nights and we will be refreshed. That is good news."

"Yes," Joseph responded "Two days and perhaps two nights. Can we last that long?"

"We will just have to," Mary stated.

Jesus joined with his mother, "Yes father we can," he said enthusiastically!

Salomé offered, "I think it would be would be a good idea if you send us off to our slumbers, with one of your stories."

And so he did.

"When last I spoke to you about Moses," Joseph began, "he had the Israelites crossing the Red Sea, leaving the pharaoh's forces behind. Well about thirty days between Elim and Mount Horeb. . ."

At the end of the second day, weak, famished, and dehydrated, they entered Fayum's outskirts. A camel herder noticed their condition and offered them a goat skin canteen of water.

"Don't be shy," he urged, "I have several others." As the others drank, Jesus walked over to the camel herder. "May I pet your camel?"

Without saying a word, the herder had the camel kneel on its front two legs. As he approached, Jesus was conscious of the terrible smell of the beast. The herder picked Jesus up and put him on the camel's back. He made a clicking noise and the camel got to his feet. Jesus was completely unafraid, in fact, his face was lighted up with one big smile.

Joseph asked him, "Do you know where or if there is an available area for encampment?"

"*Shalom,* to you sir. There is an area just up the road and it is close to water. You can have the boy back if we can get him down from the camel. Your family is Jewish is it not?"

"Please excuse my poor manners, and yes we are Jewish."

"Once you have settled yourselves, the marketplace is a short distance to the west and if you see Jousef Eisenberg, he will help you with whatever your needs are. Just tell him that old Moise sent you."

They followed directions, found a suitable space, and began to settle in. Jesus and Joseph erected a cloak and branch enclosure, Mary and Salomé tethered the donkey and made the encampment habitable. Joseph and Jesus went to the marketplace to make some purchases for this evening. As they were doing so, the merchant said, "You two are Jewish, are you not?"

"Yes we are, my family and I have just arrived, *Shalom*. You are a keen observer."

"How can I help you," the merchant asked?

"Is there a Jewish settlement?"

"Yes, there is a rather large one. It is out there," he said pointing to the left it is six kilometers from here. Can I sell anything to you?"

Joseph and Jesus began reciting to the merchant, their list of needs. The merchant promised to fill their list and have it delivered to their encampment. Joseph paid the man his due, and when Joseph and Jesus returned, they found that Mary and Salomé had done wonders. Their encampment looked like they had been there for some time. Salomé informed Joseph that they had filled the goatskins and that small fire was already begun. A short time later the purchases arrived, food was prepared and they settled in for the night.

As they wearily made their way east, into the heart of Fayum a large temple came into view. It was large and white giving the impression that a great deal of money had been spent in its construction. This told him that the community had given a great deal in the care of their faith and where they will worship. It was surrounded by a small wall in the courtyard were shrubs, and palm trees. A priest met them at the gate.

"*Shalom* weary travelers," the priest said in greeting. "Can I help you?"

"*Shalom*. You are correct in saying that we are weary and hungry. We had a brief rest last night but not enough to correct what we need. I am Joseph, son of Jacob from the house of David with me is my son Jesus, my wife Mary and our companion Salomé. We are fleeing from King Herod in Jerusalem."

"What heinous deeds have you done," he asked.

"Somewhat over five years ago, King Herod went on an insane rampage. He ordered his troops into Bethlehem to kill all children two years of age and younger. At the same time, my wife had given birth and our child fell into that category. I was told to take my wife and child and go into Egypt and that is what I have done. We have since heard that Herod's troops were in pursuit of us."

"You said that your child's name is Jesus."

"Yes, that is so."

"Are you familiar with what the name Jesus means in Hebrew?" Without waiting for a response, he continued. "In Hebrew his name is Yehoshua which means 'Jehovah saves.' The priest looked at Joseph carefully, looking to see if there was anything meaningful here, and when Joseph failed to follow up, he dismissed it as a coincidence.

"We can satisfy two of your quests. We have food that we share with you and there is also a small one-room building where you and your family can rest for the night. My name is Matthew Gharries and I am the rabbi in this temple."

"Thank you rabbi and forgive me for not recognizing your station."

The rabbi showed them to a large dining area where he sat with them as they ate.

"Everyone who stops here has a story to tell. What is your story? Surely you are not just visitors."

Everyone was eating hungrily, along with drinking several pitchers of water.

"We lived in Bethlehem in Judea," Joseph began, "when King Herod issued an edict that all children two years of age and under were to be executed."

"Is the man insane?"

"There can be no other explanation. It is our fervent hope you have not placed you in peril by staying with you."

"Do not let that concern you," the rabbi said. "For now, what are your immediate needs?"

"We need to replenish our supplies, but for right now we need to refresh ourselves for the next leg of our journey. I am a *tektôn*, and I need work. But that also means my family needs a place to stay, and I need a place where I can work."

"We are in need of a storage facility," the rabbi said, "and I can put you to work building that. One of the elders has several vacant houses. I will speak to him in just a few minutes and secure one of them for you. The rent you will have to work out with him, but I will urge him to be generous. Is there anything else that we can take care of?"

"Yes there is. Since we have arrived in Egypt, I have been fascinated by the country and its history. Is there anyone I could speak with to learn as much as I can about Fayum?"

"You are fortunate indeed. Your landlord, Saul Meister, is probably the most knowledgeable in that area. When I speak with him, I will also tell him of your interest."

The rabbi went into the temple and returned shortly with the elder. Introductions were made.

"I will leave you to work out arrangements for the house. Saul, Joseph is also interested in the history of our city. You know anything about it?"

"I know a few things."

Saul gave Joseph directions to the house he had in mind. "Why do you not go there, and I will be there shortly. I have some things to finish up here first. We will also discuss the rent."

The Holy Family followed the directions given them, found the house which was much like the homes in Bethlehem, three rooms on the first and second floors, connected by ladders and another ladder leading to the roof. Jesus and Mary looked at one another smiling.

"This will do my Lord. This will do."

Everyone in the family had a task to perform, and they went about doing it. The two rooms downstairs we use for storage and the rooms upstairs to be their living quarters. The third row on the ground floor Mary and Salomé found that the former occupants had used it as a kitchen. They would also.

The upper rooms, they decided, one would be used for dining and sleeping, and the other as a bedroom. When they climbed the ladder to the flat roof, they determined that this too can be used for sleeping on hot nights.

Joseph went about setting up his workshop, arranging his tools and constructing a makeshift workbench. He would build a better one when there was some income. He inspected the rear courtyard and found that the ground was carved with stone to gully running out to the street, two rough hewn benches sat by two fully grown shade trees. Yes, he said to himself, this will surely do.

Saul had given them the day to get settled before he visited them. At first they discussed the rent and came to an equitable agreement. Joseph invited Saul into the courtyard where Salomé served them tea.

"What is your interest in Fayum, Joseph?"

"Only a keen interest in its history and the Temples and pyramids that seem to dot the landscape."

"I think I can satisfy some of that interest. First, some geography. We are 96 kilometers south of Cairo. It lies within a depression that has since become an oasis. Unlike the typical oasis, whose fertility lies on one from springs, our water comes from the Nile River itself through a series of canals. The diversion process has become known as Bahr Jousef. The first canal built is fifteen miles long and the water is controlled by a series of dams. These in turn provide the water to Fayum and its fertile surroundings.

"It is believed to have been built by Jousef, Pharaoh Thutmose III's vizier. It is also said that nine different viziers were also responsible for saving Egypt during seven years of famine, but that is another story. The waterway, when it was built, was meant to serve three purposes: control before the Nile, control water level of the Nile during the dry season and serve the surrounding area with water for irrigation. It has more than fulfilled its expectations.

Fayum was known to the ancient Egyptians as the 21st Nome of upper Egypt. A Nome is a substantial restraint division and has the earliest evidence of a falling in Egypt. Because of that, it became known as the breadbasket of the time.

"Something else you might be interested in, the people hereabouts not only embalm their dead, they also place a portrait of a dead person over the mummy's wrapping shroud box that they have been placed in. The mummies have been preserved by the dry desert environment resulting in the richest collection of portraits that have survived all these years."

"What a wonderful story Saul and you tell it well."

"Thank you. The rabbi has told me of your situation. "I think it is terrible that you constantly live in fear. Do you have any plans for the future?"

"For right now, we are in need of rebuilding our reserves, both material and physical. To that end, I have to find work to do and at the same time, restore our dehydrated bodies."

"The rabbi has also told me that he wishes you to build a storage facility we need. How long do you think that will take?"

"That contract will answer all of our needs. The cost to build will depend on the size you want. When we have money in our pockets, food in our stomachs and in the company of good friends, who could ask for more?"

"At the end of that time, where do you think you'll be going next?"

"My main concern is to place as many miles between us and our pursuers. I think it best that we head south. The quickest way, as far as I can tell, will be to go by boat. When that time comes, we will need to be directed to the closest facility providing boats. The money I earn will also pay for passage."

"The nearest port where you can hire a boat will be in Lisht, the western shore of the Nile. I will prepare a map for you showing you every oasis that I know of and proximate miles you need to travel. After that, you are in the hands of Yahweh."

"Thank you Saul and I will start work tomorrow. My family and I will also be attending temple services."

The first day was spent sketching out the rabbi's requirements for a storage facility. Joseph made a list of the materials that would be needed and an order was placed. On the next day in late afternoon, the materials were delivered. Later that afternoon, work was begun.

The rabbi had given him an advance in his wages allowing them to buy foodstuffs and other vital materials. Mary and Salomé went about storing the foodstuffs and Jesus was given the task of cleaning the workshop. Everyone had a job to do. Their health has been restored, and their routine returned to normal. Jesus had been enrolled in the temple school for young children, an experience he loved. In the meantime, Mary had continued her lessons with him and he had found children of his age to run around with.

At the end of forty-five days, Joseph went to the rabbi to inform him that the work was completed. His wages were paid to date and because he completed the job before the estimated time, he was given a small bonus.

"Joseph," he began, "you are more than a carpenter. You are a master craftsman. I've never seen such fine carpentry work in all my life.

"I suppose now it's time for you to prepare yourselves to continue your journey. A truly sad day. Joseph you will be in our thoughts and our prayers. *Lekh em ha-Elohim.*"

On the 46th day, the Holy Family began their trek across the desert heading for Lisht.

CHAPTER FORTY-FIVE

AT AN OASIS somewhere in the vast desert, Salomé could walk no further. Her feet were swollen, blistered, and infected. Mary went to her aid. She drew water from the well and began bathing Salomé's feet with the cool water. An elderly woman at the oasis saw what Mary was doing for the other woman. She came to them saying in Hebrew, "I am Rachob. I have been in the desert many years with my family. May I help you and your party," she asked?

Mary looked to Joseph for guidance; he nodded.

"Yes," Mary answered, "I do not know what to do for her."

Rachob returned to her group then returned with several pewter jars of ointments and balms. She handed Mary one of them. "This is a cleansing solution to wash her feet with. Cleanse your feet as well. After you have done that, massage her feet with these ointments and balms that will wake up the blood in her feet and she will be better in no time. She will have to be off her feet for a day or so. *Refu'ah shelenah,* fellow travelers."

"Thank you mother of the desert," Mary said. "Go with God."

The Holy Family stayed at the oasis for two days while they healed. Whatever ointments had been used, they had done a remarkable healing.

They could smell the river and hear the screeching birds before they saw any boats. The smell from the river was alien to them but somehow familiar.

"There is that smell again father," Jesus observed. "It is the same as the smell on the other river. The Nile must be close by."

They had completed another arduous trek across burning desert sands. They were better prepared but the hardship remained daunting.

"Well done Jesus. He picked up on that right away. Let us see if we can find a boat that is going south."

When they reached the shores of the Nile there were four large boats tied up at the docks.

"There," Jesus exclaimed, "the man with the big bushy grey beard."

Joseph and Jesus approached the man. "You with any of these boats," Joseph asked? The man passed Jesus a big smile lighting his weather wrinkled face.

"As a matter of fact I am. I am the Captain of that blue hulled felucca. I call her Manakil which means 'spring of freshwater.' What can I do for you?" As he was speaking he felt Jesus' small left arm. "You are a strong young man," he observed.

That brought a smile to Jesus' face. "We are seeking passage with you if you're heading south and if we can afford your fare."

"How many of you are there?"

"There are four of us plus a donkey."

The man pulled his beard, squinted his eyes at Jesus, and quoted Joseph a price.

"My partner and I," Joseph said with a wink, "must confer with our family."

"Always a wise move."

They left the Captain and walked over to where Mary and Salomé were waiting. Before they could speak, He called out, "The price I quoted you includes one meal a day, and the services of a tour guide will be free."

They huddled together discussing the price that was quoted. "The price is within our means, Mary. What are your thoughts?"

"The money goes into the purse slowly and leaves it very rapidly. Wherever you go my Lord, I will go."

"Me too," Jesus added.

"We have little choice Mary. We must put distance between ourselves and Herod's troops as quickly as we can. This seems like the best option."

"Well, I do not want to be left behind," Salomé said quietly, "so I will go with you."

"You are already included Salomé," Joseph said.

With Jesus holding his hand, he returned to the ship's Captain. "We would like to book passage with you." They paid him the fees asked for.

"Get your family and you go on board, we sail with the tide. There is a small stable on the lower deck you can tether your donkey, we have some feed for him, straw mostly, but it is your responsibility to clean up after him every day.

"You and your family can find space set on the lower deck, you can spread your bedding." Pointing to the front portion of the lower deck, he said, "You will notice a metal brazier anchored to the decking. That is where the meals are prepared. Joseph, for your information we cook with charcoals. When the meal is over, the cook will take the charcoals and throw them overboard. By that time there should be nothing more than hot ashes. In case there is a mishap, coals getting on the deck, there are three buckets of sand against the bulkhead. Cover the coals with sand as quickly as you can. If you do any cooking by yourself, please keep those instructions in mind.

"You and your family will have free run of the lower deck but do not go to the upper decks. That is where we will be doing all the work. Also notice that there are three masts for sails that have to be worked every day while we are traveling down river. Please have your family stay out the way of the crew. Coming up the river, we rely more on the currents than on the sails. I tell you all this is for the safety of the little one as well.

"To improve the seaworthiness of the craft, we have added a bowsprit at the front of the craft and raised the deck aft or rear the boat. Both areas are too dangerous for your son to go wandering about. A word of caution to you and your family. We raise or lower the Lateen sails, those are fore an aft, the crew is too busy tending to business to be watchful for others. I thank you for your cooperation, and we hope that you enjoy your trip down river with us. Now if you'll excuse me.

"Before we part I think we should introduce ourselves. My name is Abdul Hakeem but you can call me Captain Abdul. What is your name?"

"My name is Joseph, my wife's name is Mary, my son's name is Jesus, and the woman with us is Salomé."

"It is good for me to know. If you'll excuse me I will see to our departure."

Before he could leave however, Jesus said, "Captain Abdul, "Is that a bird attached to the front of the boat? Why is it there? Why doesn't it fly away?"

"The last Captain of the ship was an ancient Egyptian. He was very superstitious and I think he had the bird put on there to ward off evil spirits."

Once on board the ship they selected a portion of the lower deck, directly below the upper deck, away from the stall and brazier. All took part in getting settled. Once that was done Jesus began his inspection of the lower deck. He jumped when the wind caught the sails and they snapped. The ship began moving smoothly in midstream. Captain Abdul came to the lower deck to inspect the cargo lashing and to see to the comfort of his passengers. As he approached them, Jesus tugged on his tunic.

"What are those birds flying overhead," he asked. "Are they seagulls?"

"No little one they are Squacco heron and the smaller one is a black headed gull. The white birds that you see on shore are Ibis and they are sacred to the Egyptians."

"What are those fish racing in the water? They are swimming as fast as the boat is going."

"Yes, they are very fast. They are called kingfishers. This reminds me, I would like you and your father to come with me. I want to show you what your job will be while you are on board."

They moved to the sideboard of the ship where the Captain picked up a fishing pole and a bucket of chum.

"Take the fishing pole," he directed and Jesus did as he was told. "Place it in the hole, that metal piece is for oars if and when we need them." Jesus placed the pole where he had been told.

Captain Abdul reached into the pail and removed a piece of chum. "This piece of fish has been cut into small pieces as you can see, and it is what we use for bait. It is called chum. "Take this piece of chum, do not be afraid of it you will not be bitten, and run the hook through it like this," he demonstrated. "Notice that there is a weight attached to the line. That keeps the bait below the surface of the water. The fish will go after the chum and when they swallow it, the hook will dig into their mouth, and you have caught yourself a fish. The fish you will catch we will later cook and eat." He threw the line overboard.

"Hold the line loosely in your fingers," he continued. "When the fish takes a piece of chum, you will feel a tug on the line. Bring the line back on board and you will find that you caught a fish. Do you think you can handle the job?"

Jesus took the line in his hand, held it as he had been shown, and almost immediately there was a tug on the line. Joseph went to his side to help his son out.

"I got one! I got one," Jesus exclaimed excitedly! Jesus and Joseph pulled the line on board and a Kingfisher lay flopping on the deck. Joseph removed the hook and at the same time sent Jesus to get another piece of chum. He let Jesus put the hook into the bait. "Now put the line back in the water," which he did.

Jesus ran over to his mother and Salomé. "I caught a fish!" Salomé returned to the sideboard with him, cut off the head and gutted the fish. Immediately they were surrounded by birds hovering overhead waiting to get the entrails.

"Throw that stuff in the water," Captain Abdul called out to Salomé, "and watch what the birds do." When that was done, the birds began to swoop down grabbing fish as they flew by. They created quite a commotion.

"I will see you later when we cook and eat them," Captain Abdul said as he turned and left. After dinner had been eaten, and they were getting settled for the evening, all four members of the family held hands as Joseph prayed. "Beloved heavenly father you have been so good to us. We thank you, we bless you for your kindness. You are the one Lord. Good night."

CHAPTER FORTY-SIX

GENTLE BREEZES AND the movement of the boat in the water woke the Holy Family to greet morning. Joseph said the morning prayer then washed himself and Jesus under the boat's pump. When he was dried off he ran to the sideboard to watch the shoreline as it drifted by.

"Jesus, his mother called, "Come, have something to eat."

Salomé unwrapped the bread they had purchased previously on the shore. Mary made herbal tea and both women had their meal.

"This is some change from two days ago "That breeze feels wonderful."

The crewmen provided them with a bucket of water and a bar of soap. Joseph made a temporary shower from their cloaks that provided the women with some privacy. As they washed, Jesus ran around the lower deck in a loincloth. Then all of the women washed their clothing and hung them to dry.

"Abba," Jesus asked, "Can we fish now?"

"You learned something new yesterday and now today, you want to do it again. Yes we can fish. Did you scrub the deck good yesterday when we were finished?"

"As best I could."

Jesus went to the fishing pole while Joseph removed the lid from the chum bucket. He then watched how Jesus baited the hook and put the line in the water. The boy held the line loosely as he had been shown, waiting for it to tug.

"Father," he called, "look over on the shore. Water is rushing into the river."

"That is a stream from the inland rushing to meet the Nile."

"Look at those logs on the shore," he pointed out.

Captain Abdul had come down to the lower deck to see how he was doing. He overheard what Jesus had said. "Those, little one, are not logs but crocodiles bathing in the sun."

"What are crocodiles," Jesus asked?

"A crocodile is a water reptile that lives in and out of the water. They call them amphibious. That's a big word for you to remember. The crocodile has a very long jaw with rows of very sharp teeth. He also has a long tail that helps them to swim in the water. He has short feet, very horny skin and a very nasty disposition. They sneak up on their prey underwater until it is too late for the animal to escape. They will eat anything that comes close enough to the shore."

He turned to Joseph. "How is everything Joseph? Is your family comfortable?"

"Quite comfortable Captain, thank you."

"From what I have heard, I understand that you like to hear the history of our cities. Is that true?"

"Not only the cities, but structures the Egyptians have created. They are not only marvelous but I find it hard to understand how they were able to create such wonders."

"As I promised to you earlier I am not only the ship's Captain, but the onboard guide. Would you like me to tell you the history of the city's history and something about the monument and pyramids we will be passing?"

"Yes Captain please. Such information about this ancient land would be fascinating."

"Captain! Captain," Jesus called out. "I caught another fish!"

Turning to look at Jesus, the Captain said, "Well done young sailor. It looks like your family will eat again tonight."

He turned back to Joseph. "The city on our port side that is over there on the left, over the railing is called starboard. The city is called Meidum noted for its last pharaoh and the third dynasty. The pyramid architect studied under Imhotep who designed the very first pyramid. As you can see it has collapsed because of modifications the architect made in Imhotep's original design. Their modifications amounted to major construction errors."

"Captain," Jesus shouted as he pointed toward the shore, "a crocodile jumped out of the water, grabbed a big animal and dragged him back into the water!"

"That is life and death on the Nile, little one. That crocodile will take his kill to the bottom of the river, where it will then eat it. That is just the way it is. In the meantime, finish with your fish and cast for another. You have many mouths to feed." He smiled at Joseph as he left.

Joseph sensed that the Captain did not want Jesus to dwell on the cruelty he had just witnessed. He distracted him by putting him to work. The captain, Joseph felt, was more sensitive than that he had first imagined.

Before long eight fish were flopping on the deck. Salomé was busy preparing them for dinner and feeding the squawking birds and she threw the entrails overboard. Jesus got busy scrubbing down the deck with the help of the deck hand who came to join him. When the fish had been cleaned, Mary and Salomé prepared the evening meal that included the vegetables and bread provided by the Captain. He and his crew ate with them.

Instead of just telling the story this night, Captain Abdul took his place as storyteller. He regaled them with stories of the Nile and its people. "The ancient inhabitants," he began, "were closely aware of their surroundings, especially with the other living things. The nature of the country was such that there were two different kinds of plants and animals; those of the desert, and those of the fertile land and river. They saw and admired the power and beauty of the animals they lived with and use their images to represent the power and beauty of the gods.

"Some animals in the desert included jackals, this is a doglike creature that feeds on dead animals. Lions will kill their prey, and antelopes are part of their diet. Along the river's edge are very beautiful birds, hippopotamus and of course crocodiles. Along the shores as we sail on the Nile, you will see lush plants, shrubs, Palm trees and all varieties of trees were first because of the proximity to the water.

"We will be stopping for the evening at Tel el Amarna. You can go ashore and if you would like to buy anything you need, but I strongly recommend that you spend the evening on the boat. Brigands hereabouts are notorious."

"Captain," Jesus asked, "will we be sailing with you again tomorrow?"

"Yes little one you will. Tomorrow we will reach Assiut, where your father wanted me to take you."

CHAPTER FORTY-SEVEN

JESUS HAD CLIMBED onto a hatch to watch the bare footed sailors take in the sails and secure them, manhandle a large stone bound with hawser that had been their anchor. A hoist of some sort lifted the stone, swung it to starboard and dropped it into the river. Captain Abdul supervised the process as Jesus watching it, walked over to him.

"At night, when we will no longer be sailing, we reef the sails and drop the anchor," Abdul explained to him.

"And in the morning," Jesus said, "everything will be reversed and will be back into the waters sailing again."

"You are a quick learner and quick with your observations and deductions."

Joseph approached the two of them chatting. Abdul said, "You can go ashore and make your purchases I will send two crewmen with you and show you where things are and to protect you from brigands. It would also be my recommendation that you spend the night on board the boat. In the morning we will continue our journey."

At sunrise Captain Abdul took Jesus to the upper deck where he could watch the men bringing in the anchor. He was first placed well out of their way, after which he began giving orders for losing the sails. The large boat pulled away from the shore and out into midstream where a brisk breeze caught and filled the sails.

Their passage through the early morning waters flushed the birds in the trees and marshes. Crocodiles could be seen rushing into the waters as well, all of which was accompanied by a cacophony of various pleasant sounds.

Jesus returned to the lower deck, rejoined his family and ate the morning meal. The morning routine followed after which Jesus and his father returned to their fishing, Mary and Salomé cleaned up their area and then bathed.

"Abba," Jesus inquired, "last night Captain Abdul said that they were brigands on shore that we should avoid. What is a brigand?"

"Well, in addition to being very bad people, brigands are robbers and thieves who usually work within a group. They plunder the caravan, people, and sometimes villages and cities. I have only heard of them in the mountains around Jerusalem, but now Captain Abdul said they can be found in Egypt as well."

"Do you know everything," Jesus asked?

"No, by no means, son, as a matter of fact, the more I learn the more I find out how little I know. Watch your fishing pole Jesus. I think you have just caught another fish." And so he had. The rest of the morning was spent in catching fish, Salomé gutting and cleaning them and feeding the birds, while Mary was grinding flour and baking bread. At midday they called a break for the meal.

After they had eaten, Captain Abdul said, "I hear that you are a storyteller. Would you tell us a story?"

"My stories are fueled by the past of the Israelites. Do you want to hear about them?"

"Yes, a good story is always worth hearing, but now it will have to wait because a rain squall is beating down on us. We have to prepare the boat. Get undercover if you can." He no sooner had spoken when heavy rains pelted the boat. Joseph found a folded cargo tarpaulin that he used to cover his family. As quickly as the rains had come, just as quickly they passed by. A short time later, Captain Abdul and two of his crew members returned to them. Canvas was placed on the steaming deck for them to keep dry.

"May we now hear a story," he asked?

"The story is about Moses, a former Egyptian Prince who later became a prophet. He was a Jew, who as an infant, was left by his mother in the bulrushes along the Nile River. He was found by the pharaoh's daughter, brought into their palace and raised as one of them. Eventually became a Prince but along the way the injustices the pharaoh was imposing on the Israelites, sickened him. He begged the pharaoh to let his people go. It came to pass.

"Moses was leading and he was taking them to the Promised Land. They came to the country of the Amorites, a people who worshiped idols. Moses wanted to lead his people through the Amorite country and so asked the leader, Sihon, if they might pass. He not only refused passage but Sihon took his Army against them. God gave the Israelites a victory over them. They moved on to Bashan where they were again challenged, and God gave them another victory.

"After forty years of walking through the desert, still seeking the Promised Land, they came to Canaan the land they had been seeking. With the exception of Moses, all of the Israelites were able to see the Promised Land."

"This God of yours denied Moses his goal, after leading his people for forty years. It does not seem fair."

"Oh but it was. Moses did everything that God asked of him, except for one thing. God told him that because he did *not* do everything he had been asked to do, he would be able to take his people to the Promised Land but he would not be able to see enter." The Lord told him to speak to the rock but he struck it twice. We must do as He tells us!

"He is a very tough task master."

"The story tells us that we should be obedient to Him in all things and that is what we try to do."

With that the story ended, the fishermen went back to the railing. Captain Abdul came over to them and said, "Thank you for that story. . ."

Jesus interrupted. "Captain," he said, "there are a herd of black cows in the water and they are blowing smoke into the air."

"Among your many talents little one, is your keen power of observation. That is a herd of hippopotamus, they are also amphibious, living in and out of the water close to the shore. They eat only grasses and plants, there are many that call them water horses. After the elephant and rhinoceros, they are the third largest animals. As you may notice their unusual shapes, they have a large mouth with enormous teeth, they are nearly hairless, with short stubby legs but, strangely, they can run very fast. During daytime they live in the water to keep cool. They also mate and give birth in the water. They come out at dusk to graze on the grasses."

The Captain turned to return to his duties. He started up the ladder to the upper deck, Jesus called to him, "Captain Abdul, where are we going?"

"Later this afternoon we will reach Assiut. It is located in the middle of Egypt and it is noted for its carved ivory, fine pottery, and wood carvings."

"What is ivory Captain?"

"Ivory comes from elephants, the largest land animals I was telling you about. They have two long teeth called tusks. When they die, the natives removed the tusks and carve them into various things.

"Joseph, to continue your history lesson, Assiut is in a strategic location in the Libyan desert. It is situated where the Nile narrows. In the city you will find shrines to the local god Wepwawet, who guards the necropolis. Otherwise, it is an ordinary city.

"When we dock, I will introduce you to Ra'ed Nagy. He is the major merchant in the city and he can tell you where the Jewish section can be located. Also, let him know that you are an accomplished carpenter. If there is work to be had on shore, he can find it for you. He unfortunately only speaks Arabic, but we can find you an interpreter."

Later that afternoon they docked in Assiut. Captain Abdul accompanied the Holy Family to the marketplace where he introduced them to Ra'ed Nagy.

After three minutes were spoken, Abdul turn to Joseph saying, "His son, Sa'ad will be your interpreter. They are honest dealers and will work with you fairly. Good fortune Joseph. Go with your God."

"God be with you Abdul."

CHAPTER FORTY-EIGHT

A PROFILE OF Herod the Great Herod indicates a greatly *disturbed* man.[71] "When Herod heard these things (the promised Messiah), he was greatly troubled and all Jerusalem with him."

Herod was a deeply *crafty* man.[72] When he had privily called the wise men to meet with him, he inquired of them diligently at what time the star appeared. And presented to Bethlehem, and said, go and search diligently for the young child; and when ye have found him bring me word again, that I may come and worship him also."

Herod was a *brutal* man.[73] "Then Herod, when he saw that he mocked the wise men, was exceedingly wroth, and sent forth, slew all the children that were in Bethlehem, and all the coasts thereof, from two years old and under, according to the problem when he diligently inquired of the wise men."

Herod the great, was the client king of Judea, and had been for thirty-four years. His son, Antipater tried to usurp him but his plot was discovered and he was arrested, accused of being a parricide, and imprisoned within the palace.

Age and remorse over his past offenses and misdeeds, began preying on Herod's mind which in turn increased his ailments. At seventy years of age, he had had an eventful life, but now was distressed by an uprising instigated by two educated doctors in Jerusalem. They were later identified as students, Matthias who was the instigator behind the tearing down of the Golden Eagle above the temple door. They were captured, brought before Herod and burned to death before him.

Herod was, at this stage in his life, besieged from within and from without. There were attempts on his life, there are plans to take his life, primarily from

---

71   Matthew 2:3
72   Matthew 2:7-8
73   Matthew 2:16

his son Antipater, and his health began to fail. The most recent upheaval at the temple, had taken its toll.

After this however, his health rapidly worsened. He was constantly plagued by an urge to scratch himself. Distemper seized his body, he developed a fever, had pains in his colon, diarrhea, and swollen feet. There was inflammation about his abdomen, and peritonitis of his genitals that produced worms. This was followed by a convulsive cough.

He tried in vain to ease his excruciating pain and convulsions by bathing in the warm springs at Callirrhoe after which he returned to his winter capital in Jericho. From there he is carried by stretcher to the hot springs at the shores of the Dead Sea. The stay at the shore did no good and he returned to Jericho.

Racked with hopelessness and despair, Herod began thinking about suicide. Then, for some reason, he had assembled the most distinguished men from every village from one end of Judea to the other, and imprisoned in the Hippodrome. He summoned his sister Salomé to his chamber. "Salomé," he said, "Execute them at the very moment that I die."

Throughout his life, Herod suffered from depression and paranoia. Now, his sick mind reasoned that their death would dispel any joy in Judea over his own death.

He no sooner issued that directive, when a letter from Caesar Augustus arrived. In the letter Caesar left it up to Herod to either exile or execute Antipater.

By this time, he was in such pain and agony that he tried to stab himself to death but was prevented by his cousin. When the people heard of his attempt at suicide, the Palace was filled with loud cries.

Antipater, in his dungeon cell, heard the cries and thought that his father had died. He summoned his jailer saying, "My father is dead, release me from the cell and I will make you a rich man."

Instead, the jailer reported the incident to Herod who cried out in anguish and tore at his beard. He summoned his bodyguard saying, "Kill my son and bury him at Hyrcanium."

Immediately thereafter, every change had to be approved, as well as appointing Archelaus, his eldest son, as his successor; Antipas, his brother, as tetrarch of Galilee and Parea; Philip D appointed as tetrarch of Trachonitis and neighboring territories; to Caesar left ten million pieces of silver, his wife Julia (Livia) and others, he left five million pieces of silver.

Herod lived five days after Antipater's execution. He had reigned for thirty-four years when he became master of the state, and thirty-seven years from when he was declared King by the Roman Emperor. After his death, Salomé released the prisoners, the men of distinction, from the hippodrome. His will was read before the people and Archelaus declared as his successor who, in turn, spared no expense for his father's funeral. He was interred at the Herodium.

The official cause of death was listed as chronic kidney disease exacerbated by gas gangrene.

After Herod's death, his body was carried in a procession from Jericho to the Herodium which is located just outside of Bethlehem. His body was adorned in purple, a crown of gold laid on his head and a golden scepter was put in his hands. His bier was made of gold, studded with jewels.

A procession consisting of household and one hundred other slaves, school censers walked behind. The body was taken to Herodium, the gravesite he had created and looked almost like a volcano artificially shaped. His body was placed in the tomb after which it was sealed. The after effect was that it resembled an ordinary mountain.

AUTHOR NOTE: In the 1960s archaeologists unearthed artifacts in the courtyard of the burial mound, Herod's fortification towers, and palace. No trace of Herod's remains was found.

CHAPTER FORTY-NINE

RA'ED NAGY'S SON was showing the Holy Family a house that was recently vacated. It was a family home with an attached stable. They liked what they saw, and Joseph immediately had thoughts of turning the stable into the workshop. They bartered with Sa'ad, offering their donkey in exchange for money as rent. The men agreed. Sa'ad then took them to the marketplace showing Joseph where they could purchase what and other materials he needed, as well as food stuffs.

Mary and Salomé made the house habitable, Joseph and Jesus began work on the workshop. It did not take long to bring about some dramatic changes. Ra' and his son came by after a week's time to see that all was well. They were pleased with what they found.

"Joseph," Ra'ed asked as they sat on the patio, "what sort of carpentry are you capable of?"

"I am a *tektôn* Ra'ed, which means that I am not only capable of doing carpentry work but stone masonry, and metals."

When he heard of Joseph's capabilities, he said, "I will place an advertising packet in my shop at the marketplace, telling people of your skills and how to make contact with you."

"I would be most grateful to you. I can certainly use the work. I would like to ask you something that has nothing to do with the subject. How far are we from Cairo?"

"What an odd question Joseph. Cairo is some distance away but I have heard that it is approximately at least 250 miles. Why do you ask?"

"We have been told that many of the Jews have fled native homes, seeking refuge in Egypt. We are just some more of those Jews fleeing from a tyrannical King Herod of Jerusalem. He has sent troops into Egypt looking for us. Their primary mission is to kill our son and us along with him."

"By Allah's breath, Joseph. Why would he want to do such a thing? Is he afraid that one of the children in Bethlehem will take his place as King?"

"What nonsense! A workingman's son to be King of Judea?" Ra'ed sensed that there was something deeper that Joseph was telling him. "Be at ease. If any of his troops or any Roman troops coming this way, we will hear of it well in advance of their arrival."

The family settled in, Mary started Jesus with religious classes in the temple. At home she taught him how to write his numbers and he began reading. In so doing, she saw that he was eager to learn and had an inquisitive mind. She tried to keep pace with his intellect.

Word had gotten out about Joseph, people began coming to his workshop giving him all the work he could handle. When people saw the quality of his work, contracts came his way.

In his spare time, Joseph began making things for their home, with Jesus assisting him. There was not very much for a youth of his years, what he was assigned to do and completed, gave him a feeling of worth and of helping out his family.

It did not take long for the Holy Family to be absorbed in the Jewish community. At the synagogue, Jesus developed a group of playmates. Whenever they went to the temple, the children would band together to play, yell, and run frantically about.

The women went into a separate room where they discussed their faith, and their place in it. The men went into the Shul with the Torah was read and discussed.

On their way home, Jesus' ever inquisitive mind, found voice to his father. "Why is everyone separated when we go to the temple? The children go one way, the women go other, and the men go a third. Why is that?"

"That is good Jesus. Whenever you have a question do not hesitate to ask. To answer your question, synagogues are typified by the separation of men, women, and children. This is a long-standing custom designed to keep men from being distracted by the female presence and those of the children during prayers. Females, in orthodox congregations, are often kept in a balcony overlooking the proceedings, or to the rear of the main gathering area. And this temple they use a separate room.

"You will notice that in the law men are mentioned and are not to be disturbed during their prayers. According to Jewish law, and that is our guidepost, you are not yet a man. I will give you the reason why. According to once again, when Jewish boys become thirteen years old, they become accountable and responsible for their actions and become a bar mitzvah, a man."

Halim Ghati and his wife Nadia became close friends. Halim was a skilled weaver and Nadia an expert at dyeing cloth. In addition to which, they had a son named Joshua, about the same age as Jesus.

They also watch the children at play in the street as they did so, Joseph and Mary were amazed to see how quickly Jesus was growing every day. With regular healthy meals, plenty of exercise, fresh air and sunshine, his body showed his development.

One day, Halim asked Joseph, "You have no doubt noticed the pagan gods that are on display about the city. Since you have an interest in history, I could take you to a location where some of the great gods are on display."

"Thank you that would be interesting."

"I will show you only three that I consider to be the most significant. It is purely subjective on my part.

RA the most important god. Swallowed at night by sky god and is reborn in the morning.

ISIS is the protective goddess who uses powers to help people.

PTAH is the chief god of Memphis and god of craftsmen.

"There are of course others taking these symbols that deal with the beliefs of ancient Egyptians."

"Thank you Halim. Is it odd that some people can believe in pagan symbolism but not in the one true God. I suppose it is possible that his teachings not yet reached the ancient Egyptians and they turn to something else. It is a shame that they had not yet come to know him."

The men returned to the others.

At a meeting of the elders during Hanukkah, Joseph was usually called upon to tell them of their life in Jerusalem and Galilee. At this particular meeting, Rabbi Isaac Iskander asked Joseph, "Can you describe the temple in Jerusalem for us; you have seen it often and some of us, have never seen it."

"I can certainly try. I just hope that I can do it adequately enough."

"The entire complex is bounded by a wall estimated at 840 feet long on the south, 945 feet long on the north, 1410 feet on the east, 1455 five feet long on the west, and covers almost 30 acres. The walls are 16 inches thick.

The temple in Jerusalem is built on Temple Mount, a stone base strong enough to support the great weight it bears. Approaching the temple is an inlaid stone flooring on two sides by colonnades. The entrance leads to a semicircular staircase which in turn, turns to the temple doors. The doors are made of inlaid gold.

"All walls and double doors to the two-story sanctuary are covered in gold with clusters of golden vines and topped with clusters of golden grapes.

Suspended before the door of the sanctuary is a tapestry supposed to have been woven in Babylon, it's multicolored design a panorama of the universe. There is an offer for incense, a golden *menorah* on the table for the holy shrew bread. The entrance of the *Holy of Holies* is covered by a double veil, and into this empty room, that life will never be allowed to enter. I am told that within this room there is a pot for *manna, a mercy seat, Aaron's Rod,* and the *Ark of the Covenant.*"

During his recitation, the elders sat around transfixed.

"Joseph," Rabbi Iskander said quietly, "you have been blessed to have been there and to have seen all."

"I am blessed rabbi, in more ways than you know. I must tell you that I have never been beyond the veils. I was only told what was there."

"Is it heavily guarded," Halim asked?

"King Herod, has his praetorian guards within the temple walls. So in answer to your question, Halim, yes it is generally guarded."

"Thank you for sharing with us your knowledge," the rabbi said. "All is well with your family? Do you need for anything?"

"Yes, rabbi thanks. All is very well. Except for the fact that we live in fear daily, it also diminishes daily. Who knows, if this trend continues, one day will be no more."

"Before you leave Joseph, I must tell you. I hear from the teachers in the temple and from some of the elders, that your son, Jesus has wisdom beyond his years. You and your family must be teaching him well at home."

"That is his mother's doing. I can only teach him carpentry."

"And something more I am thinking," the rabbi opined.

Six months past that were fruitful for everyone. One day after a hard day's work, Joseph slept deeply. An angel of the Lord appeared to him in a dream saying, "Arise, and take the young child and his mother, and go into the land of Israel; but they are dead which sought the child's life."[74]

At breakfast the next morning, Mary noticed a deep concerned look on Joseph's face. "Joseph," she inquired, "something has happened. Pray tell us what it is."

Jesus and Salomé were still at the table and they all looked at him quizzically.

"During the night an angel of the Lord appeared to me and spoke with me."

"He did, what did He have to say?" Joseph reached out and took Mary and Jesus by the hand.

"He said that we can all go home. King Herod is dead!"

Mary bowed her head. "God be praised!"

"Jesus," she said embracing him, "You are no longer in danger. We can return home."

---

[74]"Matthew 2: 19-20

"The angel also said," Joseph amended, "that I should take you and Jesus and return to Israel." Joseph turned his attention to Salomé. "When we leave Salomé, will you be leaving with us?"

"It has been more than three years," Salomé observed. "After all that time of living in fear, it is ended. The Lord is good! Yes Joseph, I will be returning with you, at least as far as Hebron where I can rejoin my family."

"We must give thought," Mary said aloud, "about how we should return home. What are your thoughts Lord?"

"Before we left the boat, Captain Abdul sketched us a map of the possible routes we should take. I have that parchment in a chest in the workshop. Jesus, would you go and get the parchment and bring it back to us? When you return we can all look it over together?"

Jesus returned quickly the parchment in his hands. He handed the parchment to Joseph who opened it and laid it on the table. The family hovered over it.

"This," he said indicating, "is the Nile River running northward and this is the way we should go. We can make a stop, for about three days at Fayum Oasis, up here [indicating] just west of the Nile. After that, and if we have enough strength, we will move on to Saqqara, Giza, and then into Tanis. At this point we will move west and then north.

"Once on the other side of the river, we will be entering the Sinai Peninsula. At this point we will begin going north into Gaza, Hebron, then into Jerusalem. If all goes well the trip should take us about eight months. Once we have crossed the border and leave Egypt, we can wipe Egypt's sand from our clothing."

Salomé asked, "will we be traveling overland to Fayum, Joseph?"

"No, I think we should go as much of the way as possible with Captain Abdul. Back to Lisht and from there to Dashur."

"Lord," Mary said as she put her hand on his shoulder, "it is obvious that you have given this journey much thought. You have brought us here safely we trust that you will return us just as safely. When should we leave?"

"As you know from our previous departures, we need to pack all our necessary belongings, leave those in the temple, after we say goodbye to Halim and Nadia, and book passage with Captain Abdul. When he heads north, we will be with him."

Two days later, the rabbi had dinner in their honor and much of the congregation attended. With dinner over, the Holy Family prepared to leave, the rabbi prayed, "Lord God Jehovah, you are sending our friends back to their home in Jerusalem. They have been a blessing to us. We beseech you to travel with them, guard and protect them, and see them safely to their home."

Joseph shook the rabbi's hand saying, "*Shalom* rabbi," as his voice cracked with emotion.

AUTHOR NOTE: God is giving a command to Joseph, for the third time. Joseph does what is commanded of him, with unflappable obedience. What better way any demonstrate his unfailing obedience and love.

CHAPTER FIFTY

ARCHELAUS, THE OLDEST son of Herod, was full brother of Herod Antipater, and the half-brother of Philip. All three were sent to Rome as hostages, where Archelaus received his education. His father, Herod the great, was about to journey in Jericho, but before he did he became embroiled in an upheaval in Jerusalem.

In an attempt to unite the prevailing religion with the state, he had a Golden Eagle installed above the temple entrance. The Jews in Jerusalem felt it symbolized blasphemy and against the Ten Commandments prohibiting and making false idols .

To well renowned teachers of the law, Judas, son of Sepphoris, and Matthias, son of Magalis, along with forty students set about cutting down the Eagle over the temple entrance. They let themselves down from the top of the tent entrance with thick ropes they cut the Eagle down with their axes. Someone in the temple ran to tell Herod what was happening. He immediately sent troops to the site and they arrested forty students. They were brought before Herod and sentenced to death at the hands of his cohorts.

The teachers and the rabbis were also captured, taken prisoner and brought before the King. Judas had been immolated before him for the crime. Herod claimed before the people that it was these people who had committed a sacrilege, and therefore, deserve to be put to death. Soon afterward, Herod died and by acclamation made Archelaus King, Rome sent word congratulating him to take Herod's place. The people and the military pledge their allegiance and goodwill and ask God to bless his government.

Archelaus prepared his father's funeral; a bier of gold, embroidered with precious stones with Herod's body covered with purple robes, a diadem on his head, a golden crown and a scepter in his right hand. After the funeral Archelaus became Herod's successor, taking the throne before Passover in 4BC. As he ascended the golden throne, was dressed in white.

His first proclamation, the appeasing of his subjects in their unrest he promised to lower the taxes, release those prisoners who were taken soon after the calamity at the temple, and in addition, he promised to punish those responsible for the death of the teachers, Rabbis and students. The crowd of people gathered to hear his proclamation, also called for the immediate punishment of those responsible for the deaths and the replacement of the High Priests. Archelaus acceded to their wishes but became quite angry with the crowds. He appeased the crowds by saying that all would be made well as soon as he was confirmed about the Emperor.

At the feast celebrating his succession to the throne, crowds began streaming into the temple area, still wailing over the loss of the teachers, Rabbis, and students. Their threatening behavior began to escalate and worsen.

Archelaus sent a Tribune with a cohort of troops to reason with the seditionists, beseeching them to wait until he returned from Rome and Caesar, the Emperor. The cohorts were stoned by the people and many were killed. When Archelaus heard of this, he sent his entire army into the city and the temple. An estimated 3000 people were slain, He canceled Passover.

Archelaus sailed into Rome where he met with Caesar and his enemies, one of which was his brother Antipater. On his arrival, Antipater levels charges against his brother saying that he feigned grief at the death of his father, that the killing of 3000 Jews was not merely threats to worshipers in Jerusalem at Passover, but it also constituted a threat to Caesar by Archelaus acting as the King before he was confirmed.

Judea was in rebellion. When the feast of Pentecost arrived the Jews gathered to avenge the greed of the Sabine's. Archelaus hastened to Rome to secure the required confirmation of his succession from Augustus. He found that he had to encounter opposition from two sides. His brother Antipas, supported by many members of the Herodian house resident in Rome, claimed formal acknowledgment for Herod's second will, that nominated him king. Besides, the Jews of Palestine sent a deputation of fifty persons—who were supported by about 8,000 Jewish residents of Rome—and petitioned for the exclusion of the Herodians from any share whatever in the government of the land, and for the incorporation of Judea in the province of Syria. Such was the disloyalty among the Herodians, that many members of the family secretly favored this latter popular demand. But Augustus, with statesman-like insight, concluded that it was better for Roman interests to make of Judea a monarchy, governed by its own kings tributary to Rome, than to leave it a Roman province administered by Romans, in which latter case there would certainly be repeated insurrections against the foreign administration. As it would be more prudent to make such a monarchy as small and powerless as possible, he decided to divide Herod's somewhat extensive empire into three portions.

Nicolaus of Damascus, Herod's confidant, argued with Caesar that Archelaus had acted appropriately, and that Herod's will, written prior to Herod's yielding his kingship to Archelaus and not Antipater, should be seen as being valid.

Hearing arguments from both sides, Caesar stated that Archelaus was able to succeed his father and gave him the title of Ethnarch or Ruler of Judea, Samaria, and Idumea. In this way, Rome would consolidate its power. In addition, his brothers, Herod Antipas was to rule Galilee and Perea and Herod Philip was to rule Ituraea and Trachonitis.

Thereafter, Archelaus became not only a dictator but a cruel tyrant, committing numerous atrocities. He ruled so badly that the Samarians sent a delegation to Rome saying, "We do not want this man to reign over us." Archelaus was deposed and banished to Vienna.

CHAPTER FIFTY-ONE

"THE LITTLE ONE will not be returning with you, is that right?" Captain Abdul asked Joseph smiling?

"No," Joseph said running his fingers through Jesus' hair. "We are leaving that one behind. We're taking this young man with us instead."

Abdul turned to the two women, "Mary, Salomé, it's good to see you again," Abdul said earnestly as he assisted them on board.

"Thank you Captain," Mary replied. "We have waited a long time for this trip on your boat."

"I have reserved the elegant part of the lower deck for you." Abdul turned to Jesus saying, "I have an opening for an experienced seaman and fisherman. It requires long hours, a keen eye, and sturdy strong hands. Do you have the qualifications to that position, young sir?"

"I am experienced as a fisherman," Jesus replied smiling, "but I am not a seaman. Can I get the job?"

"Then we will have to train you. Yes, you can come on board and welcome." As Joseph ascended the ramp Abdul informed, "We will put ashore at Tel el Amarna and spend the night. After that we will go on to Lisht. Will you be heading to Fayum, or will you continue up the Nile?"

"That is our plan," Joseph replied, "to head for Fayum."

"Good, once we are in Lisht, I will assist you in your provision and see you safely on your way."

"We are ever grateful Captain," Joseph said as he shook the Captain's hand. On board the large boat, the Holy Family went about getting themselves comfortable. Captain Abdul started getting the ship ready to sail.

The boat left the quay, the sails filled with a strong breeze, as the sun rose in the eastern horizon. Everyone fell into the life pattern they had fashioned on their way south. Mary and Salomé cared for the living area to which they had been assigned, Joseph and Jesus returned to the sideboard and their fishing, and

---

the boat moved smoothly along. As a result, their lives were no longer hectic or stressful, but serene.

The Captain brought the boat into the quay at Tel el Amarna, but Joseph noticed that the city had changed little; perhaps more populated and industrious, but little else. Before they could go ashore, Captain Abdul's two crewmen were assigned to go with them.

"Just a precaution" he advised. The two women went with an escort and Captain Abdul gave Mary some money to buy ships stores by way of food. He introduced them to the provisionary, and bade them farewell. They purchased the necessary provisions, purchased new sandals for themselves, and then returned to the boat.

Mary and Salomé prepared the evening meal, set the table and called everyone to meal.

Without a word, everyone sat back and began to relax as Joseph started.

"Tonight there will not be a story, but an addition to Jesus' life now he is old enough to understand.

"Children, obey your parents in the Lord: for this is right. Honor thy father and mother; which is the first commandment with promise; that it may be well with thee, and thou mayest live on the earth. And ye fathers provoke not your children to wrath; but bring them up in the nurture and admonition of the Lord."[75]

"It is good advice to fathers and their children." The Captain stood, along with his crewmen and bade them good night and returned to the upper deck.

"What I meant by that Jesus, is that love and respect goes both ways. Know that we would never show you anything but love, honor and sincere respect. And well, I just thought it was something that needed to be said."

"Abba, is something bothering you?"

"Yes, we have been through great turmoil and I have not once told you how well you have borne it all. Well, I am telling you now and you too Mary and Salomé forgive me for not telling you sooner."

Mary reached out her hand to touch his face. "Joseph the pressures you have been under safeguarding us, is showing itself because some of the tension has been relieved. Well done my Lord."

Before sleep took them, Mary said, "Have you noticed Joseph, how quickly Jesus is growing? He cleans himself every day washes himself and has become quite self-sufficient."

"Yes I have Mary. You should have seen him dealing with the merchant. He is very forthright and keen of thought."

---

[75] Ephesians 6:1-4

"Do you remember when we were questioning what should be done with the Messiah in his upbringing? I have never given it a thought since. He is a boy unlike all boys, yet he is the same."

"I thought that the only lessons I could teach him was how to become a good carpenter. He watches me closely, copying my mannerisms and the way that I confront people, openly, honestly and fairly. The way my father taught me. He picked right up on that. But also keep in mind, you sent him away to school whenever we have had the opportunity. His religious training was supplemented by you and Salomé, mostly by you. I think the way we are bringing him up, is what God had in mind. We can only judge the boy we see before us."

Mary waited for a while and then spoke. "The return journey that we are about to make, as you have pointed out will be taxing on us physically. It will also be a great drain of our resources. Salomé and I have gone over our purse, and the prospects do not look good. It pains me to have to say this but I think that once we have traveled north, we will be required to make a stop for at least one month, to strengthen our larder."

"I know what a careful housekeeper you are and if you and Salomé say-so, we will find a place where I can work and try to earn enough for our needs. Think of it this way Mary, it can also count as a resting break, a place for Jesus to further his education."

Mary began to cry, tears trickling down her cheek. "I am the most undeserving of women to have a son like Jesus, and a Lord like you. Praise be to Adonai and His everlasting mercy!"

CHAPTER FIFTY-TWO

THE BOAT WAS quiet as Joseph and Mary stood at the railing.

"Lord, there's something on your mind. Please share whatever it is with me," Mary pleaded.

"This voyage down the Nile has given me time to reflect about our return home."

"I knew you were deep in thought. And I knew also that you would speak of it when you are ready. I have every confidence in you and in your reasoning."

"When we viewed the parchment prepared by Captain Abdul for us, I had determined that we should return by way of Fayum, Giza and Cairo."

"Lord an excellent way to return," Mary observed.

"No, and let me tell you why. I selected that route to satisfy my needs. However, when I saw the excitement on your face and Salomé about returning home, I had to discard that route. What I propose now is that we continue by boat to Cairo and get back on track from there, eliminating Fayum and Giza thereby reducing our traveling time by at least a month and maybe more."

"I know how disappointing that would be for you Lord. Are you certain that that is what you want?"

"Yes Mary I want to stabilize our lives as quickly as possible, returning Salomé to her home too."

"Let us go to the Lord with this Lord." They did.

Early the next morning, Lisht came into view, and shortly thereafter the boat was made fast to the quay. The Holy Family was about to go ashore, when Captain Abdul met them at the gangway.

"We will be here in Lisht for about two hours," the Captain said. We have some minor repairs to make him about, we need to take on some cargo, and after that, we sail on to Cairo. I think it's a good idea for you and your family to go into the city and stretch your legs. There is little enough exercise on board the boat, especially for young Jesus. While ashore you can make whatever purchases you deem necessary but be back on board within two hours."

As they walked to the streets of Lisht, they met with Moses Ankh, whom they had met on their previous visit to the city.

"*Shalom* Joseph. I never thought that you would be here," Moses said.

"*Boker tov*, my friend. And why not? This is my place of business. How long will you be staying this time," Moses asked?

"We have two hours before we must be back on board the boat. Not a very long time by any measure."

"Where are you going? Are you still being pursued?"

"In answer to your first question, we are no longer being pursued."

"Hallelujah!"

"In answer to your second question, with King Herod dead, we can return to our home in Jerusalem. Although your country is beautiful, filled with unbelievable monuments and pyramids, it is not our home."

"No it is not Joseph, and I understand what you're saying. While you are here, will you see any of the sites in Lisht?"

"We certainly hope to. On our last visit, I wanted to see the ruined pyramid of Amenemht, and the undisturbed tomb of Senebtisi. Do we have enough time you think?"

"Yes, but only if I take you."

Mary touched Joseph's shoulder. "Lord, you go with Moses and see those things, while we do the shopping that is necessary."

"Are you sure you do not mind Mary?"

"Not in the least. We will never be back this way again so this is your only opportunity."

He took Mary's face in both of his big hands, "I am glad that I have you."

As the two men walked away, Moses began his narrative. "Lisht has always been a necropolis, with two pyramids and twenty-one tombs and that was mostly mastabas. The more famous of the two mining complexes is that of Amenemht, the one you wanted to see since it features an offering hallway of granite, with a granite altar. And the undisturbed tomb of Senebtisi, still as it was..."

Joseph rejoined his family on board the boat, just as the crew pulled in the gangway. Captain Abdul was standing nearby watching the men at work. When it was done, and the boat began to move into midstream, the Captain walked over to them.

"Did you enjoy your afternoon," he asked?

"Yes," Mary replied. "It was good to stretch our legs."

"In the city," Jesus said excitedly, "I saw some rats running around the fruit stand."

"Yes Jesus, they are called fruit rats, and are a plague in the city. They bring disease. I'm glad you did not go near them."

"No, mother would not let me."

"Always listen to your mother. On a separate matter, and while I have the opportunity, Joseph has spoken to me about your revised plans. I will take you to Cairo as requested. And speaking of that, we will be near Cairo in about two hours, depending on the time. In point of fact, we will be in the area within Cairo called, Old Cairo. Once we get there, and knowing your interest in history, seek out someone that can fill in the gaps. It is only sixty miles upstream. We will stay there for the night and at sunrise, on our way to Tel Basta. A full day of sailing and perhaps a bit more. At Tel Basta we will again stay on board overnight. Then, you will be on your way after the morning meal."

Salomé said excitedly, "I cannot believe this is happening! We have waited so long and now, we are on our way. Thank you Captain. Would you take the time to eat with us in the morning?"

"With such fine cooks, as you two women, it would be foolish to do otherwise."

When they landed in Cairo, it was quite evident that the city was a beehive of activity. "Woven rugs were on display everywhere, fine linen was draped on racks of every color imaginable, baskets of dates and pomegranates and of the fruits displayed along the streets. Camels snorted and donkeys brayed in the voices of the Arabs calling to people to buy their wares, created a muted din. One ancient sat on a small pedestal covered by a rug, he wore a gray shawl that covered a white tunic and he wore sandals on his feet. He was selling parchment maps of Cairo and other parchment that told the story of the city. There were other parchments of old Cairo and Babylon, Joseph purchased the parchment entitled Babylon.

It read:

> "The area known as "old Cairo" is a relatively tiny portion of that
> city, but is the oldest part of Cairo and has interesting churches,
> museums, as well as the remains of Babylon. The fortress of
> Babylon was built as part of the offenses of the city of Memphis,
> on the edge of the ancient city of On. The visual fortress town
> landed here in which Emperor Augustus entered Alexandria. The
> Romans brought Christianity into Egypt and Babylon became a
> safe haven..."

There was more to read but Joseph folded it up and put it inside his tunic. They spent the remainder of that time buying a few odds and ends then it was time to return to the boat. The boat was being made ready to continue its journey of the tributary. It was not until after the evening meal, that Joseph was able to read the rest of the parchment.

"This gives us a background into Babylon that was so important to the Israelites who were fleeing Egypt. And now that great city and become a small part of the larger Cairo. That probably came about when the capital was moved from Memphis to its present location in Cairo. I'm glad that we had the opportunity to be in Cairo and to secure this parchment. Jesus was quiet for a time and then spoke. "The past is always a part of the future."

CHAPTER FIFTY-THREE

UPON THEIR ARRIVAL in Tel Basta, Mary suggested, "Would it not be a better plan to make our purchases for the journey home in Tanis? We can see how the other travelers provisioning themselves and be guided by them."

Joseph had previously suggested that they make their purchase of a donkey, for the journey home, in Tel Basta.

"An excellent idea Mary! We will do as you suggest, buy only required purchases and wait on the rest." He turned to Jesus. "Do you see what a clear thinking mother you have?"

In the heart of the city they stopped at a produce stand where Mary and Salomé saw to the foodstuffs. As they walked an animal came ambling by.

"Abba," Jesus asked, "what was that?"

"It looked to me to be a dog, but I am uncertain. It is no breed that I have ever seen."

"That sir," the wizened merchant said to them, "is a Saluki. They are ancient dogs, good hunters, and favorite of Kings and pharaohs. They are not usually seen wondering about the city. So I would imagine that it is lost or perhaps someone's pet who wandered off."

"How long have you been living in Tel Basta," Joseph asked?

"All of my life," the merchant answered. "What about you? You've visiting our city?"

"We were. . ."

"And now we are going home," Jesus cried out!

"It is always a pleasure to be going home. Can I help you?"

"We are seeking a place to stay for about a month, preferably in a Jewish community. Is there such a location?"

A smile came to the merchants face. *Atah yehudi?*

"Yes we are Jewish, and wish to abide with our fellow Jews."

"Understandable. Just north of here is a fine location. The synagogue is nearby and other travelers have also gone there. It is a good location in that there is good ground, one of two buildings that you might be able to use, and it and a deep well with clear water. I myself live there."

"Thank you sir, for your help. No doubt we will return to the market, yours will be one of the first stands that we stop at to make purchases."

Their first priority was to find a place where they could make camp. Jesus was the first to spot a suitable location. It was on a bluff, a small abandoned cave and a small stream nearby. It took them the rest of the day to make the location suitable for living.

Early in the morning of the following day, the Holy Family took a walk into town. The women did some window shopping and examining the various stands with a variety of merchandise available. Joseph stood nearby merely watching over them. They continued their walk when at last they came to the temple. It was a rather large structure with two minarets, and enclosed courtyard filled with shrubbery, and the logic temple door was surrounded by stonework.

A man, perhaps the rabbi, or an elder of the church, was tending to the garden. They entered the courtyard through the wrought iron gate.

When he heard the creaking of the gate, the rabbi turned smiling. He wiped his hands and walked to them with the right hand out in greeting.

"*Boker Tov, Shalom*. I am rabbi Isadore Ghatis."

"*Boker Tov*, and *Shalom* to you rabbi. I am Joseph of Nazareth, this is my wife Mary, our son Jesus and our companion Salomé."

"You have a fine family Joseph. What may I do to be of service to you?"

"He does fine work with wood," Mary interjected. "He also works with metals and other materials."

"The wife speaks well of you Joseph. Is she your agent?"

Joseph responded "And my best friend."

"This is most fortunate indeed. Our altar area needs to be refurbished and we have had no one to do that. If you are what your wife says you are, our prayers and yours have been answered. Is that something you can do?"

"I would have to see what is involved, what materials are needed and if it can be done, I will do it for a fair price."

"It sounds like a reasonable way to begin. I will turn you over to one of our elders, Solomon Niemann. He will find you suitable quarters, you and your family can use while you are working here. He will show you what needs to be done. *Lail tor*. Solomon will be with you shortly."

The rabbi showed them to the dining area, and as they ate, he shared a cup of tea with them. "I must tend to some of the matters and bid you good afternoon."

"Good afternoon rabbi," Joseph said. "And thank you."

When they had finished eating a short jovial man, his head covered with a shawl, entered the room. He was almost as big around as he was tall as he walked he waddled.

"*Erev tov*," he said with a smile lighting his chubby face. When he spoke, his beard bounced up and down causing Jesus to laugh. "rabbi has given instructions to seek your needs. I am Solomon Niemann but you can call me Sol." When he spoke it was in rapid-fire fashion, hardly pausing for breath. "Please follow me."

He showed them two rather large rooms with ample windows, and bathing facility. Something they had never seen indoors before.

"These rooms are for you and your family to use but we have no furniture for them. However towels are available in the hall closet.

"We break bread at sunrise. Each morning we have porridge, bread, tea and milk for the young man. I will see you tomorrow morning."

Joseph spoke to Mary privately. "Although we have made camp, where would you rather we stay indoors or outdoors. We have an option."

Mary responded, "Let us move our things into these quarters. It will be near your work and closer to the temple which Jesus can continue his education."

When Sol left them, they went to their campsite, returning with their belongings. Their straw mattresses were put on the floor, the larder in one corner of the room. That completed, they got together in the room joined hands. Joseph said, "Lord God, your humble servant thanks you for what you have done, and are doing. All praise and glory is yours Almighty Father."

As he had promised, Sol was at the door at sunrise.

"*Boker tov*, Sol," Joseph said in greeting.

"*Boker tov*. Did you sleep well?"

"Quite well thank you. My helper and apprentice, Jesus, will be coming with us. He will carry my slate and supervise the work that I do to be sure it is satisfactory."

Jesus appeared with the slate tucked under his arm, a shawl over his head cinched by a goat skin belt. He was ready to work.

"He may come with you, as long as he is your apprentice," Sol said going along with the charade.

Mary kissed both the workers goodbye. They left and walked on to the synagogue where Sol showed Joseph, and his apprentice, what needed to be done. Joseph took the slate from Jesus, made a few notations, made a few recommendations, and quoted a price.

"Will you be able to begin today," Sol asked?

"Does the rabbi except my price?"

"He has given me the authority to negotiate for him and I find your quote acceptable."

The men shook hands and Jesus stuck out his hand, and Sol shook it too.

"I will make a list of what is needed. Can it be transported here?"

"I will see to it. Is there anything else?"

"And gathering histories of those places where we have been. Is there anyone who can tell me the history of Tel Basta?"

"It so happens, that you are speaking to him. When we get everything set up for you, all materials on hand, I will begin to give the history during our meal break when we can talk together.

"The rabbi has seen fit to hire two additional apprentice carpenters to assist you, along with your son Jesus. Your contract is still for one month and if you finish before that time, he has all the work you would like to take care of. They will be with us shortly."

"May I ask what their names are?"

"Certainly, in fact here they are."

Two young men entered the dining area and were introduced. "This tall young man with broad shoulders is Micah. The other young man, his brother, is Abraham. They are apprenticed to you."

Everyone shook hands, including Jesus, and they sat at the table. Sol left them to order materials and Joseph brought his helpers up to date. In the earthen floor he sketched out what they were about to do, how it would become and how long it would take.

Joseph asked, "Do either of you have any questions?" There were none.

"My young apprentice here, Jesus is his name, and I have estimated that the work should take us about three weeks, barring delays. We are contracted for thirty days and I will see to it that you two are included in the contract. Is that acceptable?

"If the rabbi is satisfied with our work, we will see what else he has to have done. Whatever it might be, we three can handle it. However, at the end of one month, my family and I plan to leave and head north. That will leave you two to finish up. I will let you know if there are any changes to the plan."

"What are we to call you sir," Mica asked?

"A good question young man, you and your brother may call me Joseph, for that is my name. For today, we will not begin work because we have no materials to work with. You can however, help me prepare the altar for what we're going to do." And so the crew got to work.

Joseph and Jesus returned to the apartment, washed up in preparation for dinner and waited for it to be served. Jesus curled up on one of the mats and was instantly asleep.

"Villain, you have worked that child too hard," Mary said smiling!

"You should have seen him Mary. He sat in on the negotiations, on the discussions of the work, and in the work itself. If this amounts to nothing else, and I doubt that very much, he will make a fine carpenter and I think, a fine young man. So far my angel, I believe we are doing the right thing."

Salomé joined the conversation. "You know, Joseph that since the axe has been removed from our necks, and armed with the knowledge that we can return home, our anxiety to do so has increased."

"We are all of one accord. My responsibility is to get you there, along with Mary and Jesus, safely and physically well. To take the trip that we are about to undertake, has certain requirements, all of which takes money. The stopover that we are making now is to allow us to increase our purse so that we can reach our goal. Please understand."

They woke Jesus to have the evening meal in the cafeteria.

As the meal was coming to an end, Rabbi Ghatis spoke. "Joseph, Mary tells me that you are a teller of tales and that each night you favor them with one of your stories. Would you include us in your stories tonight?"

"Yes, I will tell you a brief story about the Israelites of old and how quickly they forgot everything that God had done for them. Moses went to the top of the Mount Sinai and was talking with God. Joshua, one of the elders, waited for him. From the tents the Israelites looked at the mountain. It looked as though it was on fire because flames flew up in the night and day. They know also that God was with Moses on that mountain top. The days became weeks, but Moses did not return. The Israelites wondered if he would ever return. They soon forgot how terrified they had been when God's voice thundered from the smoking mountain. They also forgot having promised Moses that they would obey the words of the Lord.

"One day the people said to Aaron, "We know that something dreadful has happened to Moses because he has not returned. Make us gods to go before us and show us the way. Aaron did in fact relent the idols because he was afraid of their wrath. In so doing, they brought the wrath of Moses who broke the Ten Commandments.

"I tell you the story tonight to demonstrate how quickly some people can lose their faith. It takes a strong faith in the Lord our God to see us through those difficult times. Let us not forget that God is with us always."

"Thank you Joseph," Rabbi Ghatis said. "That was a short story with a powerful message." The work on the altar was nearing completion. As they sat partaking the afternoon meal, Sol said, "I have not yet told you some of the history of Tel Basta. It was at one time the capital of the 18th Nome because it was the key territory on the route from Memphis to the Sinai, and into Asia.

"It was destroyed by the Persians and was built by Herodias. It was identified as a popular place of refuge for religious pilgrims who came here for the annual Goddess Festival, one of the grandest in all of Egypt. Of course, that was thousands of years ago.

"You may have noticed when you entered the city, there is a marble column that bears the image of pharaoh Osorkon II, from Tanis. However following that, we had a number of capitols the last of which is Cairo. That is about the extent of my knowledge. I hope that is enough."

The work was over, the job completed. rabbi Ghatis inspected the work and expressed his delight at how well it has been done.

"We are sorry to be losing you Joseph and your family. We have all gained from the experience. Here are your wages with the hope that this is enough to see you safely home. After services tonight the congregation would like to say goodbye. Please allow us the privilege."

"We thank you for the work that you have given us and we would be honored to say goodbye to the congregation.

"We will pack our things after the morning meal; purchase a donkey to use on the long trek home, and head to Tanis, the first stop of many. Thank you rabbi and May you always walk with God."

CHAPTER FIFTY-FOUR

THE NIGHT BEFORE they left the rabbi, they purchased another donkey. When the animal came over to muzzle Mary palm she explained, "This is the one Lord. Her name will be Chloe."

Chloe bore her burdens well. She was a little over four feet tall, was very surefooted, and her tail kept the flies from being too annoying. The occasional flick of her ears was also used to keep the flies away from her face. She was loving, especially to the one who fed her and easy to handle. The only negative was the aroma that she gave off; bearable but not pleasant.

Chloe's companions on the trip across the alluvial plain were dressed similarly. The women and men wore tunics with light robes draped over them, because around their heads were covered with a square cloth like a turban, folded into a triangle, called a kuffeyah with a fakal around the top holding the cloth in place. Mary had woven the headpiece from twisted goat's hair. Headpieces were not usually worn except for crossing the desert and then it was worn to protect them from the sun and sand. For his part, Jesus wore the same attire but in a small size.

As they walked across the plain, Joseph walked to one side of Chloe, either Mary or Salomé rode on him and when not riding they walked on the other side, and Jesus was at the rear holding Chloe's tail especially during the sandstorms. The land they were walking on now was not as harsh as the sandy desert, but the sun was just as hot.

Along the way they came across another family group who had stopped under the shade of some trees. The Holy Family stopped deciding this was the place to have their afternoon meal. Mary and Salomé had baked some bread that they broke now and dipped it into some olive oil. They each had a small portion of a watered down wine; sufficient unto their needs.

Joseph, who still wore the wood chip pinned to his tunic, was easily identified as a carpenter. The man spoke first. "I see by the wood chip that you are wearing, that you are a carpenter. Where is your place of business?"

"I am Joseph of Nazareth son of Jacob, and Nazareth is our home. With me, is my wife Mary, my son Jesus, and our companion Salomé. What is your name and what do you do?"

"Forgive my bad manners. Blazing sun has fried my brain. My name is Mikel, my wife is Sophie and our two daughters are Hanna and Leah. I too am a carpenter specializing in woodworking and we live in Beersheba."

"Have you taken your family on a holiday or did you have a special task in mind?"

"And a promise of work in Tanis but when we got there, the job was no longer available. So it is back to Beersheba where I will start again."

"We have been traveling throughout Egypt for more than three years. It is now time for us to return home."

"You are welcome to share our shaded area, but I apologize for not being able to offer you food, nor will we seek any from you."

"Companionship at meal is good enough. Our families can chatter away together."

After a brief respite of food and drink, both families traveled together.

On the outskirts of Tanis they searched for a location to make camp. Jesus' keen eyesight came to the rescue.

"Abba," he said, "over there by the oasis is an empty area where we can make camp."

"Good spotting Jesus! It is a good thing that we have you with us."

They went to the area and began to get themselves settled. When that was completed Mary and Salomé went about preparing the meal. Mary began kneading the dough and Salomé went to fetch some water. Joseph and Jesus walked to a larger encampment.

"Abba," Jesus observed, "there is another of those strange animals. I believe they were called camels."

They had a penned in area where six of the beasts were tethered. They were guarded by a filthy Arab, dressed in rags. A dirty turban sat akimbo on his head. Joseph approached him.

"*Shalom*," Joseph said in greeting.

"*Boker tov*," the man responded.

"These are your camels, are they not," Joseph asked?

"I work for the Emir but these camels are for the hire."

"Could you tell us something about them," Joseph asked?

"I can tell you something. They are over six feet tall, they weigh over a thousand pounds, their tails are over three feet in length, they shed their thick woolly coats every spring of course back fur and in the autumn they shed it. We lead them by a rope that is passed through a hole in his nose."

"What is that large mound on his back," Jesus asked? "Does he store water there?".

"No, that is fat that is stored there by the animal. When food is scarce, the fat stored provides energy to the animal. They are capable of carrying large amounts of weight, over long distances and have earned the nickname 'ships of the sea.'

"How can they walk in the sand," Jesus inquired?

"Cattle and horses walk on their hooves. Camels walk on broad pads and they have two toes. The pad spreads and supports the animal and that it amounts to weight distribution."

The men arose from a squatting position. It was obvious that he did not want to say anything more.

Joseph said, "Thank you for the information you have shared with us. We saw some camels inland and my young son rode on one. He enjoyed the experience."

"In sandy areas like this, camels are the most economical form of transportation. It is not a surprise to me that you saw one in the interior."

They returned to camp, Jesus told his mother and Salomé what they had learned about the camel. They ate the meal that the women had prepared for them and, as usual, sat waiting for Joseph's storytelling.

"Instead of telling you a story, allow me to go to the Lord in prayer in order that we thank Him properly."

"Almighty and everlasting God, you have seen us through our times and through your strength, have seen us safely here.

"On the morrow, beloved Lord, we will be out of Egypt and on the road to Pelusium. We pray for your intelligence and guidance to Israel and to our home in Nazareth. This we pray."

"Please Joseph," Salomé implored, "tell us a short story this one time."

Joseph looked around the anxious faces. He could not resist. "I will tell you a story about how this all began, and I will recite it as I remember it."

"In the beginning God created heaven and earth. And the earth was without form, and void; and darkness was upon the face of the deep. And the Spirit of God moved upon the face of the waters. And God said let there be light; and it was light. And God saw the light that it was good: God divided the light from the darkness and God called the light day, and the darkness he called night.[76]

"Jesus if you recall, some time ago you asked what a day was and I gave you a long drawn out story that describes the day and the night in terms that we know today. Actual fact it was just described to you in the first book of the Old Testament, God created a day and night. It is as simple as that.

---

[76] Genesis 1:1-5

"From now on, whenever we have the opportunity, I will tell you about the scriptures in order that you have some familiarity with them. Every Jew must know the scriptures it is part of our reason for being. I learned them from my father, now you will learn them from your father.

"Tonight I began with the creation, tomorrow, I will continue from there.

"Do you have any questions about what I have said?"

"You always tell interesting stories, Abba."

CHAPTER FIFTY-FIVE

THE HOLY FAMILY entered Tanis where, Joseph explained to the others, Moses was found in the marshes of the Nile River, located in Tanis.[77]

Joseph was following directions to that location in the city where caravans were being put together. They heard and smelled the location before reaching it. It was most unpleasant. Thousands of people were milling about an open tent where a caravan master was located. When Joseph looked inside the tent, he saw that it was the same master that had taken them south all those years ago.

Joseph left the others and the tent and approached the table where the caravan master sat. He looked up, saw Joseph and stared at him quizzically.

Finally he said, "I know you from somewhere. I haven't seen your face for a long time ago."

"I am pleased that you do recognize me," Joseph said. "I am Joseph, son of Jacob and you allowed us to travel with you going from Ashkelon to Egypt."

"Welcome Joseph. Do you wish to make a return journey from whence you came?"

"If it pleases you to allow us to join your company," Joseph replied.

A voice from the crowd spoke out. "This man has two women and one child who fled into Egypt to elude King Herod, and you allowed him to come with you."

Joseph turned and immediately recognized Aziz, who had in fact traveled with them all those years ago.

Joseph raised his right arm in greeting saying, "Shalom Aziz. *Ma shelomkha?*

"I am well Joseph and it is good to see you," Aziz replied.

"Now that King Herod sleeps with his ancestors," the caravan master spoke, "is it your wish to return to your home?"

"Yes it is," Joseph replied. "We have been away for far too long a time."

---

[77] Exodus 2:3-5

"How will you fare under the tyrannical thumb of his son, Herod Archelaus? We hear that he is worse than his father."

Joseph was stunned at what he heard, he asked, "Archelaus is King of Judea? What happened to Antipater, his brother? I thought he was next in line for succession to the throne.'"

"From what is being spread about," the caravan master said, "Antipater had been imprisoned by his brothers and turned him over to the executioner. When that happened, Herod named Archelaus successor and was later approved by Caesar. Then, the story goes, once he was approved as Regent, he gave Antipater Galilee and Perea to rule which was also approved by Caesar."

Joseph's concern grew. He had heard, but had given no serious thought at the time, that Archelaus had presided over the massacre of three thousand pilgrims on Passover Day.

But when he heard that Archelaus did reign in Judea, in the room of his father Herod, he was afraid to go thither; notwithstanding being warned by God in a dream, he fled into Galilee seeking refuge.'[78]

Archelaus the King? Everything he had heard about the man, convinced him that he was in fact more tyrannical than his father. Judea had to be avoided.

He was too shocked to speak immediately. Finally he said, "We must return to our families before we can make a decision on what should happen next."

"Well Joseph," the caravan master replied, "we can use stouthearted men like you. If you have the appropriate fees, we leave in two days. Get what provisions you need and be ready at dawn."

Joseph left the tent with Aziz to return to the encampment. Aziz greeted Mary and Salomé warmly. However, he stood for some time staring at Jesus. He said, "Mary, where is the babe you had with you so long ago? Did you lose him?"

"Alas no. Instead he grew into this fine young man you see before you."

He held out his hand to Jesus in greeting.

"*Shalom* Jesus. I am Aziz, merchant and traitor and friend of your parents."

Jesus took his hand and shook it saying, "How do you do sir? I too am pleased to meet you."

"Well mannered as well. You have done a good job."

"Are you camped nearby Aziz," Joseph asked?

"Not too far away. Can you and your family break bread with us this evening? We can make plans to link up two day's hence for the journey north."

Mary responded, "It would please us Aziz, thank you."

Aziz had given directions and then left for home. When he had gone, Joseph said, "I have news to share." Everyone gathered around a small fire that had been used to cook their meal. They were anxious to hear what Joseph had to say.

---

[78]   Matthew 2:22

"In a dream that I have had, I was told by God's messenger, that those who seek to harm us, were dead. The messenger also said that we should return home. I shared that dream with you and we immediately made preparations to begin our homeward journey.

"This afternoon, while Jesus and I were making preparations with the caravan master to return home, he informed us that Herod was dead, that Archelaus, his son was now the King of Judea. With one tyrant gone, he has been replaced by another tyrant, only this one is worse than the father!

"Where does that leave us, Joseph," Mary asked anxiously?

"If you recall, we had planned to return to Jerusalem, or Bethlehem, preferably Bethlehem. That means that both locations present a danger since both are in Judea. That means, we must go to Nazareth in Galilee where we should be able to live in safety. Antipas is a somewhat more sedate son of Herod, and he has been appointed tetrarch, with the approval of Emperor Augustus.

"In addition to that Mary, I was told by an angel of God that we should go to Galilee, and you know that I have always placed great faith and obedience to the dreams that I have."

"Then it is settled," Mary agreed," we must go to Galilee."

Salomé spoke, "Joseph, I need to return to my home in Hebron. I have been away for so long."

"Of course Salomé! We will see you safely returned to the arms of your family. Forgive me for not mentioning it sooner."

Joseph returned to his wife. "What are your thoughts Mary?"

"What you have said about our destination, and the reasons for a change, makes sense. Besides, it will put me with my parents who have not seen their grandson."

"It pleases me that we are in agreement. For now though let us keep our own counsel. We can discuss it further in the morning."

They walked to Aziz' encampment, where they were introduced to his family. That topic of conversation dealt with heading north in two days. They chatted about the positives and negatives until it was time for the evening meal. Aziz gave the blessing and they ate. During the meal, Aziz burped and his wife smiled. Joseph thought to himself, this must be their custom to show his wife that he enjoyed the meal.

"What historical facts are you seeking these days Joseph? You have not lost interest have you?"

By way of an answer Joseph said, "We have been fortunate to be given a wealth of knowledge and lore in every city that we visited. Tanis is however, something of a mystery." "Well then, allow me to fill in the gaps in your knowledge, at least as much as I have been able to garner.

"Tanis was founded late in the twenty-first dynasty and became the northern capital of Egypt. The King of Tanis named himself as legitimate successors to the throne of Upper and Lower Egypt. There are numerous tomes and archaeological ruins, but I do not think you will have the time to visit them."

Joseph sensed that his host was running out of historical information. He changed the subject. The caravan master "You have made numerous caravan trips together. Tell us, if you will, how does the journey begin?"

"The caravan master assigns to each group a number and it shall be your identifier throughout the trip. As one group is sent out, the next one is called up and sent forward. We will follow the procedure each day that we are on this trip. If brigands attack us along the way, the lead group and those following, can be called back to encircle the brigands and annihilate them. In such an instance, little mercy is shown.

"Be assured, the caravan master knows the location of every well and oasis in the Sinai desert. We make stops along the way only at those locations."

"How long will we stop at each of these locations," Mary asked?

"We will only stop overnight. Be sure that you have enough goatskin water bags. The desert is hot and dry, so be sure you have enough water with you so you do not become dehydrated. Goatskins can be purchased from the caravan master, if you need to buy some."

The next day was spent in preparation. Extra goatskins were purchased, and filled. Chloe was exercised and fed. They were ready.

After the evening meal was consumed, Joseph gave them last-minute instructions.

"We will be entering the Sinai desert. It stands between Egypt and Israel. This is the land into which Moses took the Israelites fleeing from the pharaoh.

"Be sure to keep your heads down, wear a veil during the day to protect your face from blowing sand. No one will ride on Chloe unless it is absolutely necessary. If you have trouble with your sandals, be sure to tell me that I may make the necessary repairs. Finally, never look directly into the sun, you can be blinded.

"We have done this all before, this is just a reminder." Joseph held out his hands, inviting others to join hands with him.

"Most precious father, your most faithful servants submit themselves to you and into your care. Be with us we pray. Be our refuge and our strength. As we begin our journey is remember.

He found them in the wilderness a wasteland of howling desert.

He shielded them, cared for them, guarded them as the apple of his eye.

CHAPTER FIFTY-SIX

"Out of Egypt I called My Son."[79]

THE SUN ROSE in the east creating a shimmering site as heat waves rose from the ground. Joseph stood with Jesus on a small knoll looking back over the line of people, gathering for the journey. Joseph estimated that there were fifty, maybe more.

There were dozens of camels, donkeys, and people on foot. Bright colors were everywhere! Underlying it all was a sense of anxiety.

"Abba," Jesus asked, "are all these people going home with us?"

"No my boy, they are going to their own homes, it just so happens that all of their homes are in the north just as our house is, and traveling together as we are, increases our safety."

All at once the caravan began to move. Joseph and Jesus rushed to join Mary and Salomé who were awaiting their turn to move. As they waited a blend of various sounds could be heard, the clanking of chains and wagons, the creaking of leather, the snorting of the camels, the hubbub of various tongues, and the clacking of crickets.

At last it was their turn to leave. They were forced to walk behind Aziz and his family. Jesus went with a group of schoolchildren, who chased each other around playing tag. As the sun grew hotter, their exuberance waned. They returned to their parents without being called.

During the midday meal, Joseph checked everyone, no blisters; there was no sun poisoning and no overexposure. Joseph had purchased for each of them a kuffeyah, a combination head covering and veil. Jesus wore a white one with red dots, Joseph wore a black and gray one, the women wore pink with gray piping. They were held in place by woven goatskin thongs. The kuffeyahs were of such length that they could cover the head and also used as a veil to cover the face.

---

[79] Hosea 11:1

"In approximately fifteen days," Joseph informed them, "we will reach the city of Pelusium where will rest for a little longer period than usual. From there we will be moving on to Gaza, another major stopover and another thirteen days. In all that time, we will be crossing the Sinai desert, and you will recall the difficulties Moses had leading the Israelite across this wasteland.

"I also mention this so you can understand that we have to carefully apportion our foodstuffs and water consumption. We can do this because we have done it before."

On this, the first night in the caravan, they were invited by Aziz and his family to share the evening meal with them and they had accepted only if they could provide part of the meal. A lentil soup was served with bread that Mary and Salomé had baked in Tanis.

When the meal was ended, and they were sitting about the fire chatting, Aziz asked, "Do you have story for us tonight, Joseph?"

"As a matter of fact, I do. Tonight I will tell you about God creating everything that we see about us. He began.

"Yahweh said, it is not right that man should be alone."

"You remember when I first told you about God creating the earth, the animals, the birds of the air, the plants and flowers and trees we see about us, and after he had done all this, he created man? Well, this is a continuation of that story.

"Yahweh said, 'I shall make him a helper. So, from the soil, Yahweh fashioned all the wild animals and all the birds of heaven. Then he brought man to see what he would call them; each one was to bear the name man would give it.

"The man gave names to the cattle, the birds of heaven and all the animals. But no suitable helper was found for him.

"Then Yahweh made the man fall into a deep sleep and while he was asleep, he took one of his ribs and closed the flesh up again forthwith. Yahweh fashioned the rib he had taken from the man into a woman and brought her to the man."

By this time all those who had been listening, had become caught up in the narrative, their mouths agape. He continued.

"And the man said: This one at last is bone of my bone and flesh of my flesh! So he called her woman, because she was taken from man.

"This is why a man leaves his father and mother and becomes attached to his wife, and they become one flesh."[80]

Aziz said confused staring at Joseph.

"That was a fine story about the creation, but what was the point of it?"

"The point of it was more for my benefit than for yours. It means that we should appreciate the woman we have asked to be our partner through life. It was also meant to be a statement to my wife, made publically, our marriage has

---

[80]   Exodus 2:18-25

---

taken some unusual twists and turns that has reminded me that she is bone of my bone and flesh of my flesh."

"I can see you are a sincere man and perhaps I have taken my family for granted. There should always be reminders. Thank you!"

When everyone had retired and they were back in camp, Mary and Joseph sat quietly by their fire until Mary spoke. "Joseph what was your point beside what you have told Aziz. I know how you think. There was another message there; am I right".

"You do know me and you are right. Our marriage began with strife, confusion and disappointment. When the angel spoke with me, I was told that all that was inconsequential was inconsequential and that I should be and I should marry you. Yahweh convinced me to obey. Since that time, I have seen you through good times and through bad, and throughout, you have always been Mary; devout, loving, caring, and always there for Jesus and me. It was not until tonight, hoverer, that I found out how important that is to me. Thank you."

Mary rested her head on his shoulder.

A day and a half later, they came to Khan Yunis, where they made a brief stop to fill their water skins and rest. The next day would bring some changes.[81]

"What do you know of this place, Aziz, Joseph asked?

"I must confess, not very much. I do know that it was once called 'Salqah' and it was once a popular resting place. In order to protect caravans, pilgrims and travelers, a huge 'khan', that is a caravansary, was constructed there by Emir Yunis. The place flourished and soon became known as Khan Yunis and became an important center for trade."

"Thank you once again, Aziz."

---

[81]   Hosea 11:1

CHAPTER FIFTY-SEVEN

THE SUN HAD punished them enough for one day. It began to wane behind sand dunes and distant mountains just turning a pale purple. Pelusium came into view after two and one-half weeks of misery and thirst. The caravan master, Theo Basha, announced that they would continue their journey after a full day's rest in this oasis.

The caravan halted, the travelers spread out seeking a place to camp. Without discussion, Joseph and Aziz made camp close by to one another. As tired as they were, children still had enough energy to play kickball. The women began to prepare the evening meal, Salomé went to fetch water, and Joseph and Aziz tethered the animals and started cooking fires. After which they sat without speaking. Finally Aziz broke the silence.

"Would you like me to tell you something more about Pelusium," he asked?

"Yes I would," Joseph replied.

"Well then, the once vital city was once called Farma and it was the location where Pompey was murdered. Since that time, the city has been used as a way station for caravans providing various offerings to travelers."

"A once vital city is now a stopover for caravans," Joseph asked?

"Alas, yes. It is called survival."

"I know that our next major stopover will be in Gaza. What other cities, if any will we see?"

"We will pass a small village of al-Arish, known in ancient times as the *Brook of Egypt*. It is located at the end of a large dry river bed called a wadi. This river at one time drained the entire Sinai plateau. Then there is Rafiah, which has little to commend it. It is a swamp with brackish pools and malaria. After that we come to Gaza, a total of 217 kilometers from here. All told it should take us about two weeks.

"That is our schedule, Joseph. Now tell me something about your flight into Egypt. Whatever it was, it must have been frightening."

"And so it was. We were being pursued by King Herod's troops who wanted nothing more than to kill us. We managed to elude them, and at the same time, we have met some of the most generous people and it has been our pleasure to meet. They saw that we were in need of help, they helped.

"As a side benefit to all of our wanderings, we have learned much about Egyptian culture, the reasons for and the building of the pyramids, we have sailed the mighty Nile, and seen animals we never dreamt existed. It was quite an education on many levels for each of us."

"Everyone was like that," Aziz asked astonished?

"Not everyone, but certainly most. Under different circumstances, it could have been a wonderful experience, but with someone's hot breath on your neck, it was frightening."

Tara Aziz, said, "Your son appears to have been well educated. How did you accomplish that? And your son appears to have been well-tutored in other areas."

"His mother and Salomé taught him how to read and write and his numbers, as well as introducing him to the scriptures. Then, whenever we came to a city where we could spend some time, and Jesus was old enough to understand, he was brought to the temple where he could learn more. It certainly was not an ideal situation but when we reach Nazareth he will learn even more."

Aziz asked, "Do you have another story for us tonight, Joseph?"

"Yes, tonight will be no exception. As we were being pursued by King Herod's soldiers, so too was Moses and the Israelites, only they were pursued by the pharaoh's army. In their flight they were being led by a cloud who took them to the Red Sea where they camped. Soon after, people ran through the camp yelling, 'pharaoh's army is coming!' They were trapped between the army and the Red Sea. It was not impossible to swim the Red Sea nor could they fight the army pursuing them.

"They cried out in fear, quickly blaming Moses for leading them into this trap. Moses went to the Lord in prayer. Then Moses said, "Fear not. Stand still and see the salvation of the Lord. It will be shown to you today." The cloud went between the Israelites and the army quickly turning into a pillar of fire.

"God said to Moses, 'Tell the people to go forward, lift your rod over the sea and divide it.' Moses obeyed and God sent a strong wind that divided the waters leaving a dry path. On each side were high walls of water. All of the Israelites and their cattle crossed to the other side unharmed.

"Pharaoh's army saw the Israelites crossing the sea, they rushed to follow. About midway the dry land was no longer dry. Men and horses began sinking into the sediment. The soldiers began to cry out, 'Israel's God is against us go back!' But it was too late. The walls of water collapsed in on them and the whole army drowned.

"The Israelites saw that God had saved them."

Mary said, "A wall of water did not fall on our pursuers, but the death of King Herod accomplished the same thing."

"Well said, Mary," Joseph observed. "In both cases, it was the intervention of God that saved."

They returned to their camps, turning in for the night, but not before the Holy Family thanked the Lord for his abundant love in prayer. "Tomorrow, alas" Joseph said, we will begin another journey over scorching sand, blowing winds and a hot sun.

CHAPTER FIFTY-EIGHT

The Sinai Peninsula is triangular in shape and is situated between the Mediterranean Sea, the Gulf of Suez, the Red Sea, and the Gulf of Aqaba. It is the land bridge between the two continents. Ancient Egyptians called the land Mafkat, or "land of green emeralds" (turquoise).

It is an arid land were living conditions are hostile for plant and animal life. It is frequently identified as *Jebel Musa*[82] where for forty years Moses and the Israelites wander through the vast, barren hot sands of the Sinai desert. A saga, the Exodus, has emblazoned the Sinai on the world map.

Mount Sinai, the location where Moses received the law from God[83] is in the southern part of the Peninsula.

• •

BEFORE SETTING OFF on the last leg of their arduous journey, the holy family met to discuss what was in store for them.

"We have two days of hot sun, hot sand, and heat before we reach Pelusium, also called *Sin* for some unknown reason. From there we will go to Al Arish, then to Gaza, and from there into Bethlehem. It will be a long difficult journey, but one we have been looking forward to."

"Will we be traveling by ourselves," Mary asked?

"No, Mary we will not. It is however, a very good question. My primary concern has been, and always will be for our safety, to ensure that I think it best that we join the caravan to go north."

And so they did.

---

82   Ezekiel 30.15
83   Exodus 19-20

A caravan, a group of twelve traveling people, mules, donkeys and camels led by Kasim Kanuri, left two days later. Bedraggled and dehydrated the Holy Family entered Pelusium where, later in the day after refreshing themselves at the well, they joined with others at the evening meal.

As they ate, Kasim announced, "With the death of King Herod, his son Archelaus has taken the throne and is ethnarch (not king) of Samaria, Judea, and Idumea."

"Is that good news or bad news," someone in the group asked?

"I do not know but he is certainly the more sedate son of the late king."

Salomé turned to Joseph asking, "Do thee still want to go to Bethlehem, after hearing this news?"

"I have not had the opportunity to tell you, but I had a dream that this had taken place in answer to your question Salomé, my primary concern has been and will always be with the safety of this family. This news does this change the way that we will be the home. Rather than take the road through Idumea, Judea and Samaria, we will stay with the caravan along the Via Maris until we reach Galilee. What that means that instead of Bethlehem that was our original destination, we will go to Nazareth where Antipas is tetrarch."

"I think you have thought this out wisely, husband," Mary said. "It will lengthen the time away from home and our families but this delay will make that reunion possible."

The caravan moved out to continue on the road until they reached Al Arish where there will more sand dunes, and the humid weather became even hotter. Al Arish was a strange place, situated at the end of a large wadi that seemed to drain the entire Sinai plateau. It was however, the basic point of Via Maris. They traveled on for another day until they reached Gaza with a caravan rested itself. After the evening meal, they all were seated around the fire, Jesus said, "Father, you have not given us a story for some time. May we have one tonight?"

"As it is with your mother, I can refuse you nothing. Tonight story is about a man called Nehemiah. He worked as a cupbearer in the Palace of King Artaxerxes. His brother had gone back to Jerusalem to rebuild the walls of the temple of the Lord. When he spoke with his brother he was told, "Things have not gone well. The walls have never been repaired, the place is in ruins. The city lies wasted."

"Nehemiah wept.

"When next he went before the King, the King saw he was very unhappy. What is wrong Nehemiah? Is there anything that I can do to help?"

"Nehemiah asked for permission to return to Jerusalem so that he might repair the walls. The king agreed and gave him letters of introduction to the priests and ministers of the city giving him authority to do so. When he arrived at Jerusalem he showed them his letters and they said, "Let us arise and rebuild the wall."

"So the wall was finished on the twenty-fifth day of the month Elul, in fifty-two days. And when all their enemies heard of it, all the nations around them were afraid and fell greatly in their own esteem; for they perceived that this work had been accomplished with the help of their God. Moreover, in those days the nobles of Judah sent many letters to Tobiah, and Tobiah's letters came to them. For many in Judah were bound by oath to him, because he was the son-in-law of the mighty and powerful people and they objected to this rebuilding. In the end, he accomplished what he had set out to do.

"What can we learn from Nehemiah you might ask? We can learn what we have been learning over the three years we have been in this foreign country, go to the Lord, thrust in the Lord, have complete faith in the Lord and He will be at your side.

"What will we do when we return to Jerusalem, Abba," Jesus asked?

"We have no rebuilding to be done we have received no such mandate. My son, we will not be going to Jerusalem. Instead we're going to Nazareth where we will join with our family and worship Him jointly."

CHAPTER FIFTY-NINE

EARLY ONE MORNING before the sun rise Mary was washing Joseph's hair and trimming his beard. Before she had done that however, she ran a small wooden rake through the growth to remove anything lodged in there. When she had finished, she saved the water for another washing.

For the next fourteen days, each day was a repeat of the day before, heat, sand, and the relentless sun. Chloe kept her brood close, the blowing sand got into everything, and the canteens were running low. At night they took turns gently rubbing each others' feet to ease the pain and stimulate circulation.

A nightly story was continued and the audience increased as more people heard of the story teller.

"Abba," Jesus asked one evening, "Do numbers and the scriptures have any significance?"

"What an interesting question Jesus. Why do you ask?"

"My mother and Salomé are teaching me numbers. I wondered if the numbers were just for counting, or were they meant for something else?"

"You have an inquisitive mind Jesus. To begin with, in scripture numbers usually have more significance than their measurable indicators would lead you to believe. Usually numbers are used to indicate a certain quantity, or the individual number given may point beyond the numerical value to a symbolic significance. At other times it may represent an approximate value, to a symbolic value.

"I will tell you of their significance as it was told to me by my father Jacob. Tonight we will cover the numbers one through ten.

"*One* notes singleness. For instance, 'Hear O Israel: the Lord our God is one.'[84]

---

[84] Deuteronomy j6:6

"*Two* is the symbol for support and witness. For instance, there were two great lights of creation[85]

"*Three* signifies perfection and completion, such as three significant events happen on the third day."[86]

"*Four* is related to the earth. The four seasons: summer, winter, fall and spring, or, for north, south, east and west. Four cups of wine are drunk at Passover.

"*Five* is the number associated with power and grace. In Leviticus it says, 'and he shall kill the bullock before the Lord: and the priests, Aaron's son, shall take the blood and sprinkle it about the altar.' Here is where grace is displayed. God is allowing Moses to sacrifice a bullock instead of his son.[87] The Lord was testing Moses.

"*Six* signifies the number of men, serpents and man was created on the sixth day. Man is commanded to work six days. The sixth commandment is the sin of murder."[88] [89]

"*Seven* is the number of God, design completeness of perfection. On the seventh day God rested after completing creation.[90] God's word is pure, like silver purified seven times in the fire."[91]

"*Eight* means a new beginning such as circumcision of young Jewish boys would take place on the eighth day after their birth."[92]

"*Nine* means fullness of blessing as there are nine fruits of the spirit: love, joy, peace, patience, kindness, goodness, faithfulness, gentleness, and self-control."[93]

"*Ten* relates to the law such as the ten Commandments were the tablets of the law."[94]

"You remembered all that," Jesus asked?

"All that and other significant numbers, but that is for another day. The numbers you just heard me tell you about, are the same ones your mother and Salomé are teaching you."

As Joseph was telling Jesus of the significance of numbers, his congregation heard the meanings as well, some for the first time. As Joseph was thinking,

---

[85] Genesis 1:16

[86] Hosea 6:2

[87] Leviticus 1:5

[88] Exodus 20:13

[89] Genesis 1:31

[90] Genesis 2:2

[91] Psalms 12:6

[92] Genesis 17:12

[93] Galatians 5:22-23

[94] Exodus 20:1-17, Deuteronomy 5:6-21

the cries of the goats could be heard, their teats bloated. Salomé went to relieve them to store tomorrow's need for milk. Chloe looked on as a concerned guardian would.

Aziz said almost in a whisper, "We have been soul wrenching times. In all of my years traveling the Via del Mare, never has it been such a hardship. And yet..."

"And yet, we have survived," Joseph completed the thought. "Tomorrow you can tell me all that you know about Gaza. Tonight I would like to have your input on how we can arrive safely in Nazareth."

"Tell me what you have in mind, perhaps I can support your thoughts or suggest alternative routes of travel."

Joseph had planned to return to Bethlehem in the province of Judea, since that was his ancestral city.[95]

"With Archelaus reigning in Judea, I am uncertain about our future in Bethlehem. If he decides to follow his father's edict, that can mean death and our flight will have been meaningless. At this point in time, there is uncertainty and we cannot take the risk."

"A wise assumption. Err on the side of caution. Do you have an alternative?"

"That is where you come in. 'We had planned to leave the caravan at Gaza, travel west to Hebron and then north to Bethlehem, but that has been set aside."

"Have you thought of an alternative," Aziz asked?

"No, I have not. This turn of events is too new to come up with one."

"What you do you think of this alternative?" he continued. "Continue north with the caravan to Caesarea, then travel northwest to Nazareth. It will be less strenuous on your family, you will be out of Judea and into Galilee and under the rule of Antipas, the less violent son of Herod."

"It is an excellent alternative but there is one flaw. We must see Salomé safely to her home in Hebron, she has been with us throughout and we must return her from whence she came."

"I can understand such loyalty. Your next best alternative would then be," he drew a map in the dirt, "Travel northwest out of Hebron, bypass Bethlehem and Jerusalem and go to Emmaus, from there to Lydda and then onto Joppa where you can join with another caravan and follow the rest of the planned route we outlined, it should take you another two weeks. You can resupply at any of the cities I mentioned"

"I knew you would grasp our dilemma. Your plan seems logical and wise. Thank you."

"Tell me Joseph, where you have gotten this deep confidence in an unknown Lord? I do not think it is a bad thing, for it gives you strength. Where does it come from?"

---

[95] Luke 2:1-4

"Allow me to quote from the Psalms:

'I believe in the goodness of the Lord in the land of the living!

"Wait for the Lord; be strong, that your heart takes courage; yea wait for the Lord!"[96]

"Go with God my friend," Joseph advised. "Now get some sleep for tomorrow promises to be just as hot and just as taxing on our energies."

---

[96]   Psalm 27:13-14

CHAPTER SIXTY

JOSEPH CARVED A miniature wheeled camel. Jesus was playing with it in the marketplace of Gaza as other children gathered about to see this phenomenon. Joseph sat in the shade watching him. Aziz sat with him drinking tea.

"Is everyone getting their rest," he asked?

"Yes, thank you they are, and your family, they are well? The day has not been too much for them? I assumed that they were well, since they are out shopping together."

"What can stop women from shopping? I like that toy you made Jesus. How was it done?"

"The most difficult part was cutting the wood in the shape of the camel. Once I got that completed, I bored two holes, one in the front and one in the rear. I ran a dowel through the holes and attached a wheel to each end. A two foot dowel I attached at the rear so the toy can be pushed around."

"Cleverly done!" After a pause Aziz continued. "You have not asked me any questions about Gaza. Are you no longer interested in historical facts?"

"Yes I am. Please continue with my education. I did not ask because I thought you had told me what you knew when we first went south. Yes, please tell me all you know."

"As I recall, I did tell you a great deal, but there is more. For instance, the city is about three thousand years old, maybe older. It was a Canaanite settlement, which came under the control of ancient Egyptians. They were replaced by the Philistines who later fell under the sword of King David and the Israelites.

"This was followed by the siege of Alexander the Great who developed the city to become the center of Hellenistic learning and philosophy."

"I am unfamiliar with Hellenistic learning," Joseph said. "What is it?"

"Basically stated, those are philosophical options that devote less attention to Plato's and Aristotle's thinking about the state, but focused instead on the

---

life of the individual independent of society. In other words, a person is within the state and not as part of the state.

"But getting back to your history lesson: when the Romans ruled over Gaza and had control of the city, Pompey Magnus granted the city to King Herod who allowed the city to be populated by Jews, Egyptians, Persians and Nabateans. Their influence can be seen throughout the city.

"The reason there were so many warlike factions, here at Gaza, the Via Mares intersects with the incense route coming from Nabatean to Petra. It also has been the caravan point of strategic importance since earliest times. It has constantly been the battleground between Egypt and Syria and Mesopotamian powers.

"In addition, this is the place where Samson was imprisoned and met his death.

"And that Joseph, is the extent of my knowledge. However, on a different subject, I have often heard you speak of having dreams, and they affect your life and that of your family. How is that possible?"

"Dreams have always had an impact on our lives. I will tell you about four dreams that I had and their effect.

"In the first dream an angel of the Lord appeared to me telling me that I should marry Mary, she would have a child, and that we should call him Jesus. So it was said, so it was done.

"In this second dream, I was again told by an angel of the Lord, to take Jesus and his mother and flee into Egypt. I was told to remain there until he, the angel, said that it was safe to return, and I did as I had been instructed. The angel said in the third dream that it was safe to return since those who wanted us dead, were they themselves dead.

"Then, in the fourth dream God told me to avoid returning to Bethlehem. He said nothing further so I took the dream as a warning."

"So," Aziz said, "here in Gaza is where you and your family will leave the caravan to go to Hebron and return Salomé to her people?"

"That is our plan."

"I have been giving your exit some thought and after discussing it with others, without giving them particulars as to who or when, we have come up with another, safer route for you to consider. It would also save you several days of travel."

"By all means we are interested," Joseph exclaimed!

"I have written it out for you." He removed a piece of parchment bearing the writing. "In broad terms, we are in the province of Philistia. When you leave here, you will enter Judea to bring Salomé to her people. It is 83.6 kilometers distant. When you leave there, you will enter into Samaria, then Galilee where

Antipas is the Ethnarch and where you should be safe. Your only real danger is while you are in Judea.

"From Hebron to Nazareth is, roughly, 1851 kilometers away or perhaps three days and I have tried to keep you on the lee side of the Judean Mountains. I have also listed several large villages where you can resupply, if you need and rest. Then, once you are past Mount Carmel, you are almost home.

"This route is not the one you would usually take returning from Jerusalem, but one that would keep you off the beaten path."

"Thank you Aziz, appreciate all your efforts."

"You and your family have been dear to us and we want you to get home safely."

"Thank you again, Aziz. Please have the evening meal with us. The story for tonight will be about Samson since we are where it all took place."

The families shared the foodstuffs and all ate in celebration. Joseph blessed the food eaten, the people gathered to share it, and the Lord's blessing on both families.

"Tonight's story is about Samson. He was noted for his great strength. Although he knew the Philistines hated him, he went in and out of their country to see Delilah with whom he was in love.

"The Philistine high priests went to Delilah and promised her eleven hundred pieces of silver if she could get Samson to tell her the secret of his strength. She went to Samson and asked him the secret of his strength. He said if he were tied with seven moist cords, his strength would be like anyone else. He went to sleep and she tied him with seven moist cords then yelled, "The Philistines are coming?"

"Samson immediately awoke burst his bonds, ready to do battle. He asked what had happened and Delilah accused him of making fun of her. She again asked him the secret. He said if he were bound by new ropes, his strength would be like the others.

"When he slept, she tied him with new ropes. She again said, 'The Philistines are coming! Once more he burst his bonds with ease.

"During his next visit, she once again coaxed him to tell the secret of his strength. This time he said, 'Because I am a Nazarite, my hair has never been cut. If my hair was cut my strength would leave him. When he slept his hair was cut and, for the third time Delilah called out, 'the Philistines are here!"

"Samson opened his eyes and saw the Philistine rulers in his room. He struggled to get away but found that his strength had left him. He was taken prisoner.

"And that is all for tonight. The ending will be told another time."

His audience began to scatter, each to their own camp. Joseph asked Aziz to stay behind. They sat by the fire, Salomé brought them tea.

Joseph allowed them to get comfortable when he said, "Aziz, my friend, you have been less than honest with us. You say that you are a merchant trader, yet you have knowledge and wisdom far beyond that of the office you hold. I do not mean to offend you but my curiosity has gotten the best of me. Would you please tell me where you gained your knowledge?"

Aziz paused for a time before answering.

"Joseph, I am being pursued as you were. I was an educator in Alexandria for about twenty years. I taught history, natural science, and philosophy. In order to keep current I frequently went on digs where I also spoke to people familiar with the area in which I was doing my research. At one such dig I came upon an ancient relic in one of the tombs. My assistant, the son of a very wealthy man, claimed that the discovery was his and we fought. He stumbled, fell and struck his head. He was dead.

"When his father heard of it, he accused me of killing his son and sent to have me taken prisoner. I thought it best to seek friendlier environs. Since that time, I have been fortunate enough to find a loving woman who has borne me two sons and shares my camp wherever I go. I have no regrets since the incident was accidental and I bear him no malice."

"Were there witnesses to these events, "Joseph asked?

"Yes, but the father was too rich and powerful to speak against. I do not know if the pursuit is still going on, it has been eight years."

"I shall not bear witness against you. My father Jacob taught me not to judge and I have not. Thank you for sharing your secret with me. Be assured that it will remain so."

"Good night, Joseph. We will see you off in the morning."

CHAPTER SIXTY-ONE

WHEREAS IN THE past, the Holy Family had walked the paths footsore and weary, as they left Gaza, today their mood had changed; they were going home! Their donkey, Cleo, somehow sensed the way she needed to go, the goats trailing after her, their little tails wagging excitedly.

As soon as the sun made its appearance, the day began to get warmer, more uncomfortable.

"Abba," young Jesus asked, "why are we being punished by the sun and heat every day?"

"For a very good reason Jesus. Do you remember when we left earlier this morning? The rising sun brought light, the horizon began to take on various colors, yellow, orange, grape white that gathered together to chase off the gray of night. Later today, the sun is tired and ready for bed, the sky blue once again take on many different colors. This is done in order that we might enjoy the colorful displays. We need the sun Jesus, to bring light and life to our day."

"It certainly does make it warm though," Jesus commented.

"Joseph," Salomé asked, "how far must we travel before we reach Hebron?"

"Are you getting anxious Salomé? When we started out, and traveled this route, I was told that it was fifty-two miles, or about five days."

"Five days," Salomé sighed? How I have missed my kinsmen, but I would not have missed these years with you, and your family for anything."

"You came to us," Mary observed, "when I needed you most! I asked myself frequently, what if? What if you were unable to come with us, what if we were unable to enjoy your companionship, what if Jesus did not have you to teach him, what if . . . They go on and on. Blessed are you Salomé."

"And we all agree," Joseph and Jesus cried simultaneously.

Suddenly, there was a tremor in the earth, the ground shook for about two minutes, stones fell from clefts in the mountains, and the trees swayed. The animals brayed in fear, and Joseph gripped Mary and Jesus to hold them close.

"That was an earthquake Lord," Mary cried out!

"Everyone stay where you are. It should end quickly." Then, as suddenly as fast as it had started, it was over. Everything took on a calmness and quiet. Joseph stood and inspected the surrounding area. The animals seemed to walk to him seeking safety. He petted and reassured each one.

"Abba," Jesus asked, "that was a terrible experience! What is an earthquake?"

At first Joseph thought it was easiest to say it was an act of God. He thought back to an earlier age but Jesus would ask questions about physical and natural phenomena. Telling him that it was an act of God or the devil, but that only provoked even more questions. He decided early on that if he did not know the answer to one of his questions, he would say so.

"My son, I really do not know what causes an earthquake."

Jesus accepted that.

That night, when their terror had subsided, and before they were to enter Hebron, they sat around the fire after the evening meal chatting together. It was the time of day when Joseph usually told them a story. That night however, Salomé took over the storytelling.

"Hebron," she said, "is one of the oldest, continuously inhabited villages in the world dating back to almost the beginning of time. Ancient Canaanites' name for the city is Abria derived from the word four, so-called because the city is surrounded by four mountains.

"After the Exodus, while the Israelites were still in search of the Promised Land, Moses sent spies into the city to see what lay before him. Later, Joshua fought the battle of Aijalon where it is said the sun stood still.[97]

"Nearby is the ancient city of Kiriath Arba, the suburb of four, because four couples are buried here: Adam and Eve, Abraham and Sarah, Jacob and Leah, Isaac and Rebecca. In the book of Genesis, it tells of the patriarch Abraham purchasing the site for 400 silver shekels.[98]

"Still later, King David and Samuel, was ordered by God to come to the city of Hebron where he was anointed King of Israel and he made the city's capital.[99]

"And then, King Herod built a wall around Machpelah to preserve the tombs of the patriarchs. Even the tomb of Yistrai and his wife Ruth, grandparents of King David, can be found here."

Salomé looked at Joseph and said, "Some more history for your collection Joseph."

"Perhaps while we are here," Joseph suggested, "we might visit Machpelah before we leave."

"Perhaps," Salomé answered.

---

[97]   Joshua 10:12-14

[98]   Genesis 23-16

[99]   Samuel 2:16

The next day they entered the ancient city of Hebron. Salomé directed them to her home. In route, Joseph was amazed at the number of pillars and mosaic floors, many of the buildings possessed.

Upon arrival at her home she was excited and at the same time warmly greeted. The scene was utter chaos, people kissing on another, hugging one another, shaking of hands and dancing in their excitement. It was quite apparent that Salomé had been missed.

Everything returned to normal, Salomé's sister, Rebecca, compelled them to share the midday meal with them.

The animals were tethered and the Holy Family accompanied Ruth to her home. They went through to the courtyard in the rear where the meal was being laid out. As they ate questions followed one another in quick succession. The three of them, Joseph, Mary and Jesus did their best to answer each question.

Joseph politely interrupted. "Salomé will not be going on with us. She can provide you later with all the details. In the meantime, may we just visit with you, and catch our breath, and prepare ourselves for our journey home?"

Immediately after eating, Jesus ran off with the other children to play.

Joseph wondered if they would be asked to stay the night. He determined that Salomé's kinsmen lived in close proximity to one another, the family members were in and out of the houses such that it gave the impression of one large residence. It was also quite evident that the families were close and loving.

As they began to walk away, Joseph turned to say, "May the good bountiful Lord shower his blessings upon you."

CHAPTER SIXTY-TWO

THE FAMILY WAS having the morning meal before departing on this long journey. They sat together enjoying the sunrise.

Mary spoke, "I know you have sought different ways for us to get home, and I know that you have our safety and well-being as your major concern. May I be so bold to suggest another alternative?"

"You certainly may, Mary. What I have sketched out for us is not etched in stone. I always will listen attentively to hear what you have to say. You have a way of cutting through the excess to get to the gist of the matter."

"However, taking the roads and paths we are familiar with, seems to me the fastest way to go and, at this point in time, the faster we are home among our family, the better I would feel. I see no safety issues. If I am mistaken please correct me."

"I cannot guarantee our safety, brigands prey on travelers. Mary taking the way that you suggest", there is always the possibility. However, a small party such as ours, should represent no great pickings."

"Nor any more than the way you outlined," Mary urged. Please consider this, we have been in flight for more than four years, we are no longer being pursued and the roads home are those

NOTE: Mary speaking out as she did, indicates the bond she has with Joseph. Jewish law directs something different. "And so train the young women to *love their husbands and children*, to be self-controlled, pure, *working*, cooking, sewing and other household chores that we are familiar with and have traveled on many times in the past."

And Joseph pondered Mary's recommendation as they cleaned up after the meal and their encampment preparing for bed.

He gathered Mary and Jesus to him saying, "Mary, your recommendation has merit on many levels. Then, taking that as a given, as I see it we will be relatively safe until we reach Jerusalem, Once inside the city we can avoid the palace and marketplace, where we would most likely be recognized. We can just mingle among the crowd, blend in. We will make a stop before entering the city and another one when we are outside the city's gates.

"Once we pass through the city's gates, however, we will be in Samaria and outside Archelaus' jurisdiction. Then, in another two weeks we will be in Galilee, Nazareth and home."

"Lord," Mary said with warmth, "you are kind and understanding."

They began their homeward trek.

"Jesus," Joseph began, "as we walk, I will continue talking to you about the early books of the bible. We have completed the book of Genesis so now we will examine Exodus, most of which we have spoken of in the past. With that in mind, I will begin with the Israelites being in Egypt and how they got there.

"It began in Genesis with God's promise to Jacob. He said, "I am God the God of your father: fear not go down to Egypt; for I will make thee a great nation;[100] And I will go down with thee . . . [101]

"And I will also surely bring thee up Moses did as he was told. With him came the twelve tribes that totaled seventy souls. And they were fruitful and multiplied and waxed exceedingly mighty; and the land was filled with them."[102]

"Are you saying that seventy people went into Egypt without knowing what they were in for," Jesus asked?"

"A new word for you Jesus is 'faith.' God told them to go and in faith and they knew He would be with them because He said He would be.

"It was similar to those five years ago when an angel of the Lord came to me in a dream and instructed me to take you and your mother and go into Egypt. He said that Herod was seeking to kill you because you represented a threat to him. We had faith that the angel was from God and so we went into Egypt.

"Faith then is a powerful force," Jesus asked?

"Yes it is. Look how far faith has taken us. It is ours, it is yours. Never be without it. If you have faith nothing is impossible!"

They passed hurriedly through Jerusalem avoiding the palace and the marketplace. Speaking to no one nor did they meet anyone who knew them. As they passed through the city's gates there was a sense of relief. They were out of imminent danger and relatively safe. At the outskirts of the city, and within the boundaries of Samaria, they made camp for the night.

"Jesus, we are very close to home. From now on we will be in Samaria and the hill country. Our first major city will be Lebanah, our next will be the Great Plains, Gilboa, and then Nazareth. Your mother will be able to see her parents,

---

[100]   Genesis 46:8

[101]   Genesis 46:3-4

[102]   Exodus 1:1-7

your grandparents and reunite with them, and be able to greet my children and your brothers and sisters."

Mary made another lentil stew that she served with bread she had previously prepared and baked in Hebron.

As they ate their stew, Joseph observed, "We have, as I've said, about 149 kilometers to go or about ten or eleven more days. We are familiar with the roads and should make good time.

"Sometime in the future, I don't know exactly when, we will be traveling this road again going to and from the temple on high holy days and special feast days.

"Your mother and I made this journey a number of times before and we are familiar with its twists and turns. Because of that, your mother was right in saying this was the best way to go."

"Will there be a story tonight, Lord," Mary asked?

"Yes, as a matter of fact there will be. The story will be from Exodus where God told Moses, and the elders on Mount Sinai, what had to be put in the temple, only God called it a tabernacle where you could dwell among them. Dimensions were given and He described what was to be placed inside: an ark of testimony that he would be given, a mercy seat where they could speak together, a table for showbread, it's utensils and bowls that were always to be filled, a golden candlestick and seven lamps to give light."[103]

"When we are back in Nazareth, I will one day take you to the temple in Jerusalem where you will see everything that God told Moses to put there and that I have described to you. These items are used in worshiping the Lord from that day on Mount Sinai the present."

"Now let us join hands in prayer and thanksgiving.

"Holy Guardian angel, ask the Lord to bless this journey which we are about to undertake, that it may profit the health of our souls and bodies; that we may reach its end, and that, returning safe and sound after so many years, we may find our families well. Guard, guide and preserve us."

Jesus asked, "Do you really believe that someone will come and watch over us?"

"Jesus, we have spoken of this before. Your mother and I have faith and belief. It is our treasure. I am surprised that you should ask such a question, or are you testing us?'"

"I seek to learn the depth of your faith and belief."

---

[103]   Exodus 25: 1-40

CHAPTER SIXTY-THREE

THE HISTORICAL CONTEXT of the Old Testament and in the 400s BC with Israel under the authority of the Medo-Persians; who allowed them to return to Jerusalem to rebuild the temple and the city.

In the 300s BC, Alexander the great conquered the Western world for Greece. After his death his empire was divided up by four of his generals and Greek became the official language of the Western world is preparing the way for the efficient spreading of the Old Testament into Greek - a volume called the Septuagint (LXX), which was the Bible of jerk of Jesus' day.

In the 100's BC, the Jews were captured by the Syrian/Greeks and persecuted. This led to the rebellion under the Maccabee family who really captured Jerusalem. With the aid of an Edomite named Antipater, the Jews convinced the new Roman Emperor Augustus to allow a modified self-rule under the Jewish Sanhedrin, while paying taxes to Rome and being policed by Roman soldiers. Antipater convinced Augustus to appoint Antipater's son, Herod the Great as king of the Jews.

Within this environment most people work physically odd jobs and were not extremely poor. Many of the residence of Judea were shepherds, the most traditional job of Israel. Many were farmers, fishermen, builders and various tradesmen, merchants, managers of the business of rich men, and vine growers.

Individual homes were the primary social points of the village. People discuss politics, religion, and social issues often over meals. The Jews spoke Aramaic in the homes-a combination of hero and Babylonian which the Jews acquired during the seventy years of captivity, however, who also educated Greek, since that was the language of business, politics and society in the Roman world.

Religion dominated every phase of life in Jesus' day. The major religious groups included: the Pharisees. At the end of the Old Testament[104] and during

---

[104]   Malachi 3:16

the inter-testament, there were conservative Jews zealous for the law called Hasidaeans or loyalists. They join the fight for independence against the Syrian/Greeks, but when the Maccabeans set up a non-Levitical priesthood in the temple, they separated from them and were called Pharisees (separatists). Unlike the Sadducees and Herodian's, the Pharisees opposed and relations with or pay taxes to Rome.

CHAPTER SIXTY-FOUR

THE HOLY FAMILY approached Nazareth, which lay in a sheltered basin some 1300 feet above sea level. They delighted in seeing the hills that surrounded the village that was part of a limestone ridge defining the southernmost border of Galilee.

"What is that strange smell," Jesus asked?

"That, my son, is Nazareth!"

Small eddies of smoke could be seen rising from the homes as people went about their everyday lives.

Joseph had often delighted in the view that could be seen from the summit above the village. To the west he saw Mount Carmel on the Mediterranean coast, to the east was Mount Tabor, to the north and with its brown, snow-covered Mount Hermon, and to the south stretch the fertile plains.

"Lord, we are home," Mary whispered!

"I know Mary, why are you whispering?"

"To keep from shouting and dancing around in circles."

Now their pace quickened.

"Why does smoke rise," Jesus asked as they rushed homeward?

He asks the strangest questions, Joseph thought, at the oddest times.

"A fire as you know makes things hot. And from what I have seen, above a fire you get quite a lot of hot air. Hot air is not as dense as the cooler air, and so it rises. Because there is quite a lot of hot air, it makes quite a big wind current as it rises, and that drags the smoke particles upward with the air, in much the same way as wind can raise dust. Some of the smoke particles are very small indeed, so they can be held up in the air for quite a long time, and they do not settle out from the air until a long time after they leave the fire and usually some distance away from the fire. The color of the smoke depends on what is being burnt. Paper and parchment usually have white smoke. Wood, tar and other such materials will burn black."

Once within the gates Joseph took hold of Mary and Jesus and spun them around doing the dance that Mary wanted to do a short time ago.

"Praise be to the Lord," he shouted! "He has seen us safely home!"

"Yes Adon, His will has been done!"

"Mary, I have asked you not to call me Adon because I am not your master and never will I be."

"May I continue to call you Lord," she asked?

"Yes but privately please call me Joseph as you did before we were married."

As they walked through the narrow streets, few people were out and about and none seemed to know them. As they approached his workshop, James looked up, recognized them and shouted out to the others. "Joseph and Mary are home and they have a young man with them!"

A cry went out throughout the neighborhood, "Joseph and Mary are home and they have a young boy with them!"

People came from their shops, from their homes, to greet their returned neighbors and friends. Joseph's children and grandchildren hugged them and cried over them. They crowded around Jesus, the newest member of their family.

Tables appeared in the marketplace along with benches and chairs. A variety of foods and fruits decorated the table tops, and in the background music could be heard. James took the animals and tethered them, Leah took their clothing bundles, and Judas took them to the village square.

The Holy Family was stunned, bewildered and thrilled at the outpouring of friendship erupting around them. Many questions were asked: where have you been, why did you leave, what have you been doing...?

The spontaneous celebration continued until dusk. People returned to their shops and homes, only the family members remained.

Joseph began to speak "There is too much excitement tonight for any decision- making. We know that our return has disrupted your lives and that changes must be made. For now, know that your life will go on just as before. We just have to find out what we can do to fit into them.

"For tonight, Mary, Jesus and I, will put our mattresses on the roof of the workshop to rest. If everyone is agreeable, we will meet tomorrow morning to discuss what is to be done.

"The outpouring of love and affection has touched us deeply. Please allow us to go to the Lord in prayer of thanksgiving.

"Heavenly Father, we come to you in praise and thanksgiving for seeing us through our travels, for your blessing by allowing us to be reunited with our family. We beseech thee to give us thy guidance in plotting the course for our future. We are most grateful to thee for having blessed our family. All praise and honor to you."

They stooped as they entered the mud brick house, climbed the ladder to the roof and laid out their mattresses. The roof, Joseph recalled, was flat, made of Birchwood branches that had been woven together, laid out on the rafters. They had covered everything with a thick layer of clay that filled the space between the branches to form a smooth, hardened plaster layer. He was pleased to see that their work had endured. Joseph spread a goat's skin mattress on the roof, they covered themselves with their cloaks and robes then slept. Jesus awoke early before the others, looking over the parapet at the hubbub in the street below. Mary was sound asleep, attesting to her exhaustion from their arduous journey.

Joseph called out, "Good morning Mary, good morning Jesus, I hope you slept well."

"The rest was made even better," Mary replied, "knowing that we were home. Was that not a pleasant surprise we had yesterday?"

Jesus observed, "Everyone was so caring about our well-being. Is this to be the family?"

"Not *to be* my son, *they are* our family."

Joseph's family were poor craftsperson's, living from day to day. Their meager diet was made up of bread, olives (fresh or pickled in salt water), olive oil and wine. They had beans, lentil stew season vegetables that were fresh and ladled onto flat bread, on occasion there was salted fish, meat was reserved for special occasions, fruits, nuts, eggs, cheese and yogurt. As they descended for the morning meal, the Holy Family wondered what the morning meal would consist of.

The Holy Family found the meal was already laid out on the table in the patio, the area chosen to accommodate everyone who would soon be arriving. When they had finished eating, Joseph sensed there was tenseness among his children.

Justus was the first to speak. "Father," he began, "this house and workshop are yours by right. If you are going to continue using the house, we must decide on what the rest of us will do. It is our wish that you continue to use those of us you need doing your work. Also . . ."

"My children," Joseph interrupted, "when we left, Mary and I had given you all that had belonged to us. We wanted that then, it will not be changed. We would ask however, we be allowed to remain in the house until other quarters can be found."

"That is your right," Judas said.

"I want to work with you in our workshop, and at the same time seek work elsewhere."

"What is to become with Jesus," James asked?

"His education will continue here at home. Mary has been teaching him to read, write, his numbers, ands to speak and be understood by other languages. I am teaching him basic Greek and a trade.

"Lydia and Assia, of you have the time, you could assist her until such time that he can go to the synagogue with the other children, and further his education there."

"Father," James said hesitantly, "you tell us that our little brother is the Messiah who has come to save the world."

"That is so James. I know that it is difficult to come to grips with that, but we have the honor of having him within our family. The gracious Lord has blessed us."

"Then why do we not go abroad and announced him to everyone that this is so?"

"I am glad that this is been brought to light and it also pleases me that everyone is present. Listen to my words my children and carry them in your heart. What we know must remain with us. It is not to be shared with anyone! I believe that it is not for Jesus to go abroad. Jesus must prepare himself for the mission his father has sent him on. We do not know what that mission is nor do we know what he will be ready to go out and be his father is emissary In the meantime we must, recognize what is going on, allow him to be a young boy, and at all times treat him with all of our respect.

"Mary and I have borne that information for all these many years and we have struggled in learning how to handle it. Now we ask you to join us.

"I will not ask you to swear allegiance to us. The belief in your brother as the Messiah is something that each of you must decide for yourselves. You are no longer in mortal peril as you once were, since the death of King Herod and later his son Archelaus, have eliminated that threat. Your brother Jesus is not ready for his mission and so I would ask you to keep this information among yourselves and said until such time that he is ready.

Joseph spread his arms, dazed heavenward saying, "Almighty and heavenly Father, we your children beseech you for understanding in carrying out Your will. Give us the strength and courage to do Your will."

They spent the rest of the day sorting out their things.

Mary set out to fetch water and then went about household chores along with Assia and Lydia, Jesus went out into the streets to play to greet and play with the other children, Joseph and his sons discussed what had been accomplished, what work needed to be done, putting off future work discussion.

"I did not see the synagogue doors," Joseph said. "Was there any problem finishing them? And did the rabbi pay your fee without grousing?"

"In answering your first question," Judas spoke out, "no, there were no problems. The way we outlined the work and the order of completion, worked out as planned."

Judas joined the discussion, "And yes, the rabbi thought we overcharged him for our work but when he heard the praises the panels brought, he gladly paid us in full."

It was James' turn to have a say. "Wait until you see the fourth panel. We had not selected a theme before you left. Well, Simon came up with the perfect theme. Wait until you see it."

The following morning Joseph walked with his sons to the synagogue. He stopped in his tracks stared at the synagogue doors in wonderment.

"My sons, I cannot believe my eyes. What I see before me is what we discussed and plotted out. Yet, it is nothing like what we did originally. It is more, so much more. You have humbled your father. I cannot wait until Mary and Jesus see this masterpiece you have created. It is no wonder that rabbi Lowe paid so quickly for what you have done. Well done all of you!"

One day, toward the end of summer, Joseph called for a family council meeting to discuss their future.

Joseph began the discussion. "Our family," he said," had been growing without need for extra money or space. We have adapted to our situation admirably. With three extra mouths to feed and shelter, our situation has been and will be strained."

There was a murmur among family members about money-saving methods, specific reductions in outlay, but none offered a solution to their financial shortfall.

"As I am sure you are aware, Tetrarch Antipas has begun a major renovation rebuilding Sepphoris eight kilometers to the north. There is also work in Cana, Mage, Dale, Nais, Capernaum and Ender. There is work to be had, we just have to leave Nazareth to find it.

"It is my recommendation that I go seeking work. And of these areas offering work, I think Sepphoris is the most logical because of its proximity and the abundance of work opportunities. Its further appeal is that when Jesus is old enough, and he has no schooling, he can go with me to learn his trade."

Simon asked, "We are already operating two workshops, is that not enough?

"For the time being we have enough space for work purposes. However, our house needs at least one room added, but more importantly, we have not made provisions for growth."

Changing the subject, Joseph turned to Simon and Judas who had taken additional work shepherding for Claudio, a neighbor and shepherd.

"Claudio, is very near the end of his days," Simon began. "He is getting on in years and Judas and I have been helping him wherever he needed it."

"That is as it should be," Joseph said, "Helping those that are in need."

"In our recent discussions with him he has offered to sell us his flock of sheep at a very reasonable price and we can pay it off over a period of time. He has no family or kinsman interested in buying the flock. The sale will include a small house with one bedroom and a dining room. With your permission we would like to go forward with the purchase."

"Do you feel you are capable of handling this undertaking and the sale," Joseph asked concerned?

"Claudio has been most generous and is willing to work with us. He added that should our debt not be paid in full before he passes on, the flock will be ours debt free."

Judas continued, "There are 64 sheep, 15 of which soon will be kidding. He has introduced us to the buyer for the wool and has told him of our purchase agreement."

"He has called in a scribe to record his contract with us," Judas said. "his wish is to eliminate any possible questions that may arise when he passes."

Judas added, "We will sign the document in the scribes' presence once it is drawn up."

"Remember the dear man in your prayers," Joseph advised.

Turning his attention to his daughters, he said, "What have you to offer to the family council?"

"The goats are still giving fresh milk," Lydia reported.

"You may have noticed, Lord, "Mary said softly, "we had fresh eggs for our morning meal."

"Yes I did and I also heard the cackling of chickens in our courtyard. Where did they come from?"

We, Lydia, Mary and I thought that an addition to our dietary supplement was called for. James built the coop, fenced in a portion of the yard to house them, and we purchased fourteen chickens. They are producing eggs daily and are capable of reproducing which enables us to add chicken and eggs to our diet"

"Did you think to purchase a cock to assist in reproduction?"

"Father," Lydia said with mock exasperation, "of course we purchased two of them to help. You should also know that we will keep the area clean to prevent sickness."

"There might be a use for their guano. As I think about it, I must have been deaf, dumb and blind not to have noticed these goings on. Congratulations to one and all, you have done well!"

Jesus was anxious to be part of the family asked, "Me too Abba?"

"You also my little scholar, you also!"

Joseph joined hands with the others saying, "O Lord what a blessing you have bestowed upon us. I thank you for my children and for my wife. We sing your praises forever!"

CHAPTER SIXTY-FIVE

WITHIN A WEEK of their return, Joseph would find work as a master craftsman in Sepphoris. Mary, for her part in the family equation, continued in her role as teacher to their son. She recognized that he was different, since he was also the son of the Holy Ghost, but continued in the roles she had defined for herself, his mother and teacher.

On his return that first evening, and had eaten a meal, the family began to assemble in the courtyard in anticipation of the usual storytelling. Before Joseph began his story, Jesus had a request, "Father, none of us had been to Sepphoris. Please tell us about that great city. What does it look like, how does it smell and tell us about the people who lived there."

"Oh yes Abba," Lydia asked anxiously. "What do the women look like? How do they dress? How do they go about on the streets?"

"It pleases me that you are interested in my work. To begin with, Sepphoris is 50 minutes away on foot, or about 6.5 kilometers. I went to the city of Nain which is 18 kilometers away, and I went to Japfia, 3 kilometers distant. By far gap Japfia the closest but there is no major construction going on. The last place I visited was Sepphoris. The city had the most to offer. Historically King David declared the city to be the Capital and ruled here for seven years.

The city was destroyed but is now being rebuilt under the auspices of Galilee's ruler, Herod Antipas. Major construction and building is going on throughout the city.

"From what I was able to observe, the population of the city appears to have money. In fact I was shown a list indicating the following: the professional scribe, the teacher, the lawyer, the hand worker, mason, carpenter, or cooper, the small shop keeper, the family farmer, the banker or money-changer, fisherman (on Lake Tiberias), tax collectors, foremen, the money lender, the master of a household, the manager of a household or steward, the ironsmith, coppersmith, silversmith, or goldsmith. To these one may add from other sources, whose status we do not know, the caravaneer, peddler, charcoal maker, lime maker,

---

tanner, leather-worker, soldier, healer, exorcist, physician, herbalist, and actors and entertainers.

"Children move at the bottom of the social structure in terms of wealth and birth, as well as in terms of historical circumstances, one found tenant farmers, day workers, agricultural workers, reapers, guards for prisons, shepherds for sheep and goats, slave children, slaves, beggars, thieves, lepers, the poor or jobless, prostitutes, and the rebel or bandit. What it amounts to is that the Jewish society has three levels: the ones who are usually landowner and entrepreneurs; the poor, who worked the land or survived by begging.

"If I had to place us within those three groups it would have to be in the middle group. We are neither rich nor poor.

"Many of the streets aligned with colonnades, while the streets themselves are paved with crushed limestone, many of the buildings and some of the houses and public buildings had beautiful mosaics, which is the art of creating images with a collection of small pieces of colored glass, stone, or other materials put together to make a picture.

"Beyond that I had very little time for sightseeing. But it pleases me and where I work and what I do. Some of the other things I said I saw was a wonder of wonders 260 meter elongated water reservoir and I was told that there is a synagogue but I did not see it."

"Jesus," Joseph turned his attention to the young man, "you are of an age where I think I can take you with me every morning to work as my apprentice."

Jesus was very excited at his selection, "Your apprentice, Abba?"

"Yes but you have to start at the bottom of the workforce. It will be your job to see that the men have the materials they need, you'll see that they have enough water so that they do not become dehydrated, and other menial tasks you are asked to do. Is that something you think you can handle?"

"Oh yes Abba!"

"Understand my family, I am not yet ready to go to work every day. I think it is my duty, and in our mutual best interests, that we strive to make things secure here at home. It is not for lack of trust, you have proven yourself repeatedly, but grant me this caution, I have our best interests at heart."

The years passed joyfully. In addition to working and running the household, they made their annual trips to Jerusalem for the Passover celebration. The entire feast was celebrated at home or in the synagogue, and in so doing they were becoming a closer family. They had been living a blessed life and at the same time they were active members of the community, and people of Israel observing the precepts of the Law of Moses.

Word quickly spread through Nazareth that Archelaus had been banned by the Roman Emperor Augustus. The result of this made Judea a Roman province. What this meant to Joseph and his family, they had nothing further to fear from Jerusalem. In addition, Nazareth became one of 24 priest centers of the Hebrew nation with Galilean priests notably more liberal in their interpretation of Mosaic Law than were the Judean Rabbis and scribes. With all the goings on Jesus and Joseph, in their hilltop discussions, began placing matters within the realm of Mosaic Law.

These trips to the hilltop afforded him the opportunity to speak together in the setting that gave them a panoramic view. The scriptures were the usual topics of discussion but Joseph quickly learned that whenever Jesus asked a question the subject could be on any topic whatever. Today for instance. . .

"What causes a shooting star?"

This was one of those questions.

"A very good question Jesus, Ancients tell us that they are not shooting stars but a streak of light that we can see that marks the path about a heavenly body when it comes to the earth. Many people fear this phenomenon for leading them to be coming from an angry God."

Jesus, like all young Jewish boys learned to read, write, and do their numbers at home. The only known book at the time was the Bible. Now he was able to join with the other boys at the synagogue, which he attended every day dressed in his *tallit,* where they were taught the history of the Jewish people hearing the rabbi's commentary on the readings of the last Sabbath. Jesus found this be very beneficial since he could compare these commentaries with those he had with his father.

Young Jewish boys being taught the Galilean school were better educated in the Bible than most Jews. Galilean teachers for the reverence, the Scripture and the passionate desire to be faithful to it.

Jesus also learned the promises that had been made, the covenants, the gift of the land and the Law of Moses. He learned how to sing the psalms:

> "Praise the Lord for his care.
> Blessing on a man who fears the Lord.
> God's mercies are many.
> God's power is demonstrated in the Exodus.
> Trust in God not idols.
> Praise his deliverance from death.
> The truth of the Lord endureth forever.
> Thanksgiving for the Lord's salvation."[105]

Jesus was also required, as were the other boys to recite the Sharma Israel. Jesus absorbed it all.

---

[105] Deuteronomy 6:4-9

In addition to the three more mouths to feed and shelter, these became additional strains on the family. Eventually, things began to improve. Joseph had all the work he could handle, the purchase of the sheep had gone well, the work in the shop was prospering and the women kept everything humming.

As he grew older Jesus wore his phylacteries as all young male men his age did.[106] He did not shave his head at the temples, as prescribed in the Bible. In Midsummer, the third year of the return, Joseph saw the necessity to build another workshop that was closer to the spring and the caravan way-station. It was his intention to promote business locally as well as for travelers going between Sepphoris in the east and Jerusalem, in the south. Once the workshop was completed, he was inundated with orders for work, making and fixing yokes and plows, leather harnesses and various other woodworking projects.

In the meantime, with the help of his mother and his aunts, Jesus mastered the Galilean dialect of the Aramaic language. Joseph supplemented his language skills by teaching him some Greek, although he was not quite that fluent.

While this was taking place behind the scenes, the Ethnarch been replaced and Rome had taken over control of Palestinian business. Rome appointed a new Prefect-Procurators and Ethnarch who administered affairs of the new sub-province. The administrators had been invested with the powers of taxation, as well as judiciary and military powers. Unaffected was the autonomy of religious affairs. However, the procurator had the authority to appoint high priests and control the duties of their office.

The affect of this was that Galilee became part of the Tetrarchy of Herod Antipas who undertook the rebuilding and fortification of Sepphoris declaring it to be the capital of Galilee. All of this brought about additional hardships and higher taxes.

Joseph called his family together to discuss the current political situation and its impact on them. They would have to be some belt-tightening but they could and would survive.

"There is another matter which needs to be discussed. Mary and Jesus and I have lived with this for over a decade and you have not been made privy to it until tonight. If you recall the family council we had that many years ago, we were fleeing for our lives and we turned everything over to you so that you might sustain your families."

"Is it now time for a reckoning father," James asked?

"Indeed it is not! When we look about us we can see the fruits of your labors. You were however, not told everything and this too was done on purpose. I am going to tell you those things that were withheld. The last time we got together

---

[106] Phylacteries, a set of small black leather boxes containing scrolls of parchment inscribed with verses from the Torah, which are worn by observant Jews during weekday morning prayers.

we, and by extension you, were under the penalty of death from King Herod because the two prophecies any of this and both. The first prophecy," and thou Bethlehem in the land of Judah, art not the least among the Princes of Judah: for out of them shall come a Governor that shall rule my people Israel."[107] The second prophecy says: "for unto us a child is born, unto us a child is given: and the government shall upon his shoulder: and his name shall be called Wonderful, Counselor the Mighty God, the Everlasting Father, the Prince of Peace.

With that fixed in his mind, plus the fact that that Herod did not want a competing ruler in Jerusalem, he promptly issued a decree ordering the death of all male children, two years of age and younger to be slaughtered. . ."

"Surely father," Justice interrupted, "that our little brother cannot be the Messiah, the one who has come to save the world."

"Two words come immediately to mind, belief and faith. We are true believers and we have faith in the Lord God Jehovah. If I may continue with our narratives, Mary was visited by an angel in a dream who told her that she was going to have a child, by the Holy Spirit and she was to call him Jesus. She became pregnant. When I found out that she was, the angel visited me in a dream and he instructed me to marry Mary, that she was with child and we were to call him Jesus.

"Following the birth of Jesus we were visited by shepherds who came to pay homage to Jesus the Savior. You saw them come here and you saw them pay homage.

"Almost two years later we were visited by magi, princes from foreign lands who followed the start to Bethlehem to give the Messiah, Jesus, gifts of gold, frankincense and myrrh.

"Shepherds came here following a star to see the Messiah. Magi came here, following a star to see the Messiah, the infant that Mary had given birth to.

Now, and once again in a dream, an angel has instructed me to take Mary and the child and flee into Egypt since it is Herod's intent to have him killed and this I cannot allow.

"Your brother has a mission, the reason that all this is taken place. What that mission is in what form it will take, and what ramifications will follow, are unknown.

Joseph turned his attention to Jesus. "You Jesus, like the shepherd's bell ringer sheep. One sheep in the flock is chosen to wear a bell about its neck. Wherever that sheep goes the others will follow. It is a rough analogy but an appropriate one. You must learn what your mission is going to be and then have the people follow you to our Heavenly Father."

---

[107] Micah 5:2

The family sat around wondering how to treat the sibling, how we should be addressed, how they should. . . So many things were discussed. They had spoken of these things previously but the true facts had not been established. This new knowledge changed everything. He was finally agreed that nothing should change.

"We are a family," Joseph said," we must continue to love and respect one another selflessly. Be assured that Jesus loves you, and he is our family member."

"Why were you and Mary chosen to have this child," Judas asked?

"I have often asked myself that question. Mary was chosen for a purity, devotion and great love. I was chosen to be the guardian, protector, husband and father. An honor I will fulfill until I can do so no longer."

CHAPTER SIXTY-SIX

ONCE THE FAMILY had settled into their familiar surroundings, the Holy Family made a trip to see Joachim and Anne, Mary's parents, Joseph's in-laws, and Jesus' grandparents. On arrival joyful reunion took place. Smiles lighting everyone's face and it was obvious that the grandparents were thrilled at the sight of their only grandson. It was some slight hesitation at first, not knowing how to treat Jesus' presence since they were well aware of the origin of his birth. The smiling gleeful young boy put them at their ease.

Anne insisted that they stay for the evening meal and stay the night with them. Joachim had dozens of questions and just wanted to hug his grandson.

"I will tell you the highlights, Joachim of our adventures and misadventures. There were sites we never saw before, animals we did not know existed, and strangest of all resale pyramids that are engineering feats. There were Jews everywhere having fled into Egypt for one reason or another."

Anne said, "We have heard that the desert sands are very hot and the sun can be equally so. Is that an exaggeration or is it as described?"

"Mother," Mary responded, "hot is not an adequate word to describe the desert. It blinds you; it drains you of your energy, and saps your strength. You know that you cannot go on but you do. More importantly, there is never enough water to quench your thirst or wash yourself. On those occasions when we did find water we quenched our thirst, wash our clothes and then ourselves."

"My poor children," Anne moaned, "how did you ever survive?"

Joseph answered her, "Our blessed Lord gave us the strength to bear those hardships and to carry on. Without his grace we could not have survived. All praise to God our Father!"

Mary and Joseph continue to regale Joachim and Anne with their adventures. They retired for the evening and slept soundly. The following morning they shared the morning meal with Joachim and Anne, and were back on the road to Nazareth. When they arrived the sun had set and they fell onto their pallets completely exhausted.

CHAPTER SIXTY-SEVEN

AFTER THE SABBATH service, Jesus and Joseph were seated on their favorite hilltop overlooking Galilee, surrounded by fig trees and olive groves.

After sitting in the shade for a time, each within their own thoughts, Jesus said, "You have often told me to have nothing to do with drawing or making graven images."

"Yes I have Jesus they are sinful in the eyes of the Lord, and they are used for idolatrous purposes."

"If that is true, and I have no doubt that it is, please explain to me the Jewish custom of touching a piece of parchment, nailed to a doorpost each time the enter or exit the house, and then kiss the finger that touched the parchment. In addition to that they say, "The Lord shall preserve thy going out, and thy coming in from this time forth and even forevermore.[108] Is that not "dolatrous?"

"There are two concepts to be considered, one is tradition, second is consistency. Jews have been following the ritual for centuries. It dates back to Egypt and the Exodus.

"The parchment is a ritual image with verses from the Torah[109] and following that line of thinking that is not an act of deference or even homage.

"Answering you by saying, 'we have always done it,' is not an adequate answer. It is a very good question that you have raised and one that I will have to think about going to the Lord in prayer seeking an answer."

Jesus and Joseph were working were working together every day and building construction in Sepphoris. He is still considered an apprentice but he would very soon become a tektôn. Jesus was well able to anticipate, Joseph thought, what was needed by a worker or what needed to be done before being told to do so. This is an accomplishment for an 11-year-old on the cusp of becoming a man.

---

[108]   Psalm 121:8

[109]   Deuteronomy 6:4-9 and 11:13-21

Continuing along that line of thinking Joseph reminded himself that Jesus would soon be taking his rightful place among the adults in the temple. He will no longer be required to be confined with the children in the Women's Court -a large open area inside the walls of the synagogue and or temple.

Soon, too soon, he will assume the status of the men and have the privileges and responsibilities this book bestowed upon them. One of the privileges, Joseph thought that Jesus would enjoy was the right to converse with scholars.

Where to begin? Joseph was having problems balancing the fact that Jesus was the son of God, and at the same time, his foster son. What could he possibly teach him? Jesus had expressed an interest in this coming-of-age, this transition. Perhaps that was the best way to go. If there were any problems that might arise, he was certain that Jesus would address them.

As they were walking home one evening Joseph told Jesus what his educational was for him.

"When we walk home at the end of the day, I want to get you started on the preparation for your rite of passage."

"I have heard the other boys in our classes at the synagogue talking about their transition. I think your idea of going over the process let me is a good one. That way I can tell the others what we are doing."

"Then let us begin. We live within the framework of Jewish law," Joseph continued. "That law requires that every Jewish boy when he becomes 13 years of age, be accountable for his actions as he becomes a son of commitment.

"Your mother and I have had and will continue to have that responsibility for your actions until you reach the age of 13. In less than two years that responsibility becomes yours. Besides the religious perspective that undertaking, it may be counted toward a *minyan,* a quorum of ten men over the age of 13 required for traditional Jewish public worship, as well as community services."

Jesus asked, "will I be required to do something or do things just happen?"

"The custom in our synagogue is that on the Sabbath, early in your 13th year, you will be called upon to read from the weekly portion of the law, or the five books of Moses, either as one of the first seven men, or as one of the last. If you are chosen to be one of the last you will be reading the closing versus of the haphtarah, a selection from the book of the prophets. You also give a *varTorah,* which is merely a reading from the Torah."

"Is that all there is," Jesus asked?

"No, there is more but that is for another time."

When they arrived at their home in Nazareth, they found Mary preparing the evening meal. Joseph and Jesus washed up before they ate. As they were eating Jesus began telling his mother about how Joseph was going to prepare him for his coming-of-age.

"How do you feel about that," Mary asked?

Jesus knew why she was asking the question. "The other boys my age are talking about this transition. By conducting this preparation, I can speak with them as a member of their group."

"My little boy," Mary observed, "O, what is a mother to do?"

"Do not be afraid gentle mother," Jesus said as he reached across the table and took her hands. "I will always be with you."

Mary smiled then turning to Joseph said, "You might also get him started on the Sabbath celebration. We want our young son to be prepared for his day."

"As we speak of coming-of-age," Jesus asked, "who do people say that I am?"

Joseph was the first to reply, "Some say that you are Jesus the carpenter's son."

"Some say." Mary said, "You are Jesus of Nazareth."

"But who do you say that I am?"

Mary answered, "You are my son and You are the Messiah!"

"I would reply as your mother has. You are my foster son but first and foremost You are the Messiah. We are now preparing You for the coming-of-age, and at the same time, we will help You, prepare for your mission."

Several days later after the Sabbath services, Jesus and Joseph climbed their hillock. No sooner had they seated themselves when Jesus asked one of his 'where did that come from' questions?

"Why do plants and trees lose their leaves when it gets cold?"

Joseph mused, the older Jesus becomes the harder it is to answer his questions. "You are very observant. Yes some plants and trees lose their leaves whenever it gets cold rather than stay with color throughout the year. Many times they say goodbye by providing a radiant show of color before the leaves fall off. This happens to allow the plants and trees to conserve their energy and prevent damage by preserving the water that is within them, called sap. As the weather gets warmer the leaves reappear, their natural color is restored, and the water had been contain circulates throughout the plant or tree. To a lesser extent, grass behaves in the same manner."

They watched for a time as the sheep moved over the countryside munching on grass. When one or more of them wandered away from the flock, one of Jesus' brothers went after it and brought it back to be with the others."

Jesus had another question, "When the men enter the synagogue, what do they do besides pray?"

"If you remember from our earlier talks, much of what is done is ritual, traditional, and historical. But first let me tell you a story that is called the Pesach Tradition. It is a story about four sons whose name were Wise, Wicked, Simple and Young. The Wise son, interpreted as the *Chacham'*, is a genuine individual with intellectual curiosity and is not at all rebellious. Like a religious Jew, the wise son understands the laws of the Passover festival and follows them faithfully. The Wicked Son represents Jews who are not respectful of their heritage nor their religion and reject them completely. The Simple Son is indifferent to all religious activities, and makes no attempt at understanding. While the Young son does not know how to ask questions and he is unaware of their culture and traditions."

"Which one are you Joseph," Jesus asked? Jesus had dropped the familiar reference of 'Abba' when specking with Joseph. They both understood their place.

"You have known me for some time now, which one do you think I am? "I think that you are the Wise Son. In my view you know and understand almost everything."

"I work on that every day and I pray daily for the Lord's blessing and guidance. When we return home I will prepare a list of things that are involved in the Passover. You can use it as a ready reference."

Day after day father and son walked to Sepphoris, and worked side-by-side on the construction of a warehouse. Joseph hired six master carpenters and six laborers. The work was moving swiftly and expertly which pleased the rabbi. He made weekly visits to the site to see for himself how the work was progressing.

The rabbi set with Joseph and his crew at the midday meal. "Joseph," he said," I am most pleased with the way you have overseen this project. No one has to be told that the work is being done professionally. Thank you. Even your workers let it be known that they are goal oriented, they work hard and are content in their work. You are a tektôn at many levels."

"The work rabbi is its own reward. The money you pay them is a bonus. Providing this food at the midday meal has added greatly to their contentment, and we thank you."

"How does your apprentice enjoy the work," the rabbi asked?

"He has become quite efficient and professional at keeping everyone supplied with the materials that they need and keeping the workplace clear. He is a fast learner. In a few days I will elevate his position and make him part of the work crew."

As they walked home that night Joseph said, "Your mother has instructed me to tell you about the Passover. You have been with us in Egypt where the Passover was celebrated. He did not take part in the celebration but I am sure that you have heard your mother and I talking about feast. You know about the Seder meal and you did take part in that ritual. Now you need to be familiar with each segment of the ritual and the traditions behind them."

"During my transitional," Jesus asked, "will I be asked to name the segments, father."

"About that I am uncertain but you should have a thorough knowledge of what takes place. To begin, Passover is celebrated in the spring, from the 15th to the 22nd of Nisan where we believe that the true experience of freedom that our ancestors gained leaving Egypt.

"Passover is divided into parts, the first two days and the last two days. The last two days commemorates the dividing of the Red Sea. In celebration Jews do not work, they do not write, but they do however light holiday candles at night. During that time they drink wine and eat delicious meals.

"Then comes the *Chametz*, that is, food that's made of grain and water that have been allowed to ferment and rise and is the food the Israelites the night before Passover. The next ceremony is the eating of the matzo which is, as you know, flat unleavened bread. This is eaten during the Seder meal and a meal consists of 15 steps which are ritually based. The spoken of rituals before. The focal points however are only four: eating matzo, eating bitter herbs to remind us of the bitter slavery endured by the Israelites, and drinking 4 cups of wine. "You and I think would drink grape juice with us in celebration of our freedom and we will recite the Haggadah that describes the Exodus."

"I remember most of that father," Jesus said.

"I thought that you would. I must tell you that other traditions include gold and silver being placed on the Seder table to remind us of the gifts that Egyptians gave the Israelites. The doors will be left open during the draining of the 3rd cup of wine allowing the poor to come in."

Jesus asked, "As I recall four questions are asked."

"Good memory my son, yes there are four questions that are read from the sheet of parchment." Joseph recited the questions from memory: "Question one: On all other nights we eat bread or matzo, while on this night we eat only matzo.

"Question two: On all other nights we eat all kinds of vegetables and herbs, but on this night we have to eat bitter herbs.

"On all other nights we don't dip our vegetables in salt water, but on this night we dip them twice.

"On all other nights we eat while sitting upright, but on this night we eat reclining.

"As you can see, Jesus, each of the questions refer to an aspect of the Passover Seder meal. Leavened bread is forbidden throughout the holiday, bitter herbs are eaten to remind us of the bitterness of slavery, and vegetables are dipped in salt water to remind us of the tears of slavery."

"That does not seem difficult to remember," Jesus observed.

"Then Jesus you are prepared."

CHAPTER SIXTY-EIGHT

JOSEPH SAID GOODBYE to Mary and Jesus before sunrise. At the door he lifted Jesus, who was now eight years of age saying, "you are the man of the house while I am gone. It is a serious responsibility and I know you can handle it."

"When can I go to work with you," Jesus asked?

"You are serving as my apprentice here at home. By next year you will have to come with me and finish your apprenticeship. You should have enough practical experience. I will see you and your mother this evening when I return."

Joseph walked east towards Sepphoris and into the sunrise. Across his shoulder he carried a leather purse with a strap. Inside the purse Mary had fixed him a light meal and a small earthen jar filled with wine.

As he walked he tried to recall what he knew about the city. He wanted to present a knowledgeable front about Sepphoris before anyone looking to hire him he knew for instance, there was a strong Roman influence about the city's architecture. He recalled seeing a Roman theater, a bathhouse several mosaics with human figurines, a cobbled street showing ruts that had been guarded from the iron rimmed wheels of carts and carriages, a large marketplace, and he had been told about at least one synagogue. He remembered telling his family about these wonders.

When he entered the city he went immediately to the synagogue. He was greeted at the door by a man dressed in a clerical robe, sandals covered his feet and a black yarmulke was set on the back of his head and he smiled in greeting. The cleric said, *"Yom tov ani yakhol laazor lekha?"*

"*Shalom,*" Joseph replied in greeting. "Yes you can help me," he answered in the Aramaic dialect. "I am Joseph of Nazareth, son of Jacob and I have come here looking for work. *Ma shimkha?*"

"*Hashem sheli,*" rabbi Saul Wallach replied. *"Ma ata ose behayim?*

"*Ani ish meturgeman têkton,* but more than that, Joseph continued in Aramaic, "I am a master craftsman and a contractor."

Rabbi Wallach switched to the Aramaic tongue. "If you are as good as you say you are, I have a great deal of work for you. We sorely need a general contractor, one who is honest and trustworthy and has all the requisite skills. Are you that man?"

"I am that man!"

"Come inside and we will talk."

They entered a rather ornate synagogue with smooth stone walls, mosaic flooring, colonnades, and hanging oil lamps. Joseph was led into a dining area with crude benches and a rough hewn table.

"Tell me some of your accomplishments so that I might judge your work."

"I have carved the synagogue doors with scenes from the Old Testament, I have made hand hewn yokes, tables, benches, harnesses and latticework for the windows. I am a general contractor, building houses, barns and silos, I do work in silver, gold, and other precious metals, and. . ."

"Say no more I am convinced. If I put you to work will you travel to and from Nazareth each day?"

"That is difficult to say. That would depend on the work to be done, the difficulty involved time to complete the work. Ordinarily I will be traveling back and forth each day. If however the work requires that I stay in Sepphoris, other accommodations would have to be made."

"How will the work be done on site or at your home?"

"And I would have to give you the same guidelines. The nature of the work would be all important. With any large piece of work it would be preferable to have a workshop on site. That would eliminate transportation costs."

"With any large bodies of work, and you think that there would be much," Joseph asked? "If you have no objections that should be my responsibility. I think that I might be a better judge of a man's skills or the lack. I will know if that person is earning the money that you will be paying him."

"Is there anything else we should discuss?"

"Yes, materials and supplies. I have or I can make any tools required. If you give me a list of the work you would like to have done, I will draft you an accounting of the materials needed at each site.

"And rabbi this must be said, any time that you are displeased with me all the work that is being done you can discharge me."

"Joseph let us think positively. I would like you to start in this room by converting it to a formal dining room. This room alone will require a table large enough to seat 12 people, chairs for everyone, a serving table or a buffet, and a cabinet for storing dishes and appropriate utensils."

Joseph had been making notes on a piece of parchment then he asked the rabbi, "What are your long-range plans after that?"

"Sepphoris was, and to a lesser extent, is a trading center. It is located on a route in land from the Mediterranean Port of Ptolemaist, Acre to Tiberius on the western shore of the Sea of Galilee. I would like you to build a warehouse, perhaps two on that route where we own property. It will be used to store wares. The Tetrarch is encouraging business and I want to get in on a growth spurt."

"That is an ambitious course you have charted, as a seafaring friend of mine would say," Joseph observed. "When you are ready to finalize your plans I will help you make a list of everything you need along with a cost estimate."

"If this works out, and I am sure that it will, you will of course hire the help that you need. Allow me the right to question you when and if I see fit."

"I think rabbi that this project we have been discussing can be mutually profitable."

"That is my thinking too. When can you begin?"

"Let us sit down together, work up a list of what is needed and then have the materials delivered. From those estimates I will hire the people that will be required and we can begin work in three days."

The men shook hands. "I am sure that you have thought of it, Joseph would like you to walk about the town in order that you may get a sense of the city? For instance, take a look at the beautiful mosaics, Abraham entertaining three visitors[110], Isaac's sacrifice[111], the consecration of Aaron.[112]

The men prepared a list of materials, the rabbi agreed to order materials and have it delivered, and Joseph learned where he could hire day laborers.

Before the men parted, the rabbi asked, "Work of this magnitude requires a contract outlining everything that we have discussed. If you have no objections I will have one of the scribes in the synagogue draft one for your signature. Is that acceptable?"

"Yes rabbi it is."

---

[110] Genesis 18:1-6
[111] Genesis 22:1-18
[112] Exodus 29:1-26

CHAPTER SIXTY-NINE

WHEN HE REACHED home, he was greeted by Mary who told him that they would be eating outside where he could tell everyone what had happened in Sepphoris.

As promised the meal fit the occasion. Chickens had been roasted, there was a variety of vegetables, bread and sweet wine, not much was left to clean up.

"Father," Jesus urged after the table had been cleared, "tell us what happened today please."

"Let me give you a little background first. The city is located and perched atop a 900 foot hill in lower Galilee. It is a sophisticated Jewish city that has, so I have been told, 10 synagogues. At one time it minted its own coins, but no longer. It has an extensive aqueduct system, an elaborate reservoir, cemetery, building two marketplaces multi-story buildings, statuary, paved streets. . ."

"Were you able to find work," Simon asked impatiently?

A broad smile took over Joseph's face. "I went to the largest synagogue in the city where I spoke to rabbi Saul Wallach, a most congenial man. He is not too old, perhaps 50, he is not as tall as I am. He . . ."

"Father," Lydia interrupted, "you are exasperating! Did you find work?"

"You are impatient Miss Lydia. Yes the rabbi gave me work, in fact, he gave me a great deal of work as a starter, he wants me to make him a formal dining room and everything that will go with it. Following that he wants me to build a warehouse, maybe two. Oh, he made me the contractor for the work."

"Lord," Mary said smiling, "that is wonderful news! Our Blessed Lord was smiling upon you."

"The work has so much potential Mary. It could be an apprentice workshop with Jesus. . ."

"Yea," Jesus called out!

"When or if there is insufficient work around here," the rabbi has given me the authority to hire help. With that in mind. . ."

"When would you begin," James asked interrupting his excitement apparent?

"In three days James. In the meantime, you should know that I have implications for the intended warehouse; I have to work up estimates of materials and supplies. I have to interview and hire the people that will do the work, I have to work up cost estimates, and then give the rabbi a timeline when all this will be done.

"Let us now join hands in prayer. Bountiful and merciful Father," Joseph began, "we come to you in prayer of thanksgiving. Make us worthy of your love and keep us safe and ever faithful to you."

"And now," Assia asked, "Before we send the children off to bed, please tell them one of your stories. Make it a story of love and romance so that they might know something of love."

"That, I think, is a very good idea. Come everyone, up on the roof and bring your blankets and bedrolls so you can rest while you listen."

Up on the roof they spread their blankets and bedrolls to stretch out under the stars. Joseph sat on a small stool and began to tell a story.

"Many years ago in the land of Canaan, Isaac blessed his son Jacob to tell him that he was not to take a wife in Canaan, but to go to his Uncle Laban and stay with him until he found a good wife. With that charge Isaac blesses Jacob saying, "And God Almighty Bless thee. And make thee fruitful, and multiply thee, and thou mayest be a multitude of people.

"And so obedient to his parents Jacob left them leaving Canaan and went to Padam-aram, the home of his uncle. On the road, because the sun had set; and it was night, he took stones and used them for a pillow to lie down and sleep. As he slept he dreamed. Behold a ladder appeared! It was based on the ground and reached up into heaven with God's angels walking up and down the ladder.

"At the top of the ladder the Lord stood above it."

"Wait! Wait! This is supposed to be a story about love and romance not a story about angels going up and down the ladder. You tell many stories about Him but few about love and romance."

"Be a little patient Assia. The Lord is about to tell Jacob what is in store for him in the future." After a pause Joseph continued. "And the Lord said unto Jacob I am the Lord God of Abraham thy father, and the God of Isaac: the land upon which thou lieth, to thee will I give it and to thy seed; and thy seed shall be as the dust and wherever thou goest, I will be with thee."

"When he awoke in the morning he took the stone that he had been using as a pillow, set it up for a pillar, and poured oil on top of it. He called the place where he had slept Beth-el. He continued his journey until he came to an open field where he found a well and three flocks of sheep with their shepherds.

He called out to them, "Where are you from?"

"Haran," they called back.

"Do you know Laban the son of Nahor?"

They replied that they did. He stopped and they were talking together and as he was telling them who he was and asking about other members of his family - they had originally come from this area, and he was looking for them. The men obligingly pointed towards a woman off in the distance. They told Jacob she was Rachel, the daughter of his mother's brother Laban.

When Jacob saw Rachel at close quarters he was instantly smitten by her. In an act of bravado he kissed her then removed the great stone cover of the well single-handed, no doubt hoping to impress the young woman. He watered her flock.

In response, Rachel ran to her father's house and told him about the young man. Her father Laban ran out to meet Jacob, welcoming him warmly. Jacob stayed with Rachel's family for a month, and during this time he fell deeply in love with Rachel.

"Oh my goodness," Lydia gasped. "He just got there and already he's kissing her! What a brazen young man!"

Jacob told Rachel who he was and where he was from. Jacob told his uncle all that has taken place. Laban said, "surely thou art bone of my bone and my flesh. Jacob approached Laban for permission to marry Rachel. But Jacob was empty-handed, could not produce the normal bride price for Rachel. Laban agreed that, his daughter could marry Jacob, but stipulated that, as a bride price Jacob must work for him seven years - the seven year cycle was a sacred one in the ancient world. Jacob agreed, and he and Rachel settled down to spend the next seven years together. What neither of them realized was that Laban had agreed to let his daughter marry Jacob, but had not specified which daughter it would be.

Rachel had an older sister Leah, not so beautiful, and the older sister and family was usually married before any of her younger sisters.

Seven years passed, and Jacob demanded his bride.

The girl was dressed in her finest clothes, including a rich head-dress and veil that covered her face. When the drinking at the banquet was over, her father led her still wearing the veil into the bridal chamber where she and Jacob made love. By this time he had been drinking a considerable amount. When the morning came, Jacob realized his mistake. The bride in his bed was not Rachel but Leah. He had been tricked into marrying the wrong sister.

"Jacob had been outwitted by Laban. Needless to say Jacob was enraged at the trick that had been played on him.

Laban simply shrugged his shoulders saying, "to bad."

Jacob insisted that Laban correct the wrong that had been done.

It was agreed that Jacob would marry Rachel after the traditional week that Jacob must spend as Leah's bridegroom. Then, work for Laban another seven years to pay her bride price.

Jacob never forgave Leah for her part in the deception. She was the unloved wife."

"That's it," Lydia protested? "You were supposed to tell the story of love and romance, not one of duplicity."

Joseph replied, "I don't know what you mean Lydia. Jacob and Rachel loved one another. They gave each other their devotion. Jacob's devotion was such that he worked seven years to win her hand. Isn't that romantic, isn't that great love? Tomorrow night I will tell you the rest of the story and I think you'll be pleased with the outcome."

CHAPTER SEVENTY

THE DISTANCE BETWEEN Nazareth and Jerusalem is a little more than 144 kilometers. It is because of this great distance that most of the Hebrew holy days are celebrated in a synagogue in Nazareth. This year, the high holy day of Passover would be debated in Jerusalem as it was every year. And Jesus has celebrated his 12 year. Joseph felt it was time for Jesus to accompany them to Jerusalem. Toward that end he made arrangements with relatives and friends who were there. Joseph and Mary were devout Jews. The Old Testament commanded for such a trip for three festivals a year, Passover, Pentecost, and Tabernacles, represents a coming time of unprecedented harmony and peace, this annual eight-day event is conducted with a strong family focus. Accordingly, members and families take part in daily church services and a whole range of positive family-based activities throughout the Festival.

This was to be the celebration of Passover and Joseph felt it was a good opportunity for Jesus to become familiar with the temple in Jerusalem. The Old Testament commanded such a trip to Jerusalem for three celebrations Passover, Pentecost and Tabernacles, the Feast of Tabernacles represents a coming time of unprecedented harmony and peace, we conduct this annual eight-day event with a strong family focus. Accordingly, members and families take part in daily church services and a whole range of positive family-based activities throughout the Festival.

As they advanced on the city, people there and villagers joined with them to create a small caravan. This was also new to Jesus so exciting. His eyes opened wide in wonder as he beheld the temple for the first time. It was enormous! It was beautiful!

After the morning meal, the Holy Family entered the temple area. There were animals of every kind wondering loose, people wearing various costumes were chattering to one another, the streets were filled with animal droppings at the hubbub was most bewildering. Jesus knew the significance of where he was.

Jesus loved and to think about God. When he had come to the temple he watched the priests in their work. He bowed with the worshipers as they prayed and his voice and joined his son to praise.

Every morning and evening a lamb was offered on the altar, representing the death of the Savior. As the child Jesus looked on the innocent victim, the Holy Spirit taught him its meaning. He knew that he himself, as the Lamb of God, must die for the sins of men. With such thoughts in his mind, Jesus wanted to be alone.

Since the temple is an enclosed space you may wander by yourself. Jesus was allowed to wander about seeing those things his father had spoken of. One of the first things he did was listen attentively to the priests and. Unerringly he found his family at meal time. For seven days that routine was followed. On the seventh day the caravan was assembling for the trip home. Women and children left first since they were slowest, men followed later because they were faster.

When Joseph arrived in the encampment, Mary asked, "Have you seen Jesus?" Jesus had not been with them during the day, which had not caused immediate concern each feeling that he had been with the other or with relatives or friends. They went from camp to camp asking, "Have you seen Jesus?" With each negative response grew their concern and fright increased. They were miles from home, there was no one to care for him, and he had nothing to eat.

Mary felt that heartache that only a mother can feel. Her son was alone, in a strange land, he had nothing to eat and no one to take care of him. Joseph felt despair and since of loss since he had failed his family as the nutritor domini.

After a fruitless search they began their way back to Jerusalem. When Jesus had remained in Jerusalem, without telling his parents what he was doing, their fifth trial had begun and Jesus' role had changed. He had been questioning and listening to his friends and teachers who were amazed that in the depth of his understanding. To them he was showing great signs of wisdom.

The sadness, this suffering and agony, had been willed by God so that Joseph and Mary might want and understand in their own way the beginning of Jesus' teaching ministry in the years to come and his apostolic life. It was the fulfillment of Simenon's prophecy. Without a doubt a sword had pierced the hearts of Joseph and Mary and in so doing, they felt alone together.

On the third day they found him in the midst as of the church listening to and questioning them. When he asked them questions, he was teaching at the same time all that they heard from him astonished in amazement at his understanding and the answers to their questions.[113] They felt that this young man had a careful upbringing by his parents, who had saturated his brain and is mind with Scripture.[114]

---

[113]   Luke 2:46-47

[114]   Deuteronomy 6-8

Pleased yet sick at heart, Mary chided him for the first time remembering the prophecy of Simeon, "a sword will penetrate your heart."

"Son, why hast thou dealt with us? Behold thy father and I have sought thee sorrowing."

The mild parental reproach leads to Jesus' self declaration of His mission. "How is it that you sought me? Wist ye not know that I must be about my father's business?"[115]

Implicit in this statement is the question, "Where else should I be," evincing a sense of mission and self-awareness, that transcends his relationship to his earthly parents?

In response, Mary points out the consequences of his action, their anxiety and their fear. Also, for the first time, Mary calls Joseph Jesus' father when speaking to Jesus about Joseph. Also, in so doing she reveals that she truly considers Joseph as the father of Jesus and that she is his spouse. And, lest it go unnoticed, it is the only time that she asked Jesus a question.

Jesus is breaking new ground with his parents they need to understand who he is and what he is saying to them. But Mary treasured all these things in her heart.

When they return to Nazareth Jesus becomes the reader of the scriptures with his parents. In the readings he asked them questions just as he had done to the men in the temple. The next years that they spend together in Nazareth constitutes the framework of Jesus young life. It is during this timeframe that his role begins to take shape. Is a man of silence and at the same time displays his virtues and remains subject to his parents. He knows too that he must act with some authority because it of his responsibility to them.

Joseph is also a guardian, a *Redemptoris custor,* called to watch over the Redeemer. For now he remains in the background until his son is ready. Maintaining what everyone thinks that Jesus is the carpenter's son. He has never altered his life-long role. He is, he was and remains guarding and protector of his family, Joseph of Nazareth.

---

[115]   Luke 2:48-49

CHAPTER SEVENTY-ONE

MARY TOOK JESUS onto the patio at the back of the house where she washed him. She washed his body, hands and feet finishing with his hair until he almost glistened. She told him to get dressed, put on your sandals and meet her at the front of the house.

"Why have you washed me so thoroughly mother?"

"This morning I am taking you to the synagogue to enroll you in classes of Scriptures.

"Yesterday Joseph spoke to rabbi Lowe who told him that classes will be getting the boys your age into the Scriptures."

"Will other boys be going as well?"

"Oh yes, I believe there will be eight if you come." And they made their way to the synagogue.

The evening before Jesus was headed for class, Joseph and Mary had a little talk about him and his future. Initially Joseph waxed philosophical.

"From the time we removed him from swaddling clothes, to the time he began to walk, and even before that, I believe that he listened to what was being said by those around him. It was not that he understood I do not believe, but he listened. He was what the Greeks called a *tabula rasa*, a blank page. By listening those pages began to fill up.

"You gave him what he needs most of the time warmth, security and love. Later you fed him and nourished him all vital to his development. He taught him to walk and talk until he was able to do so on his own. He has always been very observant and a quick learner. He watched you and I eating and then was able to do so by himself.

"We soon found out what a quick mind along with the ability to get along well with others. You developed his mind by teaching him his numbers, how to write how to read, all critical skills. The pages on his slave were piling up rapidly. You placed him in synagogues in numerous cities throughout Egypt; valuable learning experiences. The classes he will be joining tomorrow will supplement the basic knowledge you are responsible for.

"Jesus had begun his study of the Hebrew law when he was with us in Egypt. And I recall you telling me how Jesus displayed an unusual ability and talent, not only for the text, but also the spirit of the Hebrew Scriptures."

Joseph and Mary were most influential in the character and intellectual development of Jesus, but there were other sources.

Nazareth was an old fashioned, place in Judea but its remoteness played an important part in Jesus early life. The city's location and several caravan routes brought travelers to the city, many of whom stayed overnight and some several days.

Travelers came from Samaria, Jerusalem, Damascus, Greece, Rome, Arabia, Syria, Persia, Phoenicia, and other lands who mingled with the Nazarenes. Jesus, like any other child his age, that these travelers strange, intriguing fascinating and quite different. He tried to learn as much about them and from them. Many of the travelers quickly discerned that this was no ordinary inquisitive boy.

Following the Sabbath service Jesus and Joseph retreated to their favorite place on the hilltop. The air was crisp, clear and inviting.

"Jesus, I know that you are doing well in your study of the scriptures. rabbi Lowe constantly tells me what a quick student you are and how well you understand."

"I know that he is pleased with my brother but I am not altogether pleased with his progress. He has made no mention of the 10 Commandments and I think that is important."

"And it is Jesus, but I am sure that he has those commandments schedule future plans. He just has not gotten to them yet. If I may be so bold and because you show an interest, I will tell you my version of the commandments speaking of your heavenly father in the third person.

"The 10 Commandments are the first direct communication between a people and God. He designed them to elevate our lives from mere frantic, animallike existence to the sublime levels humanity is capable of experiencing. They are the blueprints of God's expectations of us and His plan for meaningful, just, loving and holy life. They include and "I am the Lord your God, who brought you out of the land of Egypt, out of the house of bondage you shall have no other gods before me.

"You shall not make for yourself a carved image-any likeness of anything that is in heaven above, or is in the earth beneath; you shall not bow down to them nor serve them. For I the Lord your God, am a jealous God visiting the iniquity of the fathers upon the children to the third and fourth generation of those who hate Me, but showing mercy to thousands, to those who love me and keep my commandments.

"You shall not take the name of the Lord your God in vain, for the Lord will not hold him guiltless takes His name in vain.

"Remember the Sabbath day, to keep it holy. Six days you shall labor and do all your work, but the seventh day is the Sabbath of the Lord your God. In it you shall do no work: nor your son, nor your daughter, nor your male servant, nor your female servant, nor your cattle, nor your stranger who is within your gates. For six days the Lord made the heavens and the the earth, sea, and all that is within them rested on the seventh day. Therefore the Lord blessed the Sabbath day and hallowed it.

"Honor your father and your mother, that your days may be long upon the land which the Lord your God is giving you.

"Thou shalt not murder.

"You shalt not commit adultery.

"You shalt not steal.

"You shalt not bear false witness against your neighbor.

"You shall not covet your neighbor's house, you shall not covet your neighbor's wife, nor his male servant, nor his female servant, nor his ox, nor his donkey, nor anything that is your neighbor's."

Later on that evening as they sat around the fire that Joseph had started to ward off the evening chill, the conversation focused on the educational opportunities available to Jesus. Joseph pointed out that he had the rabbinical schools where he had developed a thorough knowledge and understanding of the Old Testament and the Scriptures.

From his mother he had learned to apply this knowledge to his life and from his father he had learned to deal with people wisely, with understanding, and honesty. At the same time Jesus was a natural student of the nature that surrounded him. The country around Nazareth was mountainous, rugged and quite beautiful. He delighted in breathing the fresh air, and basking in the warm sunshine. He loved the feel of rain, the smell the flowers and trees, and he took particular delight in listening to the water as it ran in the streams. Jesus learned of his heavenly father's power, wisdom and love. As he studied, he still had this knowledge in his heart to be used later when he began his public ministry. The education that Jesus received in this was of greater value than the traditions and human philosophy taught in the synagogue schools.

Although he was reasonably well educated, Joseph had to go to Sepphoris to secure work merely to sustain their lives. Now that he was old enough, Jesus joined with his father just to maintain subsistence. At best it was a life of self-denial and privatization and temptation. Apparently Jesus had been placed where his character would be constantly tested. Much depended on the foundation Joseph and Mary had made in their son bless you.

The caravan's coming into Nazareth brought not only their trade goods but an abundance of wickedness and sin. "Can any good thing come out of Nazareth?"[116]

Following the incident at the temple in Jerusalem, Jesus lived with her, was obedient to his parents, faithful and cheerful he acted his part in bearing the burdens of a household. He was a willing servant a loving and obedient son. He learned the trade of his father earning the title of tektôn working with his hands at Joseph side in the carpentry shop. He wore the simple garment of a carpenter and when he was not working, he walked about the town exchanging pleasantries with his neighbors. Everyone knew him as Jesus, the carpenter's son.

Jesus grew in wisdom and stature in favor with God and all the people.[117]

---

[116] John 1:46

[117] Luke 2:52

CHAPTER SEVENTY-TWO

"BUT MADE HIMSELF no reputation and took upon Him the form of a servant, and was made in the likeness of men."[118]

In his thirteenth year it was time for Jesus to take part in the ritual of coming-of-age. The classes in the synagogue that a dimension in preparation for the ceremony. The demeanor of the boys also underwent a change as they approached teenage years, barmitzvah and son of commandment.

When next they met at the hilltop Jesus informed Joseph the change in curriculum.

"I know that the time was near. We have previously discussed the procedures and that the rabbi will also discuss them with you, if he has not already done so. I want to review with you the inner workings. You will be wearing a *tefillin* which has two leather boxes with parchments inside inscribed with the *Sh'ma*, "Sh'ma *Israel Adonai eloheinu Adonai echad.*" Hear O Israel, the Lord is our God, the Lord is one,"[119] and so on with other biblical passages. These *tefillin* boxes have straps attached that are wrapped around the head and arms as reminders that we are to harness our intellect, our emotions and actions to the service of God.

"Then follows the aliyah, or "ascent" is the immigration of Jews from the Diaspora to the land of Israel, when the Torah is read in public. You may be called upon to read a portion.

"The Torah will first be taken from the ark by the rabbi and placed on the *amud*, or lectern by the *amud* will be several branches of the *menorah*, or candelabra that will be lighted in remembrance of the *menorah* in the temple.

"If you want to go to the *bimah,* that is the podium it will be covered, the rabbi will go to the ark to remove the Torah and he will open it to the section that is to be read. You will notice that over the ark is the *ner tamid*, or eternal light.

---

118 Philippians 2:7
119 Deuteronomy 6:4-9

"Your mother will make you the *tallit* and you will wear it over your shoulders during the ceremony."

"Will you be with me during the ceremony," Jesus asked?

"Yes I will be with you as a matter of fact I am required to recite a prayer of thanks to God that I am no longer legally responsible for you. I must tell you Jesus I have no concern in that regard. No father could ask for a better son, a more loving son, or a more loyal son. I am truly blessed!"

The families got together at the synagogue and the ceremony took place. Afterwards there was a luncheon at their home and in the village square. There was roasted lamb, chickens, vegetables and special breads which the women made. There was also various fruits and sweet wine.

"Today," Joachim announced, "my grandson has, become a man." Raising his hands and placing them over Jesus' head, Joachim said, "May the Lord God Jehovah watch over you and bless you!"

The following day Joseph and Jesus went to the temple to meet with Rabbi Lowe. The rabbi had requested this meeting indicating that he had set Jesus apart.

"Jesus," he began, "recognizing that you are no longer a young boy, the ceremony yesterday was your right of passage. Allow me to read this passage from the ceremony, that I think it bears repeating.

"God, before he created the world planned your life. You are here on this earth with the purpose of God which, through you he can fulfill, (how prophetic are his words). God made you perfect. He does not make mistakes!"

"God is with you, will see you as a man from this day forward and you will be treated as a child, Jesus," rabbi Lowe said in conclusion, "a man went to great lengths to secure the blessings of his father. He was given the blessing and he prospered. His brother did not get a blessing and he did not prosper. At the ceremony your father gave you his blessing; words carry power."

The next Sabbath Jesus went with his family to the synagogue. Joseph placed a small *tallit* across his shoulders and he was led to a small altar. He was called upon to recite the Maftir and Haftoras. Joseph was called upon to pray. When he had finished the congregation sang *Mazeltov* and *Simantor* in celebration. The ceremony came to an end when Joseph blessed Jesus once again. He thought about this and noted to himself that two life changes had taken place: we stayed behind in the temple to speak with the doctors and scribes, it was in fact the declaration of independence. And now with this rite of passage ceremony, Jesus became an independent adult. Joseph thanked God for allowing him to be part of his son's transition.

The very next day father and son walked into the sunrise heading for Sepphoris and another day of work.

Later on that year Emperor Augustus appointed Marcus Ambivius a Prefect of Judea to succeed Copmus, who had been appointed to replace Archelaus, whom the Emperor had exiled.

Herod Archelaus ruled so badly that the Jews and the unified Samarians appealed to Rome requesting that he should be deposed. Archelaus was banished to Vienna in Gaul and after a bloody revolt led by Judas the Galilean, Judaea became a province of the Roman Empire.

Joseph's steps were a little slower, his back a little more stooped, and more flex of white appeared in his hair. By this time Jesus' beard and hair were full-grown, his physique fully developed and well proportioned. He was becoming more introspective. It had become his habit, along with the help of his mother, to have a hot water waiting for Joseph at the end of the day. And now for something that he look forward to.

In 14AD Prefect Augustus died and was succeeded by his adopted son Tiberius Caesar. For six years during the reign of Augustus and two years during the reign of Tiberius, Joseph was being ravaged by infirmities. He forced himself to go every day into Sepphoris with Jesus to complete a day's work. Jesus could see the toll it was taking on his pain racked body.

One morning Joseph made his usual walk into Sepphoris. Mary had asked Jesus to stay behind and help her at home. He was celebrating being eighteen years of age.

Toward mid-afternoon a runner came into Nazareth. The runner was one of Joseph's work crew, bringing word to Mary that Joseph had collapsed at work while working on the governor's house. The worker had no idea what had caused the collapse or the serious nature of it. Jesus wanted to leave immediately to be with his father but Mary asked him to stay back and keep things in order at home. She sent for James and together they went into the city to bring Joseph home.

Several hours later they returned with Joseph on a pallet being borne by his work crew. They put him immediately to bed.

Everything was going reasonably well in his pain racked body when a runner from Sepphoris brought word to Mary that Joseph had collapsed at work while working on the governor's house. Jesus wanted to go to his father's side but Mary directed otherwise. She would hasten to Joseph and James should attend her. Jesus would watch over things at home until she returned.

Joseph arrived at home on a pallet, and was put to bed in the house his bodily strength gradually diminishing, the unavoidable end approached. Mary and Jesus were in constant attendance. A physician was called in but there was nothing he could do to relieve the pain.

Mary turned to Jesus saying, "Let his death be precious in thy eyes, as the uprightness of his life was pleasing to thee, so that he may depart in peace and the certain hope of eternal reward. Be mindful my son of the humility and love of thy servant; his exceedingly great merits and virtues; of the fidelity and solicitude by which this just man has supported thee and me, they humble handmaid."

"Mary my mother, the request is pleasing to me, and the merits of Joseph acceptable in my eyes. I will assist him and assign him a place among the princes of my people, so high that he will be the admiration of the angels and will cause them and all men to break forth the highest praise. With none of the human born shall I do as with thee spouse."[120]

Joseph was well aware that his tenure has provided, comfort and his position as protector of his family was drawing to a close. With Mary and Jesus at his bedside, he made these facts known to them. Joseph's bodily afflictions and infirmities were to become the crucible preparing him for the journey he was soon to take. His strength gradually diminished as he approached the unavoidable end of his mission. He called out praise to his Lord for honoring him with that mission.

Mary and Jesus were at his bedside continually. He looked at Mary saying, "I must leave you Mary. I want you to know that I have never had a doubt about you, our marriage or the life we have had together. You have been and are everything to me and I will honor and praise you always hoping to be worthy of you."

He turned to Jesus. "Jesus you are well prepared for the journey, the mission your Father has sent you here to accomplish. You have taken over the mantle as Nutritor to your mother and I and for that we have been blessed."

Joseph turned to Mary taking both her hands in his. "Mary, bride of my youth, when the angel told me to fear not and marry you, I did so with complete commitment. Later, when they learned that you were with child by the Holy Spirit, my future role was made abundantly clear, and I have never looked back but with you I have always looked ahead. "We have shared many trials and tribulations always guided by an angel of the Lord. When we were instructed to leave everything behind and flee into Egypt, without hesitation we made ready and left always trusting that the Lord would be with us.

"For more than three years we traveled throughout Egypt always in fear of the Roman's centurions and their threat to the child Jesus. Later, another angel of the Lord came to us and told us that it was safe to return home since King Herod, the main threat to Jesus' life and was no longer a threat.

"Again we left everything behind and returned to our native land, the home of our forbears. When we had reestablished a home the goal was to support Jesus. All lines here in Nazareth became like those of Jews throughout Judea. When Jesus was in his thirteenth year we took him to Jerusalem for the Passover celebration, we worried and we fretted when we could not find him on our way home. After three days of searching we did find him. He said words at that time that made a profound change your life and our lives forever more. How is it you sought me," you said, "Wist ye not that I must be about my father's business?"[121]

"Those words of yours Jesus told me that my role, was nearing its completion. But know this, as I can draw a breath I will support you and love you."

Joseph closed his eyes and fell asleep.

As he slept he reviewed his life since marrying Mary. They have been married nineteen years, in all that time he never thought differently about her nor his unworthiness to be with her. She was holy, she was blessed and she was the mother of the Messiah! And he was so unworthy. He worked briefly saying, "Mary my beloved wife, it is time for me to join my ancestors, place my remains in a remote location, with no marker so that I might be easily forgotten except in your memory."

Yet the Lord had allowed him to join their journey.

Joseph, son of Jacob, was so different from other patriarchs. They had been blessed and endowed with graces and spiritual gifts intended not for the increase of their personal sanctity for the service of the Most High and other souls. That is to say, gifts and graces freely given are not dependent on the receiver.

With Joseph however, all divine favors the product of personal virtue and perfection connected closely with the holiness of his life. The nearer to holiness he grew, the more worthy he became to be the husband of Mary.

For the nine days that he lingered, he had uninterrupted attendance of Mary and Jesus. In that time he was allowed to see the divine being of his Lord, all that he believed by faith was revealed to him.[122]

Requiescat in peace.

---

[121]   Luke 3:49

[122]   This excerpt was taken from "Mystical/City of God" by Venerable Mother Mary of Jesus of Agreda.

END NOTE: Nowhere is it recorded when Joseph died, the cause of his death or his final resting place. His work done he walked off into blessed obscurity.

KING JUDAH AND then became the King of Israel. The, ten decades later, from the House of David, a son, Joseph was born n to Jacob and Rachel in Bethlehem, who would be chose of God to be the early father of his Son. Such a man would have to be without blemish, a pious man. He was in fact a gracious man who kept the laws of Judaism and was well respected in his synagogue and community. He was a man of meager means but none the less, an honorable and faithful man. Skilled as a +carpenter in the small town of Nazareth, Joseph observed the Holy Days and Hebrew Feast We know that through Joseph's sensitivity and obedience to God, he fulfilled the role of protector and guardian of Jesus. He enacted the role of 'father' admirably in every way. He never questioned the role given him by his Lord but carried out each directive, but King David was born in Bethlehem. As a boy he was an armor bearer who went on to become strangely, not one word of his is recorded and yet, he is the patron saint of at least 61 organizations and authorities. His crowning achievement, he was chosen as the foster father of God's only Son!

CPSIA information can be obtained
at www.ICGtesting.com
Printed in the USA
BVHW03*0858050318
509717BV00005B/573/P